Freedom

FOR YOUNG PEOPLE

Summer

Freedom

FOR YOUNG PEOPLE

Summer

The Violent Season That Made
Mississippi Burn and Made
America a Democracy

BRUCE
WATSON

ADAPTED BY REBECCA STEFOFF

SEVEN STORIES PRESS
New York • Oakland • Liverpool

A TRIANGLE SQUARE BOOK FOR YOUNG READERS
PUBLISHED BY SEVEN STORIES PRESS

SEVEN STORIES PRESS
140 Watts Street
New York, NY 10013
www.sevenstories.com

School teachers may order free examination copies
of Seven Stories Press titles. To order, visit www.sevenstories.com
or send a fax on school letterhead to (212) 226-1411.

LIBRARY OF CONGRESS CATALOGING-IN-PUBLICATION DATA

NAMES: Watson, Bruce, 1953– author. | Stefoff, Rebecca, 1951– adaptor.
| Watson, Bruce, 1953– Freedom Summer.

TITLE: Freedom Summer for young people : the violent season that
made Mississippi burn and made America a democracy /
Bruce Watson ; adapted by Rebecca Stefoff.

OTHER TITLES: Savage season of 1964 that made
Mississippi burn and made America a democracy

DESCRIPTION: New York : Seven Stories Press, [2020] | "A Triangle
Square book for young readers." | Audience: Grades 7–9

IDENTIFIERS: LCCN 2020032394 (print) | LCCN 2020032395 (ebook)
ISBN 9781644210093 (hardcover) | ISBN 9781644210109 (trade paperback)
ISBN 9781644210116 (epub)

SUBJECTS: LCSH: African Americans—Civil rights—Mississippi—History—20th century—
Juvenile literature. | African Americans—Suffrage—Mississippi—History—20th century—
Juvenile literature. | Mississippi Freedom Project—Juvenile literature. Student Nonviolent
Coordinating Committee (U.S.)—Juvenile literature.
Civil rights movements—Mississippi—History—20th century—Juvenile literature.
Civil rights workers—Mississippi—History—20th century—
Juvenile literature. Mississippi—Race relations—History—
20th century—Juvenile literature.

CLASSIFICATION: LCC E185.93.M6 W28 2020 (print) |
LCC E185.93.M6 (ebook) | DDC 323.1196/0730904—dc23

LC RECORD AVAILABLE AT HTTPS://lccn.loc.gov/2020032394

LC EBOOK RECORD AVAILABLE AT HTTPS://lccn.loc.gov/2020032395

BOOK DESIGN AND PHOTO RESEARCH BY Abigail Miller and Stewart Cauley
ADDITIONAL PHOTO RESEARCH BY Elisa Taber

Printed in U.S.A.

9 8 7 6 5 4 3 2 1

PAGE ii PHOTO: Children pose outdoors on
and in front of a pickup truck during Freedom Summer, 1964.
Likely at the Freedom School, Priest Creek Baptist
Church, Hattiesburg, Mississippi.

Contents

MISSISSIPPI AT A CROSSROADS

ON HALLOWEEN NIGHT, A STUDENT FROM YALE University in Connecticut stopped for gas in Port Gibson, Mississippi. A hundred years earlier, during the Civil War, Union troops had entered Mississippi through this same town. Now, in the eyes of local people, a new invasion had begun. Like the Union troops, the new invader was a Yankee, a northerner. He was easy to spot: a white, blond-haired stranger in a car with a black man and woman.

Four local men took action. They ordered the white man out of the car, beat him to the pavement, then circled, kicking and pounding. After the bloodied man was finally allowed to climb back into the car, the thugs followed it for miles along dark roads.

Road running into the town of Yazoo, Mississippi, 1964.

Two days later, two of the strangers—the white man and the black man—were spotted driving north out of the town of Natchez. A shiny green Chevy Impala with two white men in it pulled up behind their car. They made a U-turn, but the Chevy followed, riding their bumper. Heading south past farms and fields, the two cars sped up. Each time the first car roared ahead, the Chevy stayed on its tail. Engines groaning, gravel flying, soon the cars topped a hundred miles an hour. Finally, the Chevy pulled even and forced the strangers' car into a ditch.

This time the locals had a gun. They ordered the driver to get out. He hesitated—then punched the gas. The car lurched back onto the road. A bullet shattered the rear window. Another tore into a side panel. A third grazed a rear tire. The driver kept going and managed to duck down a side road as the green Chevy roared past.

It was November 1963. In Washington, D.C., the nation's capital, President John F. Kennedy was not thinking about Mississippi. He was wondering whether he should pull the United States out of the Vietnam War. We will never

know what Kennedy might have done, because
an assassin's bullet ended his life later that
month in Texas. Something else happened that
month that changed the future. For one weekend
in Mississippi, thousands of bone-poor citizens
gave America a long-overdue lesson.

A Lesson in Democracy

The two men who'd been attacked and shot were
Freedom Election volunteers. They and others
like them were working to get black citizens
of Mississippi registered to vote. Many black
Mississippians had never voted—mostly out of
fear. When slaves were freed after the Civil War,
they had voted in great numbers, but in 1890
this basic right was taken away. Mississippi and
other Southern states passed laws requiring
blacks to pay poll taxes—that is, to pay in order
to vote. Few could afford such taxes. Other laws
forced any black person who tried registering to
vote to pass a reading test, or to interpret part of
the state constitution. Blacks who still insisted
on registering had their names published in
the paper. They were then beaten, or had their
homes shot into at night. By 1964, just 7 percent
of blacks in Mississippi could vote.

But an election was coming that would decide the state's next governor. Everyone knew that Paul B. Johnson would win the election. His father had been governor before him. White voters liked him. Johnson firmly supported segregation, the web of laws and practices that separated people by race and made African Americans second-class citizens. And he stood firmly against integration, the movement to make blacks and whites equal under the law, with the same rights to use schools and other public institutions. Johnson *literally* stood against integration. As lieutenant governor, the second highest office in the state, he had physically blocked a black man from entering the state university.

Mississippi had a long history of racial division and violence, as you will see in chapter 2. During those first days of November 1963, the violence erupted against black Mississippians and the students who had come from other states to help them vote. A Freedom Election worker was shot at. A rock-throwing mob broke up a Freedom Election rally. Cops closed down another. Seventy election workers were arrested on charges that ranged from disturbing the peace to driving cars too heavy for their license plates. Roughed up or just told to get out of town, the out-of-state students got a taste of how Mississippi law worked in 1963.

The terror nearly succeeded. The organizers of the Freedom Election had hoped that 200,000 African Americans would cast Freedom Votes in their churches, cafes, barber shops, and pool halls. This Freedom Election would be separate from the official state election, but under an old law, the parallel ballots of the Freedom Election would be legal. They might be used to challenge the results of the official election.

In the end, after police seized some of the Freedom Election ballots, black Mississippians had cast 82,000 votes. Not enough to keep Johnson from becoming the state's new governor, but each vote was a sign of change in Mississippi. Bigger changes were coming. Mississippi stood at a crossroads.

It's Going to Take an Army

A few months before the Freedom Election in Mississippi, a quarter of a million people in the nation's capital had heard Martin Luther King Jr. talk about his dream—that someday the

Fannie Lou Hamer
and others march
on Freedom Day,
January 22, 1964.

United States would live up to the promise in its Declaration of Independence that "all Men are created equal." Prejudice against African Americans existed across the country, but racism reached its peak in the South. Everyone knew where it was worst. Roy Wilkins, the head of the National Association for the Advancement of Colored People (NAACP), had said, "There is no state with a record which approaches that of Mississippi in inhumanity, murder, brutality, and racial hatred. It is absolutely at the bottom of the list."

In Mississippi, a black body floating in a river was "as common as a snake." Spies and informers working for the state kept files on people and organizations that supported integration. Civil rights workers were routinely arrested and beaten. Years of peaceful protest had been met with bombings, beatings, and murder. And the rest of America did not seem to care. Martin Luther King Jr. had turned the nation's eyes toward racial inequality in southern cities such as Birmingham, Alabama, and Atlanta, Georgia. Even King, though, did not dare to organize in Mississippi. It remained a neglected outpost of civil rights, too remote, too rural, too simmering with hatred to offer the slightest hope.

After the Freedom Election, its chief organizer said that "the Negroes of Mississippi will not get the vote until the equivalent of an army is sent here." And an idea blossomed. What if hundreds of college students from all over the country poured into the state and spent a summer there? Wouldn't America pay attention then?

And what if these volunteers did more than get African Americans registered to vote? They could run Freedom Schools, teaching black history and black literature to black kids who would never study such things in their segregated public schools. They could set up Freedom Houses, with libraries, day care, and evening classes in reading and voting rights. And at the end of the summer, delegates from a new Freedom Party would to go the national convention of the Democratic party. Under the spotlight of national news, they would claim to be Mississippi's rightful representatives.

The "army" arrived the very next summer. College kids from all over the country descended on Mississippi. Organizers called it the

Mississippi Summer Project, but the summer of 1964 would come to be known as Freedom Summer.

Although Freedom Summer brought out the best of America, it brought out the worst in Mississippi. When word of the summer project leaked, it sparked rage and resentment. Hadn't Northerners flooded into Mississippi after the Civil War? And now they were coming back. An "invasion," some Mississippians called it. Governor Johnson declared, "We are going to see that law and order is maintained, and maintained Mississippi style." Jackson, Mississippi's capital city, beefed up its police force with shotguns, teargas, and a six-ton tank. The city's mayor said, "We're going to be ready for them. . . . They won't have a chance."

White rural Mississippians stockpiled kerosene, shotguns, and dynamite. New life flowed into the Ku Klux Klan, the underground terrorist and racist organization that dated back to the violent years after the Civil War. One warm evening in April, the Klan's burning crosses blazed in courthouse lawns, town squares, and open fields across sixty counties. The stage was set for confrontation.

Before the summer ended, black churches would be torched. Homes and Freedom Houses would be bombed. Violence of all kinds— including murder—would erupt. The violence would indeed turn the nation's attention to Mississippi. But Freedom Summer would be more than just violence.

That summer, America began to change. President Lyndon B. Johnson signed the landmark Civil Rights Act. Slowly, grudgingly, the "Whites Only" signs began to disappear from lunch counters and water fountains across the South. Meanwhile, in Mississippi, several hundred students and their host families showed Americans, black and white, how to treat each other with uncommon decency.

For the volunteers, the summer would be a journey into an unfamiliar America of dirt roads and tumbledown shacks. They would teach in crude classrooms and learn the human cost of racism. Going porch to porch to talk about voting, they tested their faith in democracy. When it was over, shaken by violence, inspired by courage, they seemed to have aged years in a single season.

"Mississippi changed everything for anyone who was there," volunteer Gloria Clark later said. Many of the volunteers would go on to be part of events that defined the 1960s, such as the movements for women's rights and against the Vietnam War. First, though, they had to survive Freedom Summer.

CHAPTER I

A RISKY BUS RIDE

THREE HUNDRED YOUNG AMERICANS SHOWED up one June afternoon at a leafy college campus in Oxford, Ohio. They were there to launch the Mississippi Summer Project, and they came in two distinct groups.

The first group was mostly white, from states such as California, Massachusetts, and Illinois. Most had just finished a year of college. Many came from top universities. They piled out of cars with guitars slung over their shoulders, wearing the fashions of 1964—polo shirts and slacks for men, capri pants and sleeveless blouses for women. They found their way to dorms, met their roommates, and settled in to learn about the daring summer ahead.

After one week of intensive training, volunteers bid tearful goodbyes and headed south, 1964.

The second group was mostly black. They wore denim overalls and white T-shirts. Some had buttons showing a black hand clasping a white one over the letters SNCC (pronounced "Snick"). They were members of the Student Nonviolent Coordinating Committee, the organizers of the project. And although most of them were the same age as the students they had come to train, they shared no college stories. Instead, they arrived with stories of being beaten and tortured. This group had come from Mississippi.

Different as they were, the two groups shared the same goal: to help bring freedom and racial justice to a state where African Americans were oppressed. Getting to know, understand, and trust each other was the first of many challenges that they would face. They had six days to do it before getting on the buses that would carry them south to Mississippi.

United in Song

First page of memo to volunteer workers accepted to the Mississippi Summer Project, from Bob Moses, director of Council of Federated Organizations (COFO), 1964.

That evening in the dining hall, the students talked about their hopes for the summer. Most of them had been in grade school during the Montgomery bus boycott of 1955–56, when

To: Mississippi Summer Project Workers

From: Mississippi Summer Project Committee

1) We hope you are making preparations to have bond money
ready in the event of your arrest. Bond money for a single
arrest usually runs around $500. We shall assume that the
first person listed on your application as the person to
notify for your bond will be the best person to contact in
the event of your arrest.

2) There will be a series of orientation periods starting
in mid-June and running until the beginning of July at
Berea College. People will be staggered over three sessions,
each lasting about four days.

3) After July 1 there will be a series of summer long orientation sessions held at Mount Beaulah in Edwards, Mississippi.
We expect all summer workers to go through some orientation
period before going into the field.

4) A conference was held the weekend of March 21-22 at which
various civil rights people and educators gathered in New
York to work out a detailed curriculum for the Freedom Schools.
The conference broke into small working groups which discussed
the various Freedom School programs -- remedial instruction,
leadership training, cultural activities, etc. At present
various people are pulling together the results of their
sessions and sending reports to the Jackson office. By the
end of April we hope to be able to put together a compre-
hensive and detailed curriculum with working suggestions
which will be circulated to all those who are being assigned
to work in Freedom Schools this summer.

5) We are presently in a very critical financial condition.
We are trying to run a number of very important programs
this spring and at the same time we are preparing for this
summer. We are running three congressional campaigns as
well as a senatorial campaign and conducting a Freedom
Registration program -- in which we hope to register 400,000
Negroes on our own registration books -- and building a
grass-roots foundation for our delegation to the Democratic
National Convention to challenge the regular all-white party
delegation. Believe it or not, at the moment we are absolutely broke. Our workers go without eating and our bills
are piling up. While two years ago this would not have cut
seriously into our program, at the present time we can no
longer operate for extended periods without funds -- e.g.
we need money for office rent, phone, office supplies,

Dr. Staughton Lynd, director of the Mississippi Freedom Schools,
lecturing to an audience of Freedom School teachers during the
second SNCC orientation session held at Western College for
Women in Oxford, Ohio, between June 22 and 27, 1964.

African Americans in that Alabama city stopped riding buses to protest the rules that forced black passengers to give up their seats to whites. The students had been a bit older when federal troops desegregated a high school in Little Rock, Arkansas. They had been in high school when blacks and whites desegregated lunch counters across the South by sitting side by side. And just in the last year, they had seen TV images of attack dogs and fire hoses tearing into African Americans in Birmingham, Alabama.

Few of the students knew anything about the South. One later wrote, "At Oxford, my mental picture of Mississippi contained nothing but an unending series of swamps, bayous, and dark, lonely roads." Few of them had seen a pickup truck with a gun rack, or been in jail, or heard a shotgun blast echo and die in the darkness.

To help them, the SNCC group had a simple plan—to tell the truth. The Mississippi Summer Project was a death-defying roll of the dice. The SNCC trainers felt it was their duty to turn the innocent idealists into worried, even terrified realists. But only after singing.

The day ended with the volunteers standing in the cool twilight beside a circle of trees. There they learned songs of the civil rights movement, with titles such as "We Shall Overcome" and "Oh, Freedom." A stocky black woman in a flowered dress, her arms thick from a life of picking cotton, threw back her head and belted out song after song, lifting the entire group. Soon volunteers and staff were holding hands and swaying to the songs they would sing throughout Freedom Summer.

Scaring Some Sense into Them

After the singing on that first Sunday night, the SNCC staff stayed up late. Many of them were already anxious about the volunteers. These "kids" seemed naive and vulnerable. Throwing them into the hellhole of Mississippi frightened the staff members who had bruises and bullet wounds from that state.

How much should the "kids" be told? Could they understand what it was like to drive on a dark road and suddenly see headlights flash in the rearview mirror, then feel a car ramming your bumper? How would they react when a mob gathered, when a sheriff took them in, and there was no one to call for help?

SNCC field secretary Cordell Hull Reagon demonstrating non-violent self-defense procedures to volunteers seated on the grass. June 1964.

In the coming days, people with experience in Mississippi would do their best to scare some sense into the student volunteers.

Tuesday: "I may be killed and you may be killed."

Thursday: "They—the white folk, the police, the county sheriff, the state police—they are all watching for you. They are looking for you. They are ready and they are armed."

Friday: "They take you to jail, strip you, lay you on the floor and beat you until you're almost dead."

But first, on Monday, the students would hear from a white preacher—the Reverend Edwin King. He stood before the group, his jaw covered with a large white bandage. It had been shattered in a car crash when his car was run off the road near Jackson, Mississippi. Now King told the students that Mississippi was "a police state," where government, courts, newspapers, and every other social institution would stop at nothing to keep black people "in their place." He described the threats, the police brutality, the "disappearance" of black men.

After King spoke, one by one the black men of SNCC rose to speak of the terrors they had seen or endured. Volunteers who had been raised to believe "the policeman is your friend" now heard a different truth. "When you go down those cold stairs at the police station," said Willie Peacock, who had been beaten while in police custody the week before, "you don't know if you're going to come back or not." One tall SNCC staffer didn't have to say anything. There were bullet holes in his neck above his white T-shirt.

Finally, the woman who had lifted the group's singing the night before stood up. Her name was Fannie Lou Hamer. She told the students about the night a year earlier when she had been ordered away from a whites-only lunch counter. Hamer had been led to a cell and forced to lie down. Guards handed a club to one of the inmates. "That man beat me till he give out," she said. The blows had smashed her head, her back, her bare feet. Across the crowded auditorium, students looked away, hands to their mouths, holding back tears. This was Mississippi—where they would be next Sunday.

The truth about Mississippi sobered the volunteers, but their idealism was strong. "A great change is at hand," President Kennedy had told the nation in 1963 when he announced

CHRIS'S ADVENTURE BEGINS

EIGHTEEN-YEAR-OLD CHRIS WILLIAMS WAS part of the civil rights movement even before he volunteered for Mississippi. He had seen racism's face at an early age, while his family lived in Washington, D.C. After he made friends with the children of his family's African American maid, the neighbors hurled insults and racial slurs at him. Chris's family soon moved north, but he never forgot.

In early 1964, during spring break from his high school in Amherst, Massachusetts, Chris had gone to Williamston, North Carolina, to join a protest outside a courthouse. Conflict erupted, and he saw a man hit with a baseball bat. Chris wasn't injured—just arrested. After three days in jail, he went home. At a civil rights rally at nearby Smith College, he heard about the Mississippi Summer Project.

Chris's parents readily gave him permission to volunteer. His father saw the summer project as a way for his son "to actually do something worthwhile." His mother was more worried. After all, civil rights activist Medgar Evers had been assassinated just the previous fall—in Mississippi. But as she told local newspapers, "American students have finally come around to support something that must be done."

Like others at the training, Chris thought he had committed to Mississippi just for the summer. He expected to start classes at the University of Pennsylvania in the fall. He did not know that in the coming months he would be shot at, smell tear gas, and meet people he would never forget, including the woman he would marry. Above all, he did not know how the summer would change him and his plans.

Freedom Summer volunteers watching a demonstration of nonviolent self-defense procedures, 1964.

his civil rights bill. "Those who do nothing are inviting shame as well as violence. Those who act boldly are recognizing rights as well as reality." Now, just seven months after Kennedy had been killed in Dallas, the volunteers had come to Oxford to act boldly.

Throughout the spring, speakers from SNCC had toured colleges across the country, recruiting those bold students. By late May, more than 700 students had volunteered to spend their summer in Mississippi. Many of them said they wanted to "honor the memory" and "carry out the legacy" of President Kennedy.

To be accepted into the program, the volunteers had to pass interviews. They were asked whether they would find it difficult to work under black leaders. Their interviewers looked for "a learning attitude toward work in Mississippi." Guidelines for interviewers warned: "A student who seems determined to carve his own niche, win publicity and glory when he returns home can only have harmful effects on the Mississippi program." For all their idealism and sincerity, dozens of volunteers failed their interviews.

Those who were accepted were divided into two groups. Canvassers would spend the summer registering voters. Teachers would run the Freedom Schools. The canvassers had arrived first in Oxford for training. The teachers would be trained the following week.

Each volunteer was told to bring $150 for expenses and $500 for bail in case of arrest. Those younger than twenty also needed the permission of their parents—which was not always easily given. "I don't see how I have any right to stop you," a mother in New York City told her son. She then went to the kitchen, did the dishes, and cried. Some younger applicants had to drop out when their parents refused to let them go. Most parents, however, could not argue with ideals that shone so brightly. As one young man wrote on his application, "I want to do my part. There is a moral wave building among today's youth and I intend to catch it!"

A Hero in Overalls

At dinner on the second night, smiles were gone. Freedom Songs were forgotten. What the students had heard that day "just scared the crap out of us," as volunteer Chris Williams put it. There was another concern, too. Throughout Tuesday's workshops on Mississippi politics, history, and geography, tensions had grown between the students and the SNCC staffers.

Some students felt lectured to. Some felt the racial divide. One said, "We don't know what it is to be a Negro, and even if we did, the Negroes here would not accept us. . . . In their eyes we're rich middle or upper-class whites who've taken a summer off to help the Negro." Yet many of the students viewed the staff from Mississippi as heroes. These volunteers shared stories about SNCC and its organizer, Ella Baker, an African American woman who had been active in civil rights since the 1930s. In 1960, after black college students had taken part in sit-ins at whites-only lunch counters, Baker forged them into SNCC. The group became a political force with chapters on college campuses across the country.

Even among daring civil rights workers, the SNCCs stood out. In 1961 seven blacks and six whites called the Freedom Riders had traveled by bus into the South, daring the federal government to enforce the laws against blacks and whites traveling together. The Riders were arrested. They were beaten by mobs. Their bus was firebombed. They gave up in Alabama, but SNCCs came forward to continue the ride into Mississippi, where they were thrown into the state prison.

SNCCs saw themselves as organizers, not leaders. Their goal was to help local people overcome their fears and work for the civil rights movement in their own communities. No SNCC member was more important than any other. All decisions were made by agreement hammered out in meetings that seemed to last for days. But although every student volunteer being trained at Oxford knew of Martin Luther King Jr., head of the Southern Christian Leadership Conference (SCLC), a leading civil rights group, few of the students recognized the SNCCs in their midst.

Many of those SNCC staffers would become legends of the civil rights movement. One of them, a shy farm laborer's son from Alabama named John Lewis, was SNCC's chairman. He would later serve in Congress. Even in this remarkable group, however, one SNCC stood out, no matter how hard he tried not to.

Bob Moses was a small man with thick glasses and overalls. He walked slowly and spoke softly. Moses had grown up in Harlem, a black section of New York City. Scholarships had taken him all the way to Harvard, where he earned a master's degree. After his mother died and his father got sick, he left Harvard so he could work to support his family. In 1960, inspired by a newspaper photo of four black men at an all-white lunch counter in North Carolina, Moses dedicated himself to the civil rights movement. "They were kids my age," he later said about those four men, "and I knew this had something to do with my own life."

In Atlanta, Georgia, Moses worked for King's SCLC. He then volunteered for a SNCC project in Mississippi. It was 1960, a time when no other Civil Rights leaders dared to work in Mississippi, but Bob Moses volunteered to go there. Alone. There he met Amzie Moore, a gas-station owner who was an organizer for the National Association for the Advancement of Colored People (NAACP). From Moore, Moses learned that lunch counter sit-ins could not fix everything. Voting, Moore said, was the key to change in Mississippi. Yet even the smallest campaigns to register African Americans to vote had sparked shattering violence from hostile whites. Moses noticed that Moore kept a loaded rifle by his side.

By the summer of 1961, Bob Moses was back in Mississippi, where he would spend nearly four years. His work to register black voters gained him the top spot on a Ku Klux Klan hit list. One hot afternoon in Liberty, Mississippi, Moses was leading blacks to the courthouse to register. Suddenly a man jumped on him and pounded his head with a knife handle. With blood streaming down his forehead, Moses calmly got up and led his group into the courthouse. He survived the attack. Other civil rights workers were not so lucky.

Herbert Lee was a black farmer who had taken the risk of driving Moses around Amite County, talking to black Mississippians about their right to vote. On September 25, 1961, on a dusty back road, Lee was murdered by a shot to the head. His killer, a white man named E.H. Hurst whom Lee had known since they played together as boys, was a state legislator. At his trial, Hurst said that Lee had threatened him with a tire iron and that his gun had gone off by accident. He was found not guilty. At Lee's funeral, his widow had screamed at Moses, "You killed my husband!"

The killing of Lee tormented Bob Moses— and it wasn't the only one. Moses and other organizers had found a witness to Lee's murder. A logger named Louis Allen swore that there had been no tire iron, and that Hurst had shot Lee in cold blood. Local whites had threatened Allen to keep his story quiet, but he told the truth to the FBI, which did not offer to protect him. When word leaked out of what Allen knew, his business suffered. A sheriff broke his jaw. Allen finally decided to leave Mississippi. On January 31, 1964, just hours before he was going to go, he was shot to death in his driveway.

"For me, it was as if everything had come full circle," Moses said. "I had started in Amite County, unable to offer protection or force the federal government to provide it. Herbert Lee had been killed; Louis Allen had witnessed it and now he was dead." After Lee's murder in 1961, the only thing the brand-new SNCC could do was "dedicate our lives to what we were doing," Moses said. "But Louis Allen's murder

Civil rights legend Bob Moses, the
architect of Freedom Summer, inspired
volunteers with his courage and calm
throughout the summer.

happened at a moment in history when we had another option."

That option was the Mississippi Summer Project.

Whose Idea Was This?

No one knows for sure who dreamed up Freedom Summer. Some say it was Bob Moses. Other say it was Allard Lowenstein, a white college professor and political activist. After Lowenstein brought students from Stanford and Yale to the Freedom Election in Mississippi in the fall of 1963, he suggested bringing more young white activists into the state the following summer. But everyone agrees that if Bob Moses hadn't wanted Freedom Summer to happen, it wouldn't have happened.

It almost didn't happen. SNCC debated the idea for months in late 1963. Stokely Carmichael, a SNCC Freedom Rider and voting-rights activist who would later create the Black Power movement, called the idea of bringing a lot of white college kids into Mississippi "either an act of madness or a daring stroke of genius." Many SNCCs who carried scars from working in Mississippi felt that *they* should have the

claim to any progress the state might make.
They also worried about how local people
would react. People who lived in Mississippi
had been encouraged to take up the fight. As
one organizer put it, "bringing a large number
down from the North would snatch the rug
right out from under the people in the local
communities."

Race was an issue, too. Some SNCCs wanted
to limit white involvement. They feared the white
college students might take over the movement,
or cause trouble for it. One SNCC worker said,
"We've got too much to lose if they come down
here and create a disturbance in two or three
months, and they're gone." Not everyone agreed.
Fannie Lou Hamer said, "If we are trying to
break down the barrier of segregation, we can't
segregate ourselves." Bob Moses felt the same
way. Blacks and whites had to join together to
show that civil rights was more than a question
of skin color.

The debate within SNCC continued. In late
January 1964, another meeting ended in a
deadlock, with no decision about the summer
project. Then Louis Allen was murdered.
Bob Moses threw his full support behind the

summer project, and the deadlock was broken. The summer project was on. Now SNCC needed volunteers and help to make it happen.

The volunteers came from college campuses across the country. The help came in many forms. SNCC took out a full-page ad in the *New York Times* to tell people about the project, hoping to raise $200,000 to pay for it. Donations poured in (and so did some hate mail). Famous African Americans, including comedian and activist Dick Gregory and author James Baldwin, helped raise funds. People, schools, and organizations sent office supplies, equipment such as typewriters, and books for the Freedom Houses. A New Hampshire woman sent forty-five boxes of her history books and magazines, along with two dollars and an apology: "I'm sorry it isn't more but a relatively poor schoolteacher doesn't have too much."

By June, money had come in and been spent. Books were stacked up, ready to fill Freedom Schools. Dozens of beat-up old cars and a handful of new ones stood ready to drive volunteers around the state. SNCC and two other civil rights organizations—the Congress of Racial Equality (CORE) and the Council of

Federated Organizations (COFO)—had divided up responsibilities. And in spite of threats, hundreds of black Mississippians had agreed to open their homes to the volunteers. Was there anything left to be done, anything that could keep volunteers safe?

On a sweltering evening in Atlanta, Georgia, not long before the first volunteers were scheduled to arrive at the training center in Ohio, two dozen SNCCs crammed into a basement for a final meeting to discuss the looming summer.

Faces around the table were anxious and worn. The summer project was far scarier than anything SNCC had ever dared. What might go wrong? For more than an hour, the group argued over whether SNCC should stick to the "nonviolent" part of its name. At least one SNCC office had acquired a few guns. Some people claimed that the time had come to fight back when offices had been firebombed or sprayed with bullets. Then Prathia Hall, who had been jailed many times and shot once, rose to speak. "When the kids in Birmingham were killed," she said, "I wanted to pick up a gun until I realized that by destroying lives we don't preserve them."

In the end, they agreed that no SNCCs would be armed that summer.

Eleven days later, on the first day of summer, the first volunteers were welcomed in Oxford. When they heard Bob Moses speak, they began to understand what lay ahead of them.

"Flash Point"

Bob Moses broke all the rules of speech-making. He looked at his feet, he never smiled, he rarely told stories. Yet like all genuine leaders, he spoke with a truth that held everyone's attention. He gave the volunteers a dose of reality:

> Don't come to Mississippi this summer
> to save the Mississippi Negro. Only come
> if you understand, really understand, that
> his freedom and yours are one. Maybe
> we're not going to get very many people
> registered this summer. Maybe, even,
> we're not going to get very many people
> into Freedom Schools. Maybe all we're
> going to do is live through the summer.
> In Mississippi, that will be so much.

The staff was already worried about the students. The young people seemed studious in classes on subjects like the history of slavery.

They dutifully read SNCC's security handbook, which warned them, "Try not to sleep near open windows" and "No one should go anywhere alone." Afterward, though, they strummed guitars and played touch football. The SNCCs felt that the volunteers just weren't "getting it."

The breaking point came on the night staff and students watched a documentary. As the film showed how Mississippi had defied the U.S. Constitution by crushing the black vote, the students watched with anger and disgust. Then the documentary focused on a white official—a registrar, responsible for registering voters in his country, who had never registered a black voter until he was hit by a lawsuit. The image that appeared on the screen was of an extremely fat man, and laughter rippled through the audience. The audience quieted as a black man told how a shotgun fired into his home had wounded his two little girls, but when his wife came on in a funny hat, some giggled.

Several SNCCs stormed out. When the documentary ended, another SNCC jumped on the stage and yelled, "You should be ashamed! You could laugh at that film!"

"The flash point," as one volunteer called it,

had arrived. A few volunteers rose and broke the silence. They called the SNCC staffers distant and arrogant, acting superior to anyone who had not shared their suffering. A SNCC answered by talking about that fat registrar. Hundreds of activists had marched to protest him. Bob Moses was arrested and another marcher was beaten in jail. And here these kids were, safe in Ohio, laughing. Another SNCC declared, "If you don't get scared, pack up and get the hell out of here because we don't need any people who don't know what they're doing."

The confrontation went on until two in the morning. When it was over, everyone joined hands and sang. Volunteers slowly filed back to their dorms. The SNCCs stayed up late, talking. They were more worried than ever. But one volunteer, crying as he wrote home, said, "The crisis is past, I think."

Wednesday brought a debate between the Reverend James Lawson, who had written SNCC's statement on nonviolence, and Stokely Carmichael, who would later take SNCC toward Black Power, a movement that shared the civil rights movement's goal of racial equality but that had some members who believed that violence was occasionally necessary to achieve that goal. Carmichael said that nonviolence had once worked but was now useless against vicious racists. Lawson urged nonviolence, but he admitted that it had a price. "When you turn the other cheek," he said, "you must accept the fact that you will get clobbered on it." Bob Zellner of Alabama, a white man who had been brutally attacked for taking part in a peaceful protest with African Americans, told the group, "You must understand that nonviolence is essential to our program this summer. If you can't accept this, please don't come with us."

After lunch, the volunteers learned how to take a beating: how to fall, roll in a ball, and absorb the blows. Staffers showed the volunteers hate mail that had come to the campus. The letters called the students "morally rotten outcasts of the White race" and worse.

On Thursday, the volunteers learned of their legal rights—and how little these would mean in Mississippi. They were told not to argue about rights with the sheriffs, cops, and highway patrolmen of Mississippi, who already had their names and descriptions. "Go to jail and wait for your lawyer," they were told.

MURIEL'S NEXT STEP

MURIEL TILLINGHAST, A BLACK VOLUNTEER
from Washington, D.C., already knew what it was
like to stand up for her beliefs. As a sophomore
in high school, she had been part of the first
class to integrate her school, facing down the
hatred of the principal and student body. She had
just graduated from Howard University, where
she had been active in the school's Non-Violent
Action Group (NAG), a campus organization
that campaigned against segregation and racial
injustice. Muriel and other NAG marchers,
including Stokely Carmichael, had been tear-
gassed by the National Guard at a protest march
in Maryland. Now she wondered if she was ready
for Mississippi.

Once, on a visit to Florida, Muriel had been warned not to touch the clothes in department stores, and *never* to try them on. She knew that in the Deep South she would face more severe racial bigotry. From telephone conversations with Charlie Cobb, a SNCC friend in Mississippi, she knew that the daily job of civil rights workers there was "mostly staying alive." Muriel's mother had taught school in Mississippi and was "beside herself" over her daughter's decision to join the summer project.

For Muriel, though, the summer project was the next logical step. When NAG members left Washington for Ohio and the training program, Muriel was on the bus. At Oxford, she was

Freedom School teachers listening to a lecture given in a theater during the second SNCC Orientation Session at Western College for Women in Oxford, Ohio, June 22–27, 1964.

treated as a SNCC staffer because of her NAG experience. At meetings she soaked up survival tips for black people in Mississippi. She learned to walk at a slow rural pace that did not draw attention. She learned how to organize small, quarreling communities into armies united to fight together for their goals.

Horror stories from the SNCCs made Muriel realize that "some of us were not going to come back," but she tried not to think about that. Courage had nothing to do with it. "These were my friends," she said, "and they were going and I was going with them."

The next day the volunteers heard from John Doar, an assistant attorney general for civil rights in the Department of Justice. Doar had filed lawsuits against the fat registrar and had worked closely with Bob Moses. Now he had to tell the young people that the federal government would do nothing to help them during the summer. He said, "The responsibility for protection is that of the local police." This left the volunteers feeling more vulnerable than ever.

Decisions and Departures

The media swarmed over the campus as the training week drew to a close. The final workshops unfolded in front of TV cameras. College kids venturing into the perils of Mississippi to work for racial equality made a hot news story. Again and again, volunteers were interviewed: "Are you scared?" "Do you really think it will do any good?"

One volunteer explained why he was going: "Part of it is the American dream, you know, and part of it is shame. I feel a very real sense of guilt." Another said, "The injustices to the Negro in Mississippi are also an infringement upon my rights." The newspapers alerted the country that

Mississippi was in for "a long, hot summer" and "a racial explosion."

Chris Williams wrote to his family in Massachusetts:

> Dear People at home in the Safe, Safe North,
> Mississippi is going to be hell this summer. We are going into the very hard-core of segregation and White Supremacy. . . . I'd venture to say that every member of the Mississippi staff has been beat up at least once and he who has not been shot at is rare. It is impossible for you to imagine what we are going into, as it is for me now, but I'm beginning to see. . . .

On the last night, the singing began after dinner. Crossing arms and holding hands, the volunteers sang songs of jail, protest, and endurance. Between songs they shared news just announced on the radio: the Senate had passed a civil rights bill. When the president signed it into law, the South would be forced to end segregation—and the volunteers would be in Mississippi to see history happen. It would not happen easily, though. In the small hours

Photograph taken from the inside of a bus which was preparing to leave Oxford, Ohio, to go to Mississippi on June 27, 1964. Volunteers and COFO staff outside the buses sang freedom songs to those about to leave for Mississippi.

of the morning, three men—two trainers and a volunteer—left the training session and headed south to investigate disturbing news that had just arrived. A black church in Neshoba County, Mississippi, set to host a Freedom School, had been burned. No one saw the three men go, but the world would soon learn their names.

Saturday brought packing, lunch, and long goodbyes. Volunteers piled their bags and guitars into two rattletrap buses and crammed into their seats. Some of them leaned out the windows to clasp hands with the SNCCs who were staying to train the next group. Others just stared blankly, eyes straight ahead.

The buses pulled away. In Cincinnati, at the southern border of Ohio, the riders changed buses while singing "Freedom Train." They ate dinner in Louisville, Kentucky, then drove through the warm night toward Memphis, Tennessee, just across the border from Mississippi. Chris Williams fell asleep. Muriel Tillinghast was wide awake. Her self-confidence and her take-charge spirit were starting to dry up. In the black southern night, she felt fear mounting.

Muriel's bus was still rocking with song as it left Memphis. But she later recalled, "We hit the Mississippi state line at midnight, and the bus went silent. There was no turning back now." Peering through the bus windows, volunteers spotted a Welcome to Mississippi billboard. Beyond it stood several highway patrol cars.

CHAPTER 2

THE PAST IS
"NOT EVEN PAST"

ON A SPRING DAY IN '61, CONFEDERATE TROOPS
marched through downtown Jackson, the capital
of Mississippi. Five thousand proud Rebels,
rifles on their shoulders, tramped along the
streets. Brass bands played "Dixie." Crowds sang
along. Women in long dresses blew kisses from
beneath parasols. Boys stared at the officers on
horseback and the glint of bayonets. Everywhere
waved the flag of the Confederate States of
America, the Southern states that had torn
themselves out of the Union.

The parade lasted for hours—then everyone
got in their cars and went home. This celebration
of the Confederacy took place in 1961, a century
after the Confederate states left the Union and
launched the Civil War.

Unveiling of
Confederate
monument
in Carrollton,
Mississppi.
December 1, 1905.

The South celebrated and fondly remembered the Civil War. Eighty-three years after the war ended, American author William Faulkner wrote, "The past is never dead. It's not even past." Faulkner grew up in Mississippi. There the Civil War—which southerners often called the War for Southern Independence—was woven into the fabric of life. A hundred years after the war, Freedom Summer would be shaped by a past that lived on in Mississippi.

A State Driven to Its Knees

The South remembered the Civil War differently than the North. In the North, the war was remembered as a tragic but great victory. The South remembered its shattering defeat as a noble lost cause.

The war had seen Mississippi invaded, occupied, and driven to its knees. From the moment troops from the North crossed the state border in 1862, Mississippi had suffered. It was the first Confederate state to be looted and burned, the first to see its capital city destroyed.

Then came the siege of Vicksburg. Union armies surrounded the town. Its people burrowed into caves and survived by eating dogs and rats. After forty-eight days Vicksburg fell, and total war swept across the land. The troops of Union general William Tecumseh Sherman burned mansions and cotton fields. After tearing up a town called Meridian, Sherman boasted that the town no longer existed. Union gunboats patrolled Mississippi's rivers. Railroad stations were piled with rotting corpses.

Before the war, Mississippi had been America's fifth-richest state, although much of its wealth was measured in muscle—the value of 436,631 enslaved blacks, who made up more than half the state's population. After the war, Mississippi became the nation's poorest state. It has been the poorest ever since. Rising from the ashes of destruction, Mississippians made a vow *never* to forget.

A Long and Savage Struggle

For the South, the battles of the Civil War were brief compared with the struggle afterward. During the war, President Abraham Lincoln had signed the Emancipation Proclamation, which officially freed the people who were held as slaves in the Confederate states, although true freedom did not come until the Confederacy was

LIFE AND LIMB

ON JULY 4, 1863, THE SAME DAY VICKSBURG
fell, terrible news reached Mississippi from
Pennsylvania. The proud Mississippi Greys, 103
students from the state university, had led a
charge against a Union position in the Battle of
Gettysburg. Every last one of the Greys had been
killed in the doomed maneuver that came to be
called Pickett's Charge.

When the Civil War was over, Mississippi had achieved another first. Of the state's 78,000 soldiers, 28,000 had died and 31,000 were wounded. No state in the North or the South had a higher casualty rate relative to its total population. In 1866, the year after the war ended, one-third of Mississippi's budget was spent on artificial limbs for the soldiers who had been maimed during the conflict.

The Siege of Vicksburg. Print shows officers in the foreground standing near trees and bushes observing an explosion on the upper right, possibly at the Confederate Fort Hill, during a bombardment of the Union encampment and earthworks outside Vicksburg, Mississippi, with other Confederate earthworks along a ridge in the background.

defeated. When the war itself ended in 1865, the Union started enforcing new federal laws across the South. This meant that African Americans were now citizens. They could go to school, vote, serve on juries, and hold public office.

The federal government sent troops south to enforce these laws and to oversee local and state elections. Federal agencies gave land and other aid to former slaves. This period after the war was called Reconstruction. To the North, it was necessary to reconstruct, or rebuild, the shattered South—not just its buildings and economy, but also its politics and society. But to Southerners, Reconstruction was an occupation by an enemy force. It was something to be resisted, violently, if necessary.

Just as Mississippi had led the South in war casualties, it led in resistance. From simple election fraud to a full-blown race war, Mississippi's actions after the Civil War stained U.S. democracy all the way to Freedom Summer a century later.

Four months after the fighting stopped, Mississippi presented a new state constitution, which it had to do in order to rejoin the Union. This hastily written document was coupled with new state laws called "Black Codes." They worked to deny true citizenship to the freed slaves. The U.S. Congress was not fooled. Mississippi was refused statehood. It was occupied as a military district until 1870, when it finally became a state again after adopting a constitution that granted the vote to all male citizens, whatever their race.

With former slaves voting freely, Mississippi sent America's first black senator to Washington, D.C. Freed African Americans never controlled the state's politics, but they did hold office as mayor, police chief, sheriff, judge, and even secretary of state. At one point, nearly half the state legislature was black. In less than a decade, the social system of an entire state had been overturned.

But it would not last. Southern whites would soon undo the racial progress of Reconstruction with what they called "redemption." They fought now to "redeem" the South, which to them meant restoring the honor they believed they had lost. In Mississippi, redemption began in 1871 when members of a new vigilante group called the Ku Klux Klan turned the streets of Meridian into a shooting gallery. After Klansmen killed two black politicians, whites roamed the countryside, hunting Negroes and killing them in the public murders known as lynchings. They killed thirty people before federal troops arrived. Seven hundred Mississippi Klansmen were charged with crimes, but rebellion went beyond the Klan. Mississippi's remote jungle landscape gave it a Wild West lawlessness. For a few years, raw violence "redeemed" the state.

The conflict built up to the Second Battle of Vicksburg, which started on the Fourth of July in 1874. Enraged by an interracial marriage, whites took over the town and hunted down terrified blacks. When elections were held the next month, terror kept blacks from voting. Whites ruled.

The election year of 1875 became a campaign to slaughter democracy. Fierce fighting between blacks and whites broke out in town after town across Mississippi. The governor, a former Union officer, begged President Ulysses S. Grant to send more federal troops. Grant said no. "The whole public are tired out with these annual, autumnal outbreaks in the South," the president wrote back. He added that the majority of Americans now disapproved of federal "interference" in the affairs of the South.

Like Lincoln, Grant was a Republican, a member of the party that had stood for the end of slavery and for black civil rights. Yet some Northern Republicans were growing weary of the violence in the former Confederacy. Meanwhile, many Southern whites supported the Democratic party, which before the war had nominated some pro-slavery candidates to office. After the war, Southern resentment against Reconstruction and Republicans helped the Democratic party gain power in the South and hold it for nearly a century.

On Election Day in 1875, the shotgun, the noose, and the mob ended black political power in Mississippi. The state's new leaders drove the governor out of office and out of the state. He said sadly that Mississippi's blacks, so recently freed and given citizenship, would be returned to "an era of second slavery."

Over the next two years, inspired by Mississippi, other Southern states wore down the Northern will to fight for the Negro. The federal government removed its troops—and its protections—from the South. By 1877, Reconstruction was over. It was seen as a mistake by everyone but the ex-slaves. They had tasted political power, only to have it stolen.

The Jim Crow Years

In 1890, Mississippi adopted a new state constitution. It ended black voting through the use of special taxes called poll taxes, and also literacy tests, which meant that voters had to be able to read and write. These barriers to voting were fully supported by the U.S. Supreme Court. The poll tax and literacy test officially applied to white voters, too, but whites were almost never tested or asked to pay the tax.

By 1900, Mississippi had the nation's highest percentage of African Americans: 62 percent of its people. Yet the state had not one black elected official. Meanwhile, 90 percent of black Mississippians were kept in the "era of second slavery" by the sharecropping system. Under this system, former slaves picked cotton for white bosses, while falling into debt for things they needed to live and farm, such as food, seeds, and equipment.

The decades after Reconstruction are known as the Jim Crow era. The name was a mocking term for a black man, but it came to refer to a

A black man enters
a segregated movie
theater in Belzoni,
Mississippi, 1939.

whole set of laws that enforced the separation of the races. At every level of life, blacks were held down and kept out, from the all-white university to the "Whites Only" signs on restaurants, railroad cars, hotels, and water fountains. Customs enforced racial segregation, too. Blacks were expected to step off the sidewalk as a white approached. Whites called grown black men "boy" and called women by their first names, never Miss or Mrs. Racial insults and slurs were part of everyday speech.

For generations, the descendants of Confederates and of slaves lived segregated but strangely intertwined lives in Mississippi. White folks had their side of town. They had nicer homes, cars, shopping trips to Memphis or New Orleans. Black folks had their side of town and what little they could scrape together: a few barnyard animals, perhaps a mule, and dresses made out of flour sacks. Many lived in shacks barely big enough for two people, let alone the eight or ten that might be crammed inside. Life in white Mississippi was social, based on family and the comradeship of hunting trips and formal dances. Life in black Mississippi was more hopeless than anywhere else in America.

Cotton hoers move
from one field across
the highway to
another. Mississippi
Delta, 1937.

"THE TRAGIC ERA"

AS JIM CROW TOOK HOLD, HISTORIANS created a new vision of Reconstruction that favored the South.

New images of the South appeared in the decades on either side of 1900. One example was minstrel shows. These popular entertainments were based on caricatures of black people as foolish and clumsy. At the same time, songs such as "Carry Me Back to Old Virginny" were full of nostalgic affection for the "Old South" of plantations and slavery. Those decades also saw many lynchings of African Americans, often by hanging or burning.

The Southern myths about Reconstruction spread nationwide. Suddenly, it seemed, the North agreed with the South. The freed slaves

had been lazy, greedy politicians, and the Ku Klux Klansmen were liberators. Popular books such as *The Clansman* (1905) and *The Negro: A Menace to American Civilization* (1907) sold white supremacy to the whole United States. In 1900, the *New York Times* said that Northerners no longer criticized the South for keeping blacks from voting. Instead, said the *Times*, Northerners understood that "the supreme law of self-preservation" had led white Southerners to block African American voters.

In this climate, Reconstruction—once seen as the beginning of racial equality in the South—soon became known as "the Tragic Era." In 1929, a Democratic politician published a history with that title. It became a nationwide bestseller. *The Tragic Era* told of "the darkest days

Confederate veterans' reunion, 1917.

in Mississippi," when a "mulatto was Speaker of the House, a darker man was Lt. Governor." In this revised view of history, the Ku Klux Klan had heroically ridden to the rescue, protecting "women, property, civilization itself." The popular 1915 silent movie *Birth of a Nation* also made heroes of the Klan.

The South had been "redeemed" indeed! The new version of Reconstruction did more than just reflect the beliefs of many Southerners. It spread the myth that white Southerners were victims and that African Americans were dangerous. In this way, the "Tragic Era" version of history made the antiblack laws and practices of Jim Crow seem justified to many people in the North.

During World War I (1914–1918), Southern blacks fled north to factory jobs. Back home, a few blacks in each town inched ahead. They bought a little land, maybe opened a barber shop or a funeral home, and kept up their modest houses. But the vast majority lived like peasants in the Middle Ages, tied to the land. They worked in the cotton fields from dawn to dusk.

In the 1920s, a brilliant flourishing of African American art, jazz, and literature took place in Harlem. Down in Mississippi, far from New York, blacks on wooden porches played guitars with bottlenecks and table knives. Some people thought their music sounded like fingernails on a blackboard. To others, it was human anguish in the form of song. It came to be called the Delta blues.

By the 1930s, Atlanta was a bustling city. Birmingham was a center of steel production. But Mississippi remained a state of small rural towns surrounded by backwoods and linked by dirt roads. To "outsiders" riding the train through the Mississippi Delta, it seemed that the twentieth century had not arrived. Even into the 1940s, sprawling plantations were tended by black workers in overalls, stuffing cotton into bulging sacks.

Halfway into the twentieth century, a journalist named W.J. Cash explored how the Civil War still shaped the thinking of the South. Southerners did not regret that their states had left the Union, or apologize for it, Cash said. Indeed, they held a romantic view of the South before the war. Slavery had not been one of the worst crimes in history. No, it was a humane system in which whites looked after blacks like firm but loving fathers. Generations later, many white Southerners still argued that blacks had been happier or better off under slavery.

Yet this same culture turned savagely on any black who offended a white person, especially a white woman, through "reckless eyeballing." Just looking at a white woman or girl could get a black man beaten—or worse. Violence against blacks was seen as noble and righteous. Murder was self-defense. Lynchings went unpunished. More than five hundred black people were lynched in Mississippi over the years, more than in any other state.

Whites who disapproved of racial violence or segregation learned to keep quiet. Any criticism of Jim Crow was seen as disloyalty. And as journalist

Cash noted, such criticism was "so dangerous that none but a madman would risk it."

Beginning to Move

For a long time, almost no one criticized Jim Crow. Most northerners considered "the Negro problem" to be a southern problem. Only a few white southerners saw it as a problem at all. "When civil rights came along," said a white woman from the Mississippi city of Natchez, "I was shocked to find black people we knew participating in the marches, because we didn't know they were unhappy." And when Freedom Summer drew draw the nation's eyes to Mississippi, many whites there would not recognize the place as outsiders saw it.

Politicians in Mississippi used race to win elections. Because many whites continued to resent the Republican party for freeing the slaves and launching Reconstruction, Mississippi was basically a one-party state, and that party was Democratic. U.S. Congressmen from Mississippi held their seats in the Senate or the House of Representatives for generations. These Democrats became some of the most powerful people in the nation's capital. Whenever an election was at risk, politicians drummed up support by playing on white voters' fears of black people. For example, Mississippi governor James K. Vardaman said, "The Negro is a lazy, lustful animal which no conceivable amount of training can transform into a tolerable citizen."

The bigot who followed Vardaman into power in Mississippi, Theodore G. Bilbo, was more blunt. He called on "every red-blooded American who believes in the superiority and integrity of the white race" to prevent African Americans from voting. This call to arms came in 1946—when things in Mississippi were finally starting to change for the better.

World War II (1939—1945) had just ended. Black soldiers had fought overseas for their country. Now they were home, clamoring for citizenship. Technology brought change, too. The first mechanical cotton picker had recently been demonstrated on a plantation in the Mississippi Delta. It was much cheaper to pick cotton with the machine than by hand. In ten years, machines had replaced 315,000 black workers. Most headed north to states such as Michigan, Illinois, and Pennsylvania. Mississippi's racial tensions cooled a bit.

At the same time, a new generation of black leaders was speaking out. Small chapters of the NAACP started meeting in churches. Several thousand Negroes registered to vote, and no one shot into their houses. Lynching seemed to have stopped. "Segregation will never end in my lifetime, of course," people said, "but my children will see its end."

Then, on May 17, 1954, the entire South was "shocked and stunned," in the words of Mississippi's governor. The U.S. Supreme Court had just delivered its ruling in the case *Brown v. the Board of Education of Topeka, Kansas*. This landmark decision said that black and white schoolchildren could no longer be sent to "separate but equal" public schools "solely because of their race." It was the legal end of segregated public education. Racially integrated schools were on the horizon. This was too much change. The South locked down in resistance.

Leading planters, lawyers, and businessmen in the Mississippi Delta formed a White Citizens' Council. It declared, "We will not be

integrated! We are proud of our white blood and our white heritage." Similar councils sprang up throughout the state and across the South.

The Citizens' Councils were sometimes called "the uptown Klan." They did not use the night rides, white robes, and burning crosses of the KKK. Instead, they spread propaganda and rumors about black people. They also carried out economic warfare against blacks who dared to register to vote, who joined the NAACP, or who called for schools to be integrated. These African Americans soon found their credit cut off, their taxes audited, or their insurance canceled. And then the phone threats started. Blacks who kept doing what whites thought they shouldn't were handled by citizens who were less "uptown."

The poor whites of Mississippi stayed one rung up from the bottom of the social ladder by beating down the blacks below them. Shunned by better-off whites, these "rednecks" carved out an existence in shacks and hovels. Their bottled-up rage could easily explode when blacks tried to climb the ladder.

George Lee was a minister who had urged his fellow African Americans to vote. One day in May 1955, as Lee drove through Belzoni,

White Citizens Council sign on highway entering Jackson, 1964. Someone has altered the sign. "Racial Integrity" now reads "Racial Integration."

A NEW INVADER

KEEPING OLD WAYS ALIVE WAS HARDER IN
the 1960s than it had once been. A new invader
threatened to spread northern ideas about
integration. That invader was television.

In those years before cable TV, most
Mississippi towns had just one or two TV stations.
It was easy to control them because of the
people who owned and managed the media. The
manager of station WLBT in Jackson, for example,
was the director of an antiblack Citizens' Council.
So were the station's owners, who also owned
Mississippi's two statewide daily newspapers.

That's why, when African American author
James Baldwin appeared on NBC's *Today*
show, he was not seen in Mississippi. The local
stations showed an old movie instead. When
NAACP lawyer Thurgood Marshall (who would
later become the first black justice on the U.S.
Supreme Court) spoke on television, station
WLBT flashed the sign "Cable Difficulty." Soon

the announcement "Sorry, Cable Trouble" was common on Mississippi televisions. News shows were often introduced with the words, "The following program is Northern-managed news."

Opposition to "northern" media sometimes reached absurd heights. In the spring of 1964, rumors spread that the hit western show *Bonanza* would feature a "Negro cow-girl." This led to a boycott of the show and its advertisers. A few months later, Mississippi's ABC stations protested a new comedy show called *Bewitched*. They claimed that a show about a man marrying a witch could be seen as "a veiled argument for interracial marriage."

If those panicked station owners and managers had been able to see into the future, they would no doubt have been astonished—and shocked— to discover that interracial friendships, romances, and marriages are an ordinary, everyday part of entertainment and advertising in the twenty-first century.

Today show, 1962.

Mississippi, a shotgun blast shattered his windshield. He died on the way to the hospital. In August, a black veteran was gunned down on a courthouse lawn. Then came the murder of Emmett Till.

Till, just fourteen years old, had come from Chicago to visit relatives. One afternoon in the town of Money, Mississippi, he was accused of flirting with a white woman in a store. No one saw the encounter, but word spread. Emmett Till was dragged from his family's home and found the next day floating in the Tallahatchie River. The jury took just over an hour to find his killers not guilty. Writer William Faulkner said, "If we in America have reached that point in our desperate culture when we must murder children, no matter for what reason or what color, we don't deserve to survive, and probably won't."

"There's open season on Negroes now," a white man had said after the Till trial. He was right. Ten more Mississippi blacks were murdered by whites within four years. No one was found guilty. But although blacks in Mississippi were living through a new reign of terror, the Emmett Till murder drove them to action. Amzie Moore, who educated Bob Moses about the state's racism, said, "From that point on, Mississippi began to move."

From the Bottom Up

Movement in Mississippi came from the bottom up. "It was the so-called dumb people," a farmer in Holmes County remembered—common laborers and farmers—who led the resistance. In town after town, the ingredients of change were simple. A few brave leaders, a chapter of the NAACP, or a place to meet were the sparks. A magazine photograph of the mangled face of murdered Emmett Till, passed from hand to hand, fanned the sparks into fire.

The state stepped in to squash black progress. New rules said that to register to vote, a citizen had to interpret part of the Mississippi constitution, a document of 285 sections. Each "interpretation" was left up to the local registrar. Blacks—even highly educated ones—routinely failed this "test." Whites rarely had to take it. The number of registered black voters in the state fell from 22,000 to 8,000.

As if getting rid of African American voters wasn't enough, Mississippi's lawmakers created a secret spy organization, the State Sovereignty Commission. It followed people, made payments to informants, tapped phones, and convinced newspaper editors to plant false stories—all to protect racial segregation. The commission used African American informers to imprison a man who tried to integrate the University of Southern Mississippi. It investigated NAACP leaders. Its reports on racial violence always blamed blacks.

Then Bob Moses and SNCC came to Mississippi. The civil rights movement finally took hold in the state. In the capital city of Jackson, black people were sitting at lunch counters, going limp as cops dragged them away. By the summer of 1962, SNCC was active in the poorest and most racially explosive spot in America—the Mississippi Delta, the northwest corner of the state, between the Mississippi and Yazoo rivers. Across the state, blacks lined up at county courthouses to register to vote. And segregationist whites felt under siege.

War at Ole Miss
Media blackouts, spies, cops cracking down, vigilantes carrying out their own form of racial justice, and Citizens' Councils pushing "right

thinking"—these turned Mississippi into "The
Closed Society." That term was coined in 1963
by James Silver, a professor at the University of
Mississippi, usually called "Ole Miss." Silver's
criticism of Mississippi's "Closed Society" made
him a target. The governor spoke out against
him. The university investigated him. He started
sleeping with a shotgun by his bed and never
drove at night.

Others at Ole Miss were harassed. The
campus director of religious life was forced to
leave. His crime? Hosting a black journalist.
Protesting the university's narrow-mindedness,
a quarter of the professors quit. Clergy felt the
same pressure. In 1963, twenty-eight Methodist
ministers signed a statement urging racial
integration of churches. Within a year, half of
them had left the state.

A few voices of reason remained. One of them
belonged to Hazel Bannon Smith, publisher
of a newspaper called the *Lexington Advertiser*.
Smith waged a one-woman campaign against
the Citizens' Councils and the Sovereignty
Commission. She said:

> Today we live in fear in Holmes County
> and in Mississippi. It hangs like a

dark cloud over us dominating every facet of public and private life. None speaks freely without fear of being misunderstood. Almost every man and woman is afraid to try to do anything to promote good will and harmony between the races.

The people of Smith's small town shunned her. Advertisers stopped buying space in her paper. Her husband lost his job. Yet Smith kept speaking up, and a month before Freedom Summer, she became the first woman to receive the Pulitzer Prize for editorial writing. Several other courageous newspaper publishers and editors also spoke up against racial hatred and bigotry. One of them had his house shot into and a cross burned on his lawn.

Ole Miss became a battleground in 1962, when an African American man named James Meredith prepared to enroll in the university. The news that a Negro planned to attend Ole Miss caused an uproar in Oxford, the charming old Mississippi town where the university is located. "Dixie" blared on radios. Confederate flags flew. White people from distant parts of the state poured in, armed for battle. Federal

James Meredith
walking to class
accompanied by U.S.
marshals, 1962.

marshals arrived on troop trucks to keep order.

As darkness fell on September 30, rioting erupted on campus. Bricks smashed cars and windows. Mississippi's highway patrolmen fled the scene. This enraged U.S. attorney general Robert Kennedy, who sent more federal marshals. All night the rioting continued. When it was over, two people were dead, twenty-eight shot, and hundreds wounded. Cars burned outside gutted buildings.

The next morning, federal troops escorted James Meredith through the rubble and into class. One of his fellow students said, "We hate violence, but we are determined to keep our way of life. Nobody can take it away from us, and I would die for it." In the hope of preventing anyone else from dying, federal troops stayed on the Old Miss campus for a year.

The Past Digs In

The news that reached Mississippi in March 1964 sent shudders through the state. Freedom Summer was coming.

Planners of Freedom Summer appealed for calm. Again and again, Bob Moses and others said the volunteers would not march, sit in, or protest. In a letter to all county sheriffs, SNCC said, "The project is concerned with construction, not agitation." Yet the Mississippi legislature quickly passed bills that doubled the number of state police and banned picketing, leafleting, and assembling. The State Sovereignty Commission told sheriffs and cops how to handle the incoming wave of what it called "communists, sex perverts, oddballs, and do-gooders."

The Sovereignty Commission also hired two black spies it called Informant X and Informant Y. The job of X—who attended the summer project training in Ohio—was to travel with civil rights workers and report on their activities. Y's job was to become part of the nerve center of Freedom Summer, which was the Jackson headquarters of the Council of Federated Organizations (COFO), an umbrella group of civil rights agencies. As the summer unfolded, X would file a series of dry reports, while Y would tell the Sovereignty Commission just what it wanted to hear.

By June 1964, Mississippi's past was digging in against the present. Rumors flew. Not just a few hundred but thirty thousand "invaders" were on their way! Gun shops did a brisk business. Cops took riot training. Police departments stockpiled tear gas, riot guns, and electric cattle prods. The county fairgrounds near Jackson became a holding camp big enough for thousands of prisoners. The Ku Klux Klan announced that it had 91,000 members in Mississippi and was looking for more. The atmosphere was ripe for violence.

Early one June evening, shots were fired into the COFO headquarters in Jackson. Six days later, a bomb hit a Freedom House. That same day, whites mauled three journalists, saying, "This is just a taste of what you Northern agitators will get."

On the last day of spring, as volunteers climbed aboard the buses in Ohio, Mississippi braced itself. Shortly after midnight on the first day of summer, young men and women sang as they rode buses toward the Mississippi line. When a blood-red sun rose the next day, Mississippi was again engulfed in wars that had never really ended—wars between North and South, black and white, tolerance and intolerance.

A report from "Informant X" including photos from the orientation in Oxford, Ohio.

July 26, 1964

    It has been learned that a new radio has been installed
at the Freedom House in Canton, Mississippi. It will be
remembered that the others were taken out because they did
not have enough range.

    The new radio was installed by two unknown white men.
It is a "Sonar" brand transmitter and receiver. A picture
of this radio is attached. The channels being used are
channels 2, 3, and 4.

    The antenna being used is 60 feet high and has been
disguised as a television antenna, to avoid detection.

    This antenna is located at the rear of the Freedom
House.

    Attached to this report are some still photographs
taken by the writer in Oxford, Ohio. Identification of
these photographs will be seen on the rear of each of those
where the participate can be identified.

    Also attached to this report is a schedule of the route
followed by Martin Luther King when he was in Mississippi.

    Information has been received that the boycott against
The Barq Bottling Company has been called off by Reverend
R. L. T. Smith, Rev. Whitney, Rev. Richardson and the negro
barber named Johnson.

    As mentioned previously this was done without any con-
cession being made by the Barq Company. It is understood
that this removal from the boycott list will be mentioned
at a meeting and in addition handbills will probably be
given out. As mentioned previously, the client is requested
to check with the writers office before making any direct
contact with the Barqs Company, if such contact is desired.

    Investigation will be continued.

CHAPTER 3

FREEDOM STREET

STUCK ON THE SIDE OF A HIGHWAY IN CENTRAL
Mississippi, eight students and two SNCC
staffers felt uneasy. They had just arrived—had
something already gone wrong? It was five in the
morning on June 21. They had been dropped off
on a two-lane blacktop that stretched out long,
straight, and empty through flat, green land.
The last sign had read "Batesville," but there was
no town. Someone was supposed to meet them.
No one was there.

A vacant Greyhound bus station and a
Mississippi Highway Patrol building stood on
opposite sides of the road. Nearby, a highway
patrolman sat in his car, sunglasses glinting.
One of the confused volunteers was Chris

Batesville,
Mississippi, July
1964.

85

Williams. Still bleary from the long bus ride, he found the situation "unpleasant, to say the least."

SNCC staffer Tillman McKellar took charge because he had been in Mississippi before. He walked to a phone booth at the bus station to call their contact, then returned to the highway and hitched a ride with the first black driver who passed. As McKellar drove away, the highway patrolman revved his engine, pulled the car over, and talked to McKellar and the driver. McKellar later said that the patrolman had told him that they would all wind up at the bottom of a river. Then the two cars drove away, leaving nine worried people alone by the roadside. They weren't alone for long.

Pickup trucks and souped-up hot rods roared past. Each muscle car was filled with young white men doing their best to look like Elvis Presley. Some of them just sneered. Others bellowed threats.

The volunteers were stunned. Had these people gotten up at five in the morning just to threaten them? Had they stayed up all night? The nine waited, slapping at mosquitoes. Suitcases and duffel bags were heaped beside them. Someone had better come soon.

It Seemed Possible

The nine stranded volunteers did not wait long outside Batesville. Around five-thirty an old truck pulled up. Its driver introduced himself as Mr. Miles, their contact. When the volunteers piled in, Mr. Miles pulled away. Then the highway patrolman quickly pulled the truck over and gave Robert Miles a ticket for running a stop sign that he had not run. A few minutes later the volunteers reached town and the Miles home, where they noticed bullet holes in the paneling. Rifles and shotguns stood behind the front door. Over breakfast, they started to get to know the Miles family.

Robert Miles had been a civil rights pioneer ever since he came home from World War II. He had helped start an organization that sued the county to open up voter registration. For his courage, he had seen his home shot into and a cross burned on his lawn. His wife, Mona Miles, seemed a little on edge. Soon the volunteers learned why. A town marshal had once badly beaten her niece because the girl's father, Mona's brother, belonged to the NAACP. After enduring a fiery cross outside his house and bullets blasting through it, the brother moved to Detroit.

As for Robert and Mona's two young sons, if they were startled to see white faces at their table, they just giggled.

Later, the volunteers went with the Miles family to their church, a small room filled with people wearing their "Sunday best" clothes. After the service, Robert Miles introduced the volunteers, then said to the congregation, "Y'all gonna hear a lot of different stories from white folks about what these people are and why they're down here. White folks are gonna tell you they're agitators. You know what an agitator is? An agitator is the piece in the center of a washing machine that spins around to get dirt out. Well, that's what these people are here for. They're here to get the dirt out."

Across Mississippi that day, a century of Jim Crow began its long, slow thaw. For this one day—at least until sundown—a sense of wonder drowned out fear. Host families took the volunteers around, showing them off like prized possessions. Hands waved from porches, smiling faces leaned out of windows. Children ran to the newcomers, asking their names, or stood shyly in the background.

"I've waited eighty years for you to come,"

the gray-haired son of a slave told one of the volunteers. Pressing a dollar into the white hand, the old man said, "I just have to give you this little bit to let you all know how much we appreciate your coming. I prays for your safety every night, son. God bless you all." The volunteers had been warned to expect the worst from white Mississippi. But none of the horror stories they'd heard in Ohio had prepared them for the warmth of black Mississippi on that first day. Whites walked through the black side of town, ate in black homes, introduced themselves to black churches, and sat on porches where no white person had ever sat before.

The opening day of Freedom Summer was a day like few others. Some 250 Americans had come to the poorest, most explosive state in the country. The day would end on a note of fear, but that first morning it seemed possible to believe that the barriers between black and white could be broken down at last.

Everyday Heroics

Nothing startled the volunteers as much as the poverty they saw around them. Most of them were appalled. Some were enraged. Where was

CHRIS'S FIRST DAY

VOLUNTEER CHRIS WILLIAMS WROTE HOME
that first day:

Dear People:

Greetings from Batesville, Miss.
The Freedom Riders, as we are called
by the locals, arrived here at 5 a.m. . . .
This morning as we waited to be picked
up at Batesville, we were greeted by the
police, sheriff, and members of the White
Citizens Council. One heckler told us,
"We're going to give you a hard time. . . ."
Another fellow said to his companion,
"We ought to kill these bastards right
now." However, the Negro community
assures us that this is the common bluff.
The people here are very friendly and
Panola County should be easy.

Late that afternoon, Chris and other volunteers dropped in at Batesville's two juke joints, places where African Americans gathered. Each had a soda fountain and general store in front, a dimly lit bar in back. On Saturday nights there would be live music, but it was Sunday afternoon, and even if these looked like the kind of places their parents had warned them against, Chris and the other volunteers went in. In their first stop, in a room that reeked of barbecue sauce and kerosene, they found a pool table and a jukebox with the best Rhythm & Blues selection Chris had ever seen. The volunteers were soon surrounded by dozens of people crowding in to meet "The Riders." It was shaping up to be quite a summer.

the pavement, the plumbing, the streetlights? The volunteers stayed with host families who had modest two-bedroom homes. These families seemed rich compared with those who lived in the shacks around the corner.

"There are people here without food and clothing," one volunteer wrote home. "Kids that eat a bit of bread for breakfast, chicken necks for dinner. Kids that don't have clothes to go to school in. Old old people, and young people chop cotton from sun up till sundown for $3 a day. They come home exhausted, it's not enough to feed their family on. It's gone before they earn it."

Ancient black hands that reached out to shake a white hand—for the first time—were callused or crippled. For every smiling face, another face on a distant porch was empty, broken, defeated. Some shacks had raw sewage behind them, or were propped up on cinder blocks. This was America, the volunteers had to remind themselves. Against these odds, what could they hope to do? And yet they were in Mississippi now. They had nothing else to do but try.

When the volunteers returned to their host homes, they found everyday heroics. In the town of Itta Bena, in the heart of the Delta, two young men marveled at their hostess, Rosa Lee Williams. She was sixty-seven years old and lived alone beside the railroad tracks that ran along Freedom Street. Limping on a leg that had been broken and badly set long ago, Williams was "a fiery and fast moving old woman." She had lost her children in a flu epidemic in 1918. Later she lost her husband. She had retired from her work as a midwife. Still she kept a spotless house, constantly sweeping the dust stirred up by passing trains.

The volunteers would get used to Mississippi sooner than black Mississippi would get used to them. College students would sit at tables piled with fried chicken, collards, even "chitlins" (spicy pig intestines) and eat their fill. They would go to the bathroom in outhouses and plunge their legs into buckets of gasoline to kill the nasty biting insects called chiggers. They would take evening "showers" out back with buckets of cold water, and wake to the sounds of roosters and barking dogs. They wouldn't complain . . . much. But on that first Sunday, everything was new, exciting, something to write home about.

"Not at Night"

Evening came late that day, the longest day
of the year. Finally adults rose from porches.
Children were called home from their games.
Fear crept over the volunteers' host homes and
over their souls. Night had come to Mississippi.
It was darker and warmer than any night the
volunteers had seen, loud with the booming of
bullfrogs and the hum of crickets.

Night had a reputation in Mississippi.
Volunteers had heard a lot about it, and none
of what they heard was comforting. Night
was when "things happened" here, when
riders in pickup trucks spread terror in the
darkness. SNCC's handbook was clear: "Do
not stand in doorways *at night*. . . . No one
should go anywhere alone, but certainly not in
an automobile and certainly not *at night*." The
volunteers were not likely to break these rules,
but the Mississippi night could easily enter their
"safe" host homes from the pitch-black streets.
Just by being in a home, the volunteer put a
bull's-eye on it. The people who'd welcomed
them during the day left the streets at night.
What other people were out, fired by century-old
rage?

Security Handbook.

SECUEITY HANDBOOK Orientation for Workers Summer, 1964

1. Communications personnel will act as security officers.

2. <u>Travel</u>

a. When persons leave their project, they <u>must</u> call their project person to person for <u>themselves</u> on arrival at destination point. Should they be missing, project personnel will notify the Jackson office. WATS line operators will call each project every day at dinnertime or thereabouts, and should be notified of changes in personnel, transfers, etc. (If trips are planned in advance, this information can go to Jackson by mail. Phone should be used only where there is no time. Care should be taken at all times to avoid, if possible, full names of persons travelling.) Checklists should be used in local projects for personnel to check in and out.

b. Doors of cars should be locked at all times. At night, windows should be rolled up as much as possible. Gas tanks must have locks and be kept locked. Hoods should also be locked.

c. No one should go <u>anywhere</u> alone, but certainly not in an automobile, and certainly not at night.

d. Travel at night should be avoided unless absolutely necessary.

e. Remove all unnecessary objects from your car which could be construed as weapons. (Hammers, files, iron rules, etc.) Absolutely no__ liquor bottles, beer cans, etc. should be inside your car. Do not travel with names and addresses of local contacts.

f. Know all roads in and out of town. Study the county map.

g. Know locations of sanctuaries and safe homes in the county.

h. When getting out of a car at night, make sure the car's inside light is out.

i. Be conscious of cars which circle offices or Freedom Houses. Take license numbers of all suspicious cars. Note make, model and year. Cars without license plates should immediately be reported to the project office.

<u>Living at Home or in Freedom Houses</u>

a. If it can be avoided, try not to sleep near open windows. Try to sleep at the back of the house, i.e., the part farthest from a road or street.

b. Do not stand in doorways at night with the light at your back.

c. At night, people should not sit in their rooms without drawn shades.

d. Do not congregate in front of the house at night.

Batesville, MS staff joining hands outside.
Left to right: Unidentified woman and
man, Claude Weaver, Geoff Cowan,
Kathie Amatniek (Sarachild), Luther
Buckley, unidentified woman, Jim Kates,
Clair O'Connor, Chris Williams (?), and
Mike Wood (?).

Across Mississippi, in villages dotting the darkening landscape, people cleaned up after Father's Day suppers. In Batesville, Chris Williams and others stood in the Miles' backyard, arms linked, singing Freedom Songs. "Get on Board, Children" and "We'll Never Turn Back" kept fear at bay. But when the songs were done, Robert Miles and his oldest son went into the house and came out carrying shotguns. They sat ready to fire at any car that entered their driveway without giving the agreed-on signal— three blinks of the headlights.

The scene was mirrored in other host homes. Dark-skinned men with guns stood guard on porches or in driveways, beneath a sparkling blanket of stars. Inside, volunteers parted curtains and peered into the blackness. Then, tired from the long and amazing day, they went to bed and tried to get a little sleep in spite of fear, sticky heat, mosquitoes, and all the sounds of the southern night.

To cope with the night, COFO had set up a warning system. Cellphones did not yet exist, but all the project offices in the state were linked to the Jackson headquarters by a telephone line that allowed unlimited calling. The offices could

MURIEL IN "THE BLACK HOLE"

NIGHT FOUND VOLUNTEER MURIEL TILLINGHAST upstairs in the project office in Greenville, Mississippi—alone. Ever since she had crossed the state line on the midnight bus that turned from singing to silence, the quaking in her stomach had gotten worse.

That morning the bus had rattled through the quiet streets of downtown Greenville. But when the bus reached the "colored" section of town, Muriel felt she had crossed into another country, one with smaller houses and broken sidewalks. Finally, when she and a half dozen others were dropped off at the building hosting the project office, sheer terror sent Muriel straight upstairs into the office. There she stayed, in cluttered rooms above a dry cleaner's—all day. While other volunteers were welcomed into homes, Muriel

huddled inside, terrified by just being in "the black hole" of Mississippi.

All her life, Muriel had heard about the Mississippi that her mother had fled. Now she was there. The idealism and solidarity that had sent her south gave way to dread. She recalled every story of lynching she had ever read, every southern horror she had ever heard of. Nothing the other volunteers said could convince Muriel to leave the office. "I was petrified," she recalled. So as night blackened the office windows, the other volunteers went to their homes, leaving Muriel alone with a sleeping bag and the mice scurrying in the walls.

Holed up in the office, she asked herself hard questions. How could she survive the summer? How could she go door-to-door helping people register to vote if she could not even leave the

office? Greenville, she knew, was less violent and risky than many other towns in the state. SNCCs said that they'd "rather get arrested in Greenville than any [other] town in Mississippi." Yet Muriel did not kid herself. For a young black woman on her own, a thousand miles from home, away from familiar well-lit streets, the night unleashed terrors inherited from her ancestors.

Night was when Muriel's grandmother, walking from Texas to Washington, D.C., had hidden from the Klan in barns. Night was when crosses were burned. All that first night in the office, the smallest details made her heart race. Each headlight that flashed across a wall startled her. Each shout from the street made her sit up. Each creak of the office stairs made her jump. Was she ready for Mississippi?

check in with headquarters every hour. That first day, only minor flare-ups had been called in. Cops had stopped a CBS camera crew. A homemade explosive had gone off in a church basement, causing minor damage. But night had just begun.

The phone network also protected workers and volunteers traveling through Mississippi. Anyone sent out from a Freedom House would give the time they expected to return, with a promise to call if they were delayed. If the traveler did not return at the expected time, COFO would call area jails and police departments. On the first night of Freedom Summer, the alarm system was put to a test that lived up to everyone's worst fears.

Into the Dead of Night

Shortly after noon on that first Sunday, three men had set out from Meridian, in the eastern part of the state. James Chaney was an African American CORE staffer from Mississippi. Michael Schwerner, also a CORE staffer, was a white man from New York. Andrew Goodman, also white and from New York, was a summer volunteer. The three had left

the volunteer training session in Ohio early
Saturday morning, before the buses started.
Now they were headed for the remote backwater
of Longdale, in nearby Neshoba County. Their
mission was to investigate the burning of the Mt.
Zion Methodist Church.

Neshoba was a rural county, with just 20,000
people spread over 570 square miles of farmland,
hills, thickets, and swamps. Three-quarters of
the people in the county were white. No African
American had registered to vote in Neshoba
County since 1955. As Freedom Summer began,
Neshoba County had a big "good ol' boy" of a
sheriff, who'd been elected because he promised
to "handle" blacks and outsiders. It also had a
White Citizens' Council. The Klan had been
active that spring, advertising for new members
and burning crosses.

Neshoba County had a reputation for being
friendly to its own people but just plain mean to
strangers—not that many strangers ventured
there. Someone who grew up in Neshoba County
might spend a whole lifetime without meeting
more than a few people from outside Mississippi.
Blacks who fled north never returned. Those
who stayed learned to be invisible. "We don't

bother no white folks and usually they don't pay no attention to us," one said. "We just live here and scratches it out." African Americans who thought differently had to keep quiet or keep moving.

James Chaney knew Neshoba County well. He had grown up in Meridian, one county over. In recent months he had spent hours driving every road in Neshoba County at night, to meet with black people and talk about voting. To avoid being stopped, beaten, or shot, he often raced at high speeds down dirt paths with his headlights off, steering by moonlight and his dim parking lights. He would turn on his headlights and slow down only after crossing the county line out of Neshoba. Chaney made these night runs all through the spring of 1964.

Before they set out for the blackened ruins of Mt. Zion, Chaney and the other two men spent Saturday night in Meridian. When they left, they told the local summer project office that they would be back by 4 p.m. If not, the calls to jails and police departments and hospitals should begin.

The hour came and went. The three men did not return. In the Meridian project office, a volunteer on her first day in Mississippi immediately called COFO in Jackson. But Bob Moses and all the other leaders were in Ohio, welcoming the second group of volunteers. Without their experience and fear as a guide, the COFO worker who took the call suggested waiting for an hour before calling jails. Maybe the men had had car trouble, or taken a longer route. They would arrive soon.

The hour was endless. The men did not arrive.

At 5:00 p.m. the calls began. Within minutes, phones rang in jails throughout Neshoba and the counties around it. No jail clerk admitted having the three in custody. There was no record of their arrest. Police said they "knew nothing at all about the case." The wait continued as night fell. More calls brought the same unhelpful answers. At this point most volunteers knew nothing about the disappearance, but dread was spreading among the SNCCs and other staffers across the state.

The evening dragged on. A visit to the Meridian jail produced no news. Pickups started circling the project office. Their engines revved, their drivers and passengers shouted racial slurs. In the office, volunteers and staffers—black and white—sat and waited for news. More calls to jails. Still no answers. Three calls to the FBI in Meridian and Jackson went nowhere. The FBI agents listened to the staffers' frantic fears but did nothing. One agent said that the FBI was not a police force. The wait continued.

When the first day of Freedom Summer ended, Chris Williams was asleep in Batesville. Muriel Tillinghast was awake and alone in the shifting shadows of the Greenville office. The rest of the volunteers were in host homes. Some of them were sleeping. Others were awake, conscious of the least whisper of the night. None of them knew that three men they'd seen back in Ohio just two days earlier were missing.

Into the morning, the calls continued: to the Mississippi Highway Patrol, to the Justice Department in Washington, D.C., and finally to the families of the missing men. No one had any answers. Michael Schwerner, James Chaney, and Andrew Goodman had vanished without a trace.

THE STUDENT VOICE

VOL. 5 NO. 15   STUDENT VOICE, INC.   6 Raymond Street, N. W.   Atlanta, Georgia 30314   JUNE 30, 1964

Orientation Prepares Summer Volunteers

OXFORD, OHIO — More than 750 volunteers have passed through two weeklong orientation sessions here preparing them for a summer's work in Mississippi.

A first group, numbering 223, arrived in Mississippi on June 21. Three are missing already, and are presumed to have met foul play.

A second group began the extensive training on June 22, and began, arriving in Mississippi last weekend.

The summer workers, 60% of them white, will work on voter registration, man community centers, and teach in Freedom Schools.

The training sessions were sponsored by the National Council of Churches, under the direction of Rev. Bruce Hanson of Washington, D.C. Staff members from the Student Nonviolent Coordinating Committee (SNCC), the group that pioneered civil rights work in rural areas of the South, helped orient the summer volunteers.

More than 60 full time SNCC workers, and some staff members from other groups, will direct the summer's work in Miss-
CONTINUED ON PAGE 4

RIGHTS WORKERS STILL MISSING

THE CHARRED STATION WAGON (left) driven by three civil rights workers last seen near Philadelphia, Miss. on last Sunday night. The tires, windows, interior and exterior were completely burned out.

MISSING CORE WORKER Mickey Schwerner (right) in the Meridian community center he and his wife Rita helped establish.

FORMAN AND DULLES MEET

JACKSON, MISS. - Former CIA head Allen Dulles was told here June 25 the Federal government must honor requests made by civil rights groups for Federal protection of civil rights workers and must stop saying they cannot offer protection for rights workers.

James Forman, SNCC Executive Secretary, who met with the ex-CIA chief and other Negro leaders here, told Dulles that President Johnson should honor three requests made by civil rights leaders for a meeting with him. Forman met with Dulles, SNCC Mississippi Project director Robert Moses, SNCC worker Lawrence Guyot, Dr. Aaron Henry, president of COFO, NAACP field worker Charles Evers, and other rights workers in the Mississippi office of the U.S. Attorney General here at
CONTINUED ON PAGE 4

PHILADELPHIA, MISS. - Civil rights workers are helping bolster a force of Federal officers in a search for three missing men, a search some rights workers say is not as concentrated as newspapers report.

The three men - Mickey Schwerner, 24, a CORE worker, and Andrew Goodman, 20, a summer volunteer, both white, from New York City, and James Cheney, 21, Negro, from Meridian - left Meridian, 35 miles away, at 9:00 Sunday morning. They were stopped in Philadelphia at 4:00 given a speeding ticket, spent six hours in jail, and released at 10:00 that evening. They have not been seen or heard from since.

Civil rights workers complained that agents from the Federal Bureau of Investigation did not arrive on the scene until at least 20 hours after they were first notified the three men were missing.

H. F. Helgesen, a Jackson FBI agent, was notified at 10:00 p.m. Sunday evening the three were missing. He told the Jackson office to keep him informed of what was happening. At 10:30, a Justice Department lawyer named Schwelb was called in Meridian by COFO workers. Jackson called Schwelb again at 11:00, but he had not left his room. At 12:00 that evening, the Jackson office called Schwelb again and gave him the license number of the missing car and requested an investigation. Schwelb said the FBI was not a police force and that he was not sure a Federal offense had occurred. He was told provisions in the U.S. Code gave the FBI author-

ity to intervene in civil rights cases. He insisted he did not have any authority. The office called FBI agent Helgesen again, and the Mississippi Highway Patrol.

At 1:00 a.m. Monday morning (one hour ahead of Mississippi time) June 22, the Atlanta SNCC office called John Doar of the Justice Department in Washington, D.C. He said they were concerned and would look into the case.
CONTINUED ON PAGE 3

CHAPTER 4

BATTLEGROUND
FOR AMERICA

IN THE NIGHTMARE HOURS BEFORE DAWN ON June 22, the news spread across the state and far beyond. Three men, all civil rights workers, had vanished in Mississippi.

SNCC headquarters in Atlanta called the FBI three times. Finally, by morning the FBI was granted power to investigate—but the FBI agent in Jackson, Mississippi, still refused to act. The Mississippi Highway Patrol was called—but without a sheriff's order, no missing person bulletin could be issued for seventy-two hours. More calls, to sheriffs, family members of the missing men, civil rights leaders, and lawyers. African American comedian and activist Dick Gregory, who was in Russia on a goodwill tour, canceled the tour and headed for Mississippi.

Student Voice, **Vol. 5** no. 15; June 30, 1964.

At 6:55 in the morning, the first breakthrough came with a follow-up call to the Neshoba County jail. Earlier, the jailer's wife had said that she had not seen the three men. Now she admitted that they had been brought into the jail at about 4:00 p.m. the day before. James Chaney had been booked for speeding. The other two had been held "for investigation." But all three had been released at 6:00 p.m., before dark.

The news sent shudders through COFO's phone network. Freedom Summer planners had expected something like this—but on the first day of the project? And what had happened after the three had been released?

Most volunteers still did not know about the disappearance. In Greenville, Muriel Tillinghast woke from a restless night of sleeping on the floor to welcome others to the project office. She would refuse to leave it all week. In Batesville, Chris Williams had another "down-home" breakfast. After that, nothing. COFO had ordered volunteers to lie low. Chris wondered when he would start the work he had come to do.

Meanwhile, in Ohio, the second group of volunteers was being trained. Bob Moses was standing on a stage in front of a map, explaining

Mississippi to them, when three SNCCs came into the room and called him over. When Moses returned to the stage, his voice was softer and his manner more serious than ever.

"Yesterday morning," he said, "three of our people left Meridian, Mississippi, to investigate a church burning in Neshoba County. They haven't come back and we haven't had any word from them." The audience rippled with alarm. In the confusion, a slender woman walked to the stage. Her name was Rita Schwerner. She asked the volunteers to group by their home states and send telegrams to their representatives in Congress, demanding an FBI investigation. Then, calmly, she wrote the names of the three men—one of whom was her husband, Michael Schwerner—on the blackboard. The clicking of the chalk was heard to the very back of the silent auditorium. Suddenly there was no need to scare anyone. Every volunteer's face showed the same fear: this could happen to *me*.

Bob Moses slipped outside and slumped down on a step overlooking a spreading lawn. Occasionally a friend walked up to hug him. One whispered, "You are not responsible for this." Moses sat there for hours.

Who Were the Missing Men?

Within a few days, photographs of the three men would be seen around the nation. Soon details of the three men's lives would spread more widely in news stories.

Michael "Mickey" Schwerner. Before the disappearance, Schwerner had spent five months in Mississippi. Some despised him for his political views, his Jewishness, and his racial activism. Those who knew him well were struck by his kindness and lack of hatred for anyone, black or white. A coworker in Meridian said, "More than any white person I have ever known he could put a colored person at ease." Schwerner would have cherished this compliment more than any other.

By the summer of 1963, Schwerner was a dedicated social worker with a degree from Cornell University in New York. He lived in New York City and rose early to work on civil rights matters with the Congress of Racial Equality. He spent afternoons helping teens on Manhattan's Lower East Side. After dinner, he made home social-work visits or attended meetings, sometimes until after midnight. His new wife, Rita, shared his dedication and also worked for CORE.

THE CIVIL RIGHTS WORKERS WHO WERE SLAIN

ANDREW GOODMAN   MICHAEL SCHWERNER   JAMES CHANEY

Andrew Goodman,
Mickey Schwerner,
James Chaney.

The searing racial violence of the summer of 1963 led Schwerner to apply to work full-time for CORE in Mississippi. "I am now so thoroughly identified with the civil rights struggle that I have an emotional need to offer my services in the South," he wrote on his application. In January 1964, the Schwerners left their cocker spaniel with friends and drove to Jackson. They were posted to Meridian. They were the first white civil rights workers in the second-largest city in Mississippi.

Sweeping, scrubbing, making curtains, repairing bookcases, the Schwerners turned a filthy old office into a Freedom House. By late February the place was bustling. A dozen or more kids showed up for Saturday morning story hours. Adults came to voter registration classes two evenings a week. Most afternoons, teenagers dropped by just to be with the Schwerners.

When the Schwerners talked about taking down "Colored Only" signs, CORE thought they were moving too fast. Still, the couple was allowed to organize boycotts of downtown stores that refused to hire black clerks. "We're actually pretty lucky here," Mickey told a reporter. "I think they're going to leave us alone."

But in "Whites Only" Mississippi, the Schwerners awoke anger and hatred. Rita was seen talking with black men! Mickey had a goatee! These things, as well as their civil rights activism, enraged some whites. Electricity and water to the Freedom House were cut off more than once. The Schwerners moved from one host home to another whenever host families' homes were targeted.

In late May, Mickey told his father that he was "a marked man." Yet he refused to leave. "I belong right here in Mississippi," he told a friend. "Nothing threatens peace among men like the idea of white supremacy. Nowhere in the world is the idea of white supremacy more firmly entrenched, or more cancerous, than in Mississippi. . . . So this is the decisive battleground for America, and every young American who wants to have a part in the decision should be here."

James Chaney. The Schwerners inspired commitment in other people, including James Earl Chaney. After being rejected from the army because of his asthma, Chaney had drifted, working odd jobs. He had been committed to civil rights since high school, so when he found his way to the Schwerners and their Freedom House, it felt like coming home. Soon he and Mickey Schwerner were inseparable comrades. "Mickey could count on Jim to walk through hell with him," said another Freedom House regular. By the time Chaney started his night runs into Neshoba County, he was a CORE staffer.

Chaney went north with Mickey and Rita Schwerner to help train the first group of summer project volunteers in Ohio. He and Schwerner agreed that volunteer Andrew Goodman was the man they wanted to start a Freedom School in Neshoba County. It would be hosted by the Mt. Zion Methodist Church in Longdale. When they heard that the church had burned to the ground, they left the training session early and headed for Mississippi.

Andrew Goodman. Goodman's mother called her son "a born activist." Like Schwerner, he came from a liberal family. In high school he had taken a bus to Appalachia to report on the lives of poor coal miners there. He was at Queens College in New York in early 1964 when Allard Lowenstein came to speak about the summer project. Goodman had been planning to spend his summer building a school in Mexico, but Lowenstein changed his mind.

He told his parents he had to go to Mississippi. When his father asked why, Goodman answered, "Because this is the most important thing going on in the country! If someone says he cares about people, how can he not be concerned about this?" His parents were concerned for his safety, but, as his father said, "We couldn't turn our backs on the values we instilled in him at home." Although Goodman's father offered to pay his son's $150 in expenses, the young man instead loaded trucks for two months to pay his way to Freedom Summer. He told a friend, "I'm scared but I'm going."

On June 21, when Goodman awoke in Meridian, he wrote to his parents: "The people in this city are wonderful, and our reception was very good." A few hours later he, Schwerner, and Chaney set off for Neshoba County in the same blue Ford station wagon that Chaney used for his night runs. Before they left, Chaney's twelve-year-old brother, Ben, cried because he wanted to go along. Chaney told Ben to be patient. When he came back that afternoon, they'd go for a drive. Ben started waiting.

Monday Heats Up

When the three men had been missing for eighteen hours, news came from the town of Philadelphia, the county seat of Neshoba County. At 9:00 p.m. on Sunday night, the men had been spotted in jail there. They looked bruised and battered.

COFO again called the FBI. Meanwhile, SNCC was growing desperate. What about an air search? Roadblocks? An all-points bulletin?

Mississippi was heating up in ways that had nothing to do with the temperature. All that Monday morning, summer project offices received hostile calls. After their warm welcome in black communities, the volunteers were finding their first encounters with whites strange and sinister.

In Clarksdale, a volunteer from Los Angeles was talking to some black people when a cop pulled up and demanded to know what he was doing. He replied that he was helping to register voters. "Don't you know that you're not wanted here?" the cop said. The cop ordered the volunteer into the car, where two snarling men cursed him. The volunteer was jailed and refused permission to make phone calls. Eventually he was released and told to get the hell out of Mississippi. Clarksdale, the sheriff said, had a hundred deputized citizens with clubs "just waiting for the signal to split some heads open. . . . Some folks are going to get hurt, maybe killed, but then things will settle down."

Things did not settle down for SNCC. All day, the FBI refused to investigate. SNCC was outraged, but not surprised. Ever since Bob Moses had come to Mississippi, SNCC had knocked on doors in the federal government, asking simply that the law be enforced. They were ignored. Attorney general Robert Kennedy wanted civil rights struggles to take place in courtrooms, not in the streets. His Justice Department had filed several dozen lawsuits charging voter discrimination in Mississippi, but none of them had gone anywhere. Bob Moses had filed his own lawsuit against Kennedy and J. Edgar Hoover, director of the FBI—and lost. He was appealing the case to a higher court.

If the federal government had done a poor job of enforcing voting laws, it had done a worse job of protecting civil rights workers. John Doar, the assistant U.S. attorney who had spoken to the volunteers in Ohio, had investigated threats against Mississippians Herbert Lee and

A SIGN OF THE TIMES AT SNCC

IN 1963, A YEAR BEFORE FREEDOM SUMMER, SNCC's frustration with the federal government threatened to sour Martin Luther King, Jr.'s March on Washington. John Lewis, chairman of SNCC, was scheduled to speak before King. Lewis planned to ask, "Which side is the federal government on?" King's assistants talked Lewis into removing the question from his speech. It was thought to be too aggressive, too angry.

By the time Freedom Summer began, SNCC distrusted the federal government and expected no help from Washington, D.C. A sign in SNCC offices throughout Mississippi highlighted the difference between words and reality:

There is a street in Itta Bena
called Freedom
There is a town in Mississippi
called Liberty
There is a department in Washington
called Justice

Before the summer project, COFO and SNCC
wrote to the Justice Department and President
Lyndon Johnson, seeking federal protection for
volunteers. There had been no answer. And now
three men had vanished on the first night. With
hundreds of potential targets now in the state,
who knew how many more people would go
down some back road and not come back?

Louis Allen, but the Justice Department had refused to protect them. Both had been gunned down. Robert Kennedy had delayed protection for the Freedom Riders of 1963, even after their bus was firebombed.

SNCC had special scorn for the FBI. SNCCs often saw FBI agents on the fringes of a violent mob, taking notes. They took notes while Bob Zellner was nearly killed by a mob, and while dogs tore at Bob Moses. FBI chief Hoover did not apologize for the agency's hands-off policy. He thought that civil rights workers did not deserve protection. Hoover was also convinced, without evidence, that the civil rights movement was riddled with communists.

The Story Breaks

Goodman, Schwerner, and Chaney had been missing for a full day when the federal government finally took action. Around 6:00 p.m. Monday evening, Attorney General Kennedy ordered the FBI to investigate a possible kidnapping. President Johnson was alerted to the situation. The Mississippi Highway Patrol issued a missing persons bulletin. And reporters in the

United States and Europe started checking maps and booking flights to Mississippi.

"Good evening," said Walter Cronkite, one of America's best-known newscasters, that night. He broke the story to the nation: "Three young civil rights workers disappeared in Mississippi on Sunday night near the central Mississippi town of Philadelphia, about fifty miles north of Jackson." While Cronkite spoke, FBI agents drove north from New Orleans. Then night fell again, and the night riders came out.

SNCC had sent no volunteers to McComb, a small town in Pike County, deep in the Deep South. The county was known to be infested with the Ku Klux Klan, and blacks had disappeared there. The events of Monday night showed that SNCC had made the right decision.

After dark, a black woman in McComb looked out her window to see a shiny new Chevy skid to a halt. A man jumped out and tossed a package. As the woman scrambled to the back of her house, the package exploded. The explosion flattened her porch, blew in her front door, and littered her bed with broken glass. Moments later another bomb, and then another, rocked the homes of people who had supported civil rights.

The following morning, African Americans in McComb surveyed the rubble. The eyes of America, though, were turned to another Mississippi town: Philadelphia, whose name meant "brotherly love." It was a place much like any other Mississippi town of five thousand people. Church steeples aimed at the heavens above a skyline of two-story buildings. Lumber mill smokestacks belched black smoke. Storekeepers swept the sidewalks, pickup trucks rolled down the streets, a farmer in overalls waved from a tractor. If they had heard that three men had disappeared in their county, they didn't seem too concerned.

Down a snaking dirt road and across the railroad tracks was another part of Philadelphia called Independence Quarters. There African Americans "scratched it out" in tiny homes with boarded-up windows. When the people of Independence Quarters heard of the disappearances, they did not doubt it. Folks said it must have something to do with that church that burned—the church that was supposed to host a Freedom School.

By 10:00 a.m., Philadelphia had been invaded. Everywhere people looked, they saw strangers with sunglasses and briefcases, wearing white shirts and skinny ties. These strangers scanned the streets and the town square, taking notes, not making eye contact. The FBI had arrived. All Tuesday morning, agents set up operations. A motel room became temporary FBI headquarters. Agents built an antenna on top of a water tower for radio contact with Washington. They then set out to visit the police, the courthouse, and the jail.

The jailer told agents that she had fined James Chaney twenty dollars and released the three men at 10:30 Sunday night. Deputy Sheriff Cecil Price said that he had arrested the men, all right. He had last seen them on Sunday night, heading south on highway 19 toward Meridian. He saw their taillights disappear over a hill. Agents were soon driving along that highway and peering into swamps. FBI helicopters swooped low, flapping laundry and scattering chickens.

In town, as the temperature approached 100 degrees, tempers flared. Enraged locals confronted the reporters who had come to town.

It was all a hoax, they said. Those three boys just took off! And if the agents and reporters knew what was good for them, they'd take off, too. The agents went from house to house, but no one would talk to them. No one would even listen.

Then, in the middle of the afternoon, news bulletins interrupted radio and television programs across the nation. James Chaney's blue Ford had been found. It wasn't south of Meridian, where Deputy Sheriff Price said he'd seen it. It was fifteen miles north of town, near the reservation of the Choctaw Native Americans. A group of Choctaw fishing in a creek had spotted the smoldering wreckage.

The car's license plate matched Chaney's. One wheel was missing and the windshield was blown out. The charred vehicle was towed into town. But there was no sign of Chaney, Schwerner, and Goodman.

The President Responds to the Crisis

Just minutes after the car was found, the news reached the White House. What would President Johnson do?

Back in April, Johnson had learned of the

summer project. He had told a senator from Georgia that it would lead to "a bunch of killings." Yet Johnson had followed advice and ignored the organizers of the project when they begged for federal protection. Now he was busy with other matters. He had to replace his ambassador to Vietnam. He also had to plan the ceremony at which he would sign the Civil Rights Act. But the subject of Mississippi kept coming up—at his press conference, in phone calls, in news bulletins.

Johnson was outraged by the suggestion that he wasn't doing enough to find the missing three civil rights workers. Still, he would not meet with Andrew Goodman's parents and Michael Schwerner's father. The president said, "I'm afraid that if I start mothering each kid that's gone down there and that doesn't show up, then we'll have this White House full of people every day asking for sympathy."

The deputy assistant attorney general, Nicholas Katzenbach, said, "I would not be surprised if they'd been murdered, Mr. President." Katzenbach also told Johnson that he had been right not to meet with the parents: "I think you'd have a problem of every future one," he said. "This is not going to be the only time this sort of thing will occur, I'm afraid."

Late in the afternoon a U.S. senator from Mississippi called the president to tell him that there was no Klan in Neshoba County—"no white organizations in that area of Mississippi." The disappearance of the three men, the senator said, was probably "a publicity stunt." That call was interrupted by FBI director J. Edgar Hoover, who told the president that the men had most likely been killed. And that evening Johnson did meet in the Oval Office with the Goodmans and Nathan Schwerner, Mickey's father. The president told them that the full powers of the Justice Department and the Department of Defense would be harnessed to search for the missing men.

Aftershocks rippled across the United States as one piece of news followed another. The attorney general was canceling a trip to Poland. The president was sending Allen Dulles, a former head of the Central Intelligence Agency (CIA), to Mississippi. More FBI agents were on their way. That night, COFO headquarters panicked at every call about harassment, every report of a volunteer who was late somewhere. Meanwhile, the terrorism went up a notch. Shots hit a black minister's home and a cafe in Jackson. In the Delta, whites chased reporters out of Ruleville— home of the senator who had told President Johnson that the disappearance was a publicity stunt. Then a mob drove through the black part of Ruleville hurling bottles and firebombs.

On Wednesday morning, newspapers all across America featured photographs of James Chaney's charred station wagon jutting out of a swamp. One headline read "Wreckage Raises New Fears over Fate of Missing Men." Protesters marched outside federal buildings in Chicago, New York, and Washington, D.C., demanding an investigation.

Closer to the scene of the tragedy, police with guns and riot clubs circled the Neshoba County courthouse in the town of Philadelphia. Locals seethed with rage and denial. People said "They had no business down here" and "This wouldn't have happened if they had stayed home where they belong." Philadelphia was just a gunshot away from a full-blown race war. Shortly after noon, a caravan of cars crossed the Neshoba County line. The trigger was cocked.

The Search

The caravan carried African American leaders, including James Farmer from CORE, John Lewis from SNCC, and comedian Dick Gregory. It also carried teenagers ready to search for bodies. All of them had been warned about Neshoba County. Still, they crossed the line.

At the Philadelphia city limit, the cars halted. Like a posse in a scene from a cheap Western movie, Sheriff Lawrence Rainey and several men with shotguns stood across the road. Rainey, an enormous man in a cowboy hat, with a wad of tobacco bulging his cheek, strode up to the lead car and asked Farmer, "Where do you think you're goin'?" Eventually Rainey agreed to meet with just four men from the caravan, including Farmer and Lewis. The rest would have to wait by the highway.

Rainey's patrol car led the four black men's sedan to the courthouse, where they walked past silent, glaring white faces. Inside the sheriff's office, the four were tense, but Rainey and his deputy seemed delighted by the attention. They smirked and joked while the county's lawyers handled all the men's questions.

Farmer demanded to visit the burned-out Mt.

Zion Church. He would need a search warrant, he was told. Lewis insisted on seeing Chaney's burned-out car. The request was refused because he might "destroy evidence." As Lewis saw it, "evidence" meant that there had been a crime. "If there has been a crime," the lawyer answered with a smile. "Those boys may have decided to go up north or someplace and have a short vacation."

His young volunteers, Farmer said, were ready to search. The lawyers' heads shook. Private property. Trespassing. Venomous snakes. "We don't want anything to happen to you down here," they said. The four African Americans were then escorted out, past the sour faces and shotguns, to rejoin the caravan waiting at city limits. All four were sure that the smug sheriff and his smiling deputy knew exactly what had happened to the missing men.

That evening, the searchers and their supporters met in Meridian as thunder rattled rooftops. The meeting crackled with anger. Dick Gregory offered a $25,000 reward to anyone finding the missing men and those responsible for their disappearance. Meanwhile, across the state, "redneck boys" roared through African American communities, shouting and throwing bottles, daring anyone to mess with Mississippi.

Whoever knew the fate of the three missing men must have been surprised to see the storm that their disappearance had stirred up. Never before had a disappearance in the Deep South sent such shock waves through the nation. The planners of Freedom Summer had been right when they figured that getting white people involved in their work would draw more attention to the cause. The disappearance of Goodman and Schwerner, who were white, got far more attention than the murders of Herbert Lee and Louis Allen.

Meanwhile, a group of searchers from SNCC sneaked into Neshoba County at dusk, making their way along back roads. The searchers examined the ashes of Mt. Zion Church and talked with local African Americans, who were sure the missing men had been killed. Then, after slamming along rough roads with their headlights off, deeper and deeper into Klan country, the searchers probed swamps and creeks, barns and wells. Pestered by mosquitoes and deer flies, they trudged on—ankle deep, knee deep, waist deep. Vines snagged their clothes. Brambles slashed their arms. They did the same thing the next night. After they heard rumors that the Klan was aware of their activities, the midnight searches ended.

Pressure mounted on the federal government not just to find the missing men but to prevent future disappearances. Parents of the Freedom Summer volunteers bombarded Congress and the White House with telegrams. The parents demanded that federal marshals be sent to Mississippi to protect their children. Debate raged in Congress and in the media. Attorney General Robert Kennedy said that law enforcement in Mississippi was the responsibility of local officials. President Johnson was strongly against sending federal troops, knowing that white Mississippi would regard them as invaders. J. Edgar Hoover of the FBI said it would be simply impossible to protect "a thousand of these youngsters going down there . . . Living in the homes of the colored population." In the end, Johnson decided to send more FBI agents but no marshals. "I'm not going to send troops on my people if I can avoid it," he said. "And they got to help me avoid it."

The families of the missing men gave television interviews. Carolyn Goodman,

"THEY ASKED FOR IT"

MISSISSIPPI SEEMED TO BE OCCUPIED BY
outsiders. FBI agents stopped cars at
checkpoints. Others motored along waterways in
boats, dragging hooks, searching for bodies. Two
hundred servicemen from the Naval Air Station in
Meridian, sent to the scene by President Johnson,
slogged through swamps, using branches to keep
snakes away.

Reporters from across the United States as
well as from France, England, and Germany
descended on Philadelphia and Neshoba County.
Mississippi was getting a black eye every night
on the national news. Walter Cronkite spoke of
"Bloody Neshoba."

But were Goodman, Chaney, and Schwerner really missing? Or was it all a hoax? That suspicion spread through white Mississippi. A newspaper claimed that Goodman had been spotted getting on a bus in Louisiana. Another rumor said that CORE had called police on Sunday afternoon, *before* the men went missing. White Mississippians told ABC News how they felt. One man said, "I believe them jokers planned this and are sittin' up in New York laughin' at us Mississippi folk." A woman added, "If they're dead, I feel like they asked for it. They came here lookin' for trouble."

Andrew's mother, appealed "to all parents everywhere" to cooperate "in every way possible in the search for these three boys." Nathan Schwerner, Michael's father, believed—like President Johnson—that the men were dead. "Don't you know we'll never see Mickey again?" he shouted at a reporter. In Mississippi, Fannie Lee Chaney, James's mother, told the press, "I'm just hoping and not thinking." This was not the first disappearance in her family. Decades earlier, her grandfather had refused to sell his land to a white man. Only his shoes, shirt, and watch were ever found.

Rita Schwerner, Michael's wife, flew to Jackson. Met by reporters, she said, "I am going to find my husband and the other two people. I am going to find out what happened to them." Then Rita and SNCC worker Bob Zellner headed off to see Governor Paul Johnson. They found him in the grounds of his mansion, where they overheard him chuckling about the disappearance. Only he and Governor Wallace of Alabama knew where the three men were, Johnson joked, "and we're not telling." Panic broke out when Zellner asked Johnson, "Is it true that you and Governor Wallace here know where the missing civil rights workers are?" Rita and Zellner were hustled off the grounds. The two next met with Allen Dulles, sent to Mississippi by the president. When Dulles offered Rita his sympathy, she said, "I don't want your sympathy! I want my husband back!"

Moving on to Philadelphia, Rita met with Sheriff Rainey, telling him she would not leave until she had seen the remains of James Chaney's burned-out car. The sheriff took her and Zellner to see it. To Rita, the wreckage was proof that she would never see her husband again. "Sheriff Rainey," she said, "I feel that you know what happened. I'm going to find out if I can. If you don't want me to find out, you'll have to kill me." After that, Rita and Zellner left Philadelphia, chased out of town by the same green pickup truck that had blocked the highway that morning when they entered town.

The Breaking Point
By the end of the week, the nation was obsessed with Mississippi. James Silver's book about conditions in the state, *Mississippi: The Closed Society*, became a national bestseller. Dozens of doctors and lawyers volunteered to spend July

or August in Mississippi to support Freedom Summer. Famous folksingers such as Pete Seeger and Judy Collins scheduled summer concerts in Mississippi, also to support the cause. SNCC offices were flooded with calls from people hoping to volunteer.

Under the national spotlight, the town of Philadelphia was near the breaking point. Local whites were horrified by the reporters and FBI agents who swarmed the area "like termites on old lumber." People huddled on street corners, talking, but their voices dropped to whispers when strangers passed. Near the courthouse, a driver rammed the car of a media cameraman. When the cameraman stepped out, so did the driver—clutching a hunting knife. Police jumped in before someone got hurt.

On the fifth night after the disappearances, Mississippi erupted. In town after town, volunteers were hounded by pickup trucks, taunted with obscenities, and arrested on trumped-up charges. Beer cans flew. A SNCC's car tires were slashed. Whites in Hattiesburg spread flyers through black communities. The flyers warned: "Beware, good Negro citizens. When we come to get the agitators, stay away."

Near Jackson, someone set a church on fire.

The most shocking news came from the Delta. Two volunteers had been kidnapped at gunpoint. Their captors had said, "Want us to do to you what they did over in Philadelphia?" The volunteers were held at a gas station, waiting for a bus on which they could be sent north. The following night, the FBI arrested three white men in Itta Bena for the crime. SNCCs could barely believe *that* news. One volunteer wrote home, "You dig it? They are in a Southern jail."

Heading into the Hot Zone

Among those who watched the news out of Mississippi that week were the second group of summer project volunteers. They were still in Ohio being trained to run Freedom Schools for the African American children of Mississippi. The mood on the Ohio campus was grim— "like a funeral parlor," someone said. Frantic parents were calling, begging their children to come home. Anxious, terrified volunteers met with psychiatrist Robert Coles, who sent eight of them home. But in the rest of the students, he saw the power of idealism.

"Suddenly hundreds of young Americans

became charged with new energy and determination," Coles wrote. "Suddenly I saw fear turn into toughness, vacillation into quiet conviction." In Ohio, the volunteers crowded around TV sets to see the missing men's car being dragged out of the swamp. They watched the ABC special *The Search in Mississippi.* "You know what we're all doing," one of them said. "We're moving the world."

Volunteers struggled to explain to their parents why they would not turn back. One wrote, "Dear Mom and Dad, This letter is hard to write because I would like so much to communicate how I feel and I don't know if I can. It is very hard to answer to your attitude that if I loved you I wouldn't do this—hard, because the thought is cruel. I can only hope you have the sensitivity to understand that I can both love you very much and desire to go to Mississippi. . . ."

On their last evening in the safe North, the volunteers filled the campus auditorium. A week earlier, the three missing men had sat in the same place, listened to the same leaders, and sung the same songs. Now this second group would follow them down. First, though, they listened one last time to Bob Moses.

Sighing, Moses asked if anyone had read
the book that was becoming trendy on college
campuses, J.R.R. Tolkien's *The Fellowship of
the Ring*. It had a lot to say about good and evil.
Then, rubbing his eyes, he said softly, "The
kids are dead." He let the words sink in. "When
we heard the news at the beginning I knew
they were dead. When we heard they had been
arrested I knew there had been a frame-up. We
didn't say this earlier because of Rita, because
she was really holding out for every hope. There
may be more deaths. . . ."

He went on, "In our country we have some
real evil, and the attempt to do something about
it involves enormous effort . . . and therefore
tremendous risks. If for any reason you're
hesitant about what you're getting into, it's better
for you to leave." After a few more comments,
Moses slowly walked out. No one said a word. No
one took the stage. Volunteers sat in the stillness.
Finally from the back of the auditorium, a
woman sang:

> *They say that freedom*
> *Is a constant struggle*

Across the auditorium, people joined hands
and joined in.

Many of them stayed up all night, talking, wandering, having final urgent phone conversations with desperate parents. The following evening they headed south.

At two in the afternoon on Sunday, the bus pulled into Ruleville, Mississippi. Twenty volunteers stepped out with luggage and bedrolls. Across the street, several white men holding beer cans stared them down. A woman with pink hair curlers drove by and waved her middle finger at them. The sheriff and the mayor showed up. So did several black families. A standoff looked likely, until Fannie Lou Hamer strode onto the scene. The stout, sturdy woman quickly matched volunteers with host families and gathered everyone at her house.

After lunch, people sat in the shade of Hamer's pecan tree and listened to shared news about how the project had been going. Some local African Americans had gone to the courthouse in Indianola to register. Fifty kids had signed up for Freedom School.

That Sunday, black churchgoers prayed next to the rubble of Mt. Zion Church. FBI agents climbed into boats to drag the Pearl River for the bodies of the missing men. In the town of

Philadelphia, other agents prepared to question Sheriff Rainey. In Washington, D.C., marchers with candles paced silently outside the White House. Rita Schwerner was on her way there to meet with President Johnson. Throughout Mississippi, white mayors talked about going to Washington, too—to protest "the invasion" of their state by the civil rights workers. Meanwhile, a few more volunteers, having driven their own cars from Ohio, arrived in their Mississippi towns. All the way down, one of them kept saying, "I don't know what all the fuss is about. It's still the United States of America."

CHAPTER 5

"IT IS SURE ENOUGH CHANGING"

ON JULY 2, 1964, PRESIDENT JOHNSON SIGNED the Civil Rights Act, making segregation by race illegal in all public facilities in the United States. All during that long holiday weekend—the celebration of the Fourth of July and the nation's independence—African Americans tested the new law. They ordered breakfast from white waitresses and got haircuts from white barbers. They checked in as guests at hotels where just a few days earlier they were welcome only as maids and kitchen help. The 1964 Civil Rights Act was a revolution in racial rights.

But in Mississippi, questions about the fate of three vanished civil rights workers hung in the hot summer air, unanswered.

SNCC field secretary Sandy Leigh (New York City), director of the Hattiesburg Project, and seventeen-year-old local African American activist Doug Smith, assistant director and youth coordinator of the project, explaining voter registration procedures to 103-year-old African American resident Sylvester Magee on his front porch, July 1964.

Four days before signing the Civil Rights Act, Johnson had visitors in the Oval Office of the White House. They were Rita Schwerner, wife of one of the vanished men, and civil rights activist Bob Zellner. Johnson shook Rita's hand and said that he was glad to meet her.

Twenty-two-year-old Rita, now sure her husband was dead, said, "I'm sorry, Mr. President, this is not a social call. We've come to talk about three missing people in Mississippi. We've come to talk about a search that we don't think is being done seriously." She asked that five thousand federal marshals be sent to Mississippi. The president replied that everything that could be done, was being done. When he abruptly left the room, his press secretary told Rita that one did not talk to the president of the United States that way.

"We do," Rita said. Then she left for a press conference.

MISSING

During that first week of July, the news from Mississippi centered on the search for Andrew Goodman, Michael Schwerner, and James Chaney. Rumors ran wild. A man looking "exactly" like

Schwerner had been spotted near the Tennessee border! Three bodies chained together had been dumped into a reservoir! The FBI tracked down each dead-end rumor. They also kept questioning people in Philadelphia and Neshoba County. Slowly they pieced together the events of June 21, when the men had gone missing.

On Sunday afternoon, a woman had seen three men—two white, one black—fixing a flat tire on a blue station wagon, with a cop and two highway patrolmen watching them. One of the patrolmen said that her story was true. He and his partner had seen the station wagon drive past them and pull off the road. Seconds later, Deputy Cecil Price raced by in his police car, with the red light flashing. He radioed for assistance. The patrolmen answered Price's call. They found the deputy watching the black man change the tire. Then the patrolmen and Deputy Price took the three men and their station wagon to the jail in Philadelphia.

A man who had been in one of the jail cells said that he had seen the three civil rights workers brought in. They had been put in segregated lockups. The man said Schwerner and Goodman had been calm. They told him that they expected to be in jail for several days. These details startled FBI investigators. Still, a blank remained between Sunday evening and the discovery of the smoldering station wagon on Tuesday. What had happened during those hours?

While the FBI investigated and the public feasted on rumors, 450 volunteers swallowed their fears and settled into their business in black Mississippi. They got Freedom Schools ready to open. They set up community centers. They sat on rickety front porches, shelling peas and getting to know their hosts. White Mississippi went about its business, too. Violence died down, perhaps because of the FBI arrests of white men in Itta Bena, or maybe because all America was watching. Yet the "calm" did not fool anyone. Each pickup truck that passed, each hateful stare, each sudden noise in the night was a reminder that raw hatred lurked within striking distance.

Threats and "Tough Towns"
Volunteers heard stories about towns much worse than those where they were posted. In the Delta, the "tough town" was Drew. When the first civil rights workers went there to talk

to African Americans about voting, an angry white mob chased them out. Volunteers were told *never* to enter Tallahatchie County, where the murdered body of young Emmett Till had washed up in the muddy river. Farther south, a reputation for savagery hung over Amite County, where Herbert Lee had been gunned down, and Pike County, where mobs had beaten SNCCs outside city hall.

Even with tough towns and violent counties off limits to Summer Project volunteers, threats and harassment kept coming. Calls logged by a volunteer at the COFO office in Jackson made white Mississippi seem as dangerous as a coiled snake. The log showed a series of scary events on June 30:

Holly Springs: . . . Threats of dynamiting Freedom House tonight. Guys driving around with guns. . . .

Ruleville: Two reports of trucks without licenses, one this afternoon. Congregating on highway 89, near city dump. . . .

Jackson, 10:45: Two guys just passed in '64 Tempest, black—with gun.

Holly Springs: A guy in gas station . . . Cursed at Larry, grabbed him by throat. Peter

FRED'S FREEDOM SCHOOL

ON HIS FIRST FULL DAY IN MISSISSIPPI, FRED
Winn tore down an outhouse and turned it into
bookshelves.

The outhouse stood behind a two-room shack
on a dusty road in Ruleville. It was full of broken
bottles, cobwebs, and cockroaches bigger than
pecans. The twenty Summer Project volunteers
were shocked and dismayed. *This* was supposed
to be Ruleville's Freedom School?

But the volunteers quickly got to work,
swarming over the house. They carried out
armloads of junk. With brooms, buckets, and
bottles of Lysol, they brought new life to the
dying building. Soon several black women arrived
with their own cleaning solutions and someone
delivered boxes of books. The volunteers stacked

the books in piles. While the piles were still small, volunteer Fred Winn started talking about bookshelves. He could build some, if he had planks—and then he noticed the outhouse. With the help of several laughing local kids, he rocked and rocked it until it fell over. The smell was paralyzing, but the boards were not as old as they looked. Winn set to work cleaning them.

By the time a late-afternoon thunderstorm skimmed over the Delta, the Ruleville Freedom School was ready for classes. Walls had been painted. The headboard of an old crib had been made into a blackboard. Fully stocked bookshelves lined both classrooms. Walking through their new school, the volunteers could hardly believe what they had accomplished, yet similar miracles were taking place in other

Adult classes held outside of the Freedom School, Priest Creek Baptist Church, 1964.

Mississippi towns. The summer's work had begun for carpenter Fred Winn and hundreds of other volunteers.

Two weeks earlier, Winn had been at home in San Francisco, where nights were deliciously cool. Now he lay in the muggy dampness of midnight on the floor of his new home—the Ruleville Freedom School—and thought about how he had come to Mississippi.

Fred had learned of the Summer Project when SNCC spoke at his college campus. Many students had given SNCC money, but Fred's friends were astonished when he decided to give his summer. A friendly twenty-year-old whose apartment was known as a "party pad" seemed like an unlikely civil rights worker. Only a few close friends knew that Fred's family had a secret. A year earlier, Fred's father, a respected lawyer,

had told his family that he had another child—a six-year-old black daughter. Fred's mother threw her husband out, but Fred was charmed by his new half-sister. "Now it wasn't just these 'Negroes' or 'coloreds' or whatever everyone was calling them," Fred remembered, "but people to whom I'm related. That's a consciousness changing thing."

Fred's mother threatened to sue his college for letting SNCC speak there if anything happened to Fred in Mississippi. The dean of the college tried to talk him out of volunteering. But Fred's father was pleased by his son's choice and signed the permission form. Shortly before Fred left for training in Ohio, the young man wrote his will. It ended, "Wherever there is a fight of equality . . . I will be there. The truth is behind me—We shall overcome."

SNCC had asked for handymen, and Fred had always liked building. He put together a toolbox and took a bus to Ohio. He was there when news of the three missing men reached the campus. He realized that there were people in Mississippi who might murder him. Fred's roommate went home, but Fred was determined to go.

In Mississippi, Fred found nights terrifying. After spending his days hanging screens, fixing toilets, and singing at meetings, he lay on the Freedom School floor and struggled to sleep. For protection, he had covered the school's windows with tin. This turned the school into a sweatbox at night. A volunteer from New Jersey slept nearby, but Fred just lay there, thinking about his broken multiracial family and wondering what he'd gotten himself into.

Cummings came back. Guy yelled at them both. "I'm going to shoot up your office."

And on it went. "Violence hangs overhead like dead air," a Ruleville volunteer wrote. "Something is in the air, something is going to happen, sometime, to someone." Police found any excuse to arrest the volunteers— for speeding, reckless driving, even "reckless walking." Meanwhile, other locals used threats and terror to drive them out. Each town may have had no more than a dozen homegrown white terrorists. But if other citizens disapproved of the violence, they said nothing.

Still, the work remained. Now that the volunteers had settled in, it was time to harvest democracy, shack by shack. Canvassers went out to talk to the people about registering to vote.

A scene was repeated all over Mississippi that week: A gravel road. A row of cabins. Black men and women slumped on porches, numb after twelve hours of cooking, cleaning, or working in the fields. As the western sky turns red with sunset, up the road come the "Riders." Their hair is combed, their shirts and blouses spotless. They have clipboards in their hands. Some of them are white pairs. Others are white and black. They step onto the porches and introduce themselves: Len and Bill, or Chris and Pam. Then they talk about the summer project and about the dream of voting.

A few African Americans answer with "Yes, sir," or "Yes'm." Most just sit and stare. The volunteers have to learn how to talk to people who are terrified and tired. Fortunately, SNCC's handbook about canvassing gives them clear instructions and smart advice.

"Know all roads in and out of town," was one instruction. Another was, "If a person talks but shows obvious reluctance, don't force a long explanation on them. Come back another day to explain more." The canvassers were told not to overwhelm people with possibilities. Instead, they should focus on just one hope. It might be a registration class, or a meeting, or a trip to the courthouse.

To Mississippi native and SNCC program director Lawrence Guyot, canvassing meant "surviving and just walking around talking to people about what they're interested in." He said, "Let's say you're riding past a picnic and people are cuttin' watermelons. You don't immediately go and say, 'Stop the watermelon cuttin' and let's talk about voter registrations.' You cut some watermelons."

As the summer went on, volunteers would have many doors closed in their faces. They would have people promise to come to registration classes, then never show up. They would hand pamphlets to old black men, only to realize that the men could not read a word. And every now and then they would be welcomed into a sharecropper's shack.

When this happened, the volunteers would try not to stare or cry. Sharecropper shacks had walls patched with yellowed newspaper and bare bulbs hanging from frayed cords. Volunteers saw barefoot children playing on the floor with bottle caps for toys. Many homes had a single picture. It might be Jesus, or John F. Kennedy, or Martin Luther King, Jr. "The whole scene," one volunteer wrote, "was from another century."

If one in twenty locals invited the volunteers inside, only one in a hundred decided that voting was worth risking a job, a home, even a life. For black people in Mississippi, registering to vote had always been risky. During Freedom Summer, that risk stalked the streets. Police cars often followed the canvassers, inching along with shotguns on display. One look at a cop was enough to send people scurrying indoors. The volunteers hated having the police on their tails—but a cop could protect them from other dangers.

As frustrating as canvassing was, it was getting results. Imagine a dozen teams going out for a dozen days in a dozen towns. Even if just one out of every hundred people they talked to was inspired to register, lines could form at courthouses as people claimed their right to vote. The canvassers came up with just enough hope to keep them going. Blacks born and raised in Mississippi could scarcely believe how things were changing.

"It's the best thing that's happened since there ever was a Mississippi," one black man said. "I just love the students like I love to eat. . . . A lot of bad smells are getting out to the outside world that never did before. And we got out-of-state FBI in here, and federal lawsuits. It's all changing, it is sure enough changing, right this summer."

CHRIS: SOUTHERN COOKING
AND SHOTGUNS

THE YOUNGEST CANVASSER IN THE SUMMER
project was Chris Williams. He had the good luck
to be stationed in Panola County.

Just a month before Freedom Summer, a
federal court had placed a one-year hold on
county laws that limited African American voting.
For one year, Panola County could not make black
voters interpret the state constitution or pay the
poll tax. Suddenly, SNCC had twelve months to
register as many black voters in Panola County
as possible. During the first week of summer,
SNCC held voter registration classes every night.
Canvassers went door to door. The number of
African Americans registered to vote in Panola
County went from one to forty-eight.

Chris was staying with Cornelia Robertson and her grown daughter, Pepper. Their home was a two-room shack with no running water and bullet holes in the front screen. Both women went early to work, so Chris made his own breakfast, showered in the sun with buckets of cold water, and then hustled to the project office. There a radio blared a Memphis soul station, playing Aretha Franklin, Wilson Pickett, and Marvin Gaye. Volunteers from northern colleges scurried around. Chris spent most of his days studying canvassing routes or running errands. In the evenings, after sharecroppers came home from the fields, he met them on their porches. Once a week, he went to the courthouse to help people register.

One afternoon Chris sat in the cool hallway outside the registrar's office with four people waiting to register. One was an elderly woman named Gladys Tolliver. A few days earlier, he had convinced her to take the risk and register. Now he was going over a copy of the registration form with her. Suddenly a sheriff stood in front of them, badge on chest and gun on hip. The sheriff began ranting about "agitators . . . come to Mississippi to cause trouble." Saying that a courthouse was no place for voting classes, he ordered Chris to leave.

In the scalding air outside the courthouse, Chris felt his confidence waver. SNCCs had told of attacks and beatings in just such places. Any minute now. . . .

Finally, Chris's friends came out of the courthouse. The sheriff followed them, still ranting. "He said they ought to send me home and let my parents teach me how to behave," Chris wrote home. "I just looked him in the eye and said nothing. He's a stupid old man."

Later that day, Chris enjoyed a big meal at the home of the Miles family, who had welcomed him on his first day in Mississippi. "I have developed a real taste for Southern cooking," he wrote to his parents. After supper, the Miles men stood guard with their shotguns out. Some things were still a long way from changing.

Suspicions

A tall, burly, middle-aged man with an eighth-grade education, Neshoba County Sheriff Lawrence Rainey was known to be hard-drinking and "hard on the Negroes." Everyone knew that he had killed two black men, both unarmed, while on duty. Mississippi sheriffs had enormous power. Each one was his county's tax collector and its agent for the sale of wine and liquor to bars, restaurants, and liquor stores. In some counties, the sheriff was also a proud member of the Ku Klux Klan. But Rainey claimed even more power. He had once bragged, after pulling over an African American driver, that he ran Neshoba County.

Now the man who boasted about running the county was becoming a suspect in the disappearance of Chaney, Schwerner, and Goodman.

A highway patrolman from Meridian had given the agents a list of seven names, saying, "I bet you every one of these men was involved in this." Two of the names were Sheriff Lawrence Rainey and Deputy Cecil Price. The agents had already learned that Rainey was in the pack that

Neshoba County sheriff Lawrence Rainey (left) and his deputy, Cecil Price, soon became suspects in the triple disappearance. FBI agents searched Mississippi for weeks, finding no bodies. Here they appear back on the job on December 5, 1964.

stormed a meeting at Mt. Zion Church—before it was burned—and beat a man unconscious. Reporters also had questions for Rainey. They had heard rumors that a white mob had been waiting outside the jail to seize the three civil rights workers. Rainey flatly said that hadn't happened.

When the agents called Rainey in for questioning, a county attorney came with him, ready to defend him if necessary. The agents showed Rainey pictures of Chaney, Goodman, and Schwerner. Never seen them, the sheriff said. Rainey then told the agents that on the night of June 21, when the men had disappeared, he had visited his wife in the hospital, then had dinner with relatives and spent the evening with them. He had made just a brief stop at the jail. There he had heard that the three men had been arrested—and released.

The agents listened and took notes. One of them asked Rainey if he was a Klansman. He said no, Neshoba County didn't even have a Klan. The county attorney could not believe what he was hearing. He knew that a flyer recruiting new Klan members had been posted on the wall near Rainey's office for days. One of the agents blurted out, "Now come on sheriff and tell us what you did with those people." Rainey said nothing. They let him leave, but they started checking his story. Rainey was shocked when the FBI called his wife in the hospital.

Two days later, the FBI heard from the attorney who had been in the room when they questioned Rainey. The attorney was stunned by Rainey's denial of Klan activity. Sheriff Rainey, the attorney told the FBI, should be their "number one suspect."

Agents also suspected Deputy Price. Like his boss, Price was a high-school dropout. His goofy behavior hid a dull rage. He shrugged off an FBI agent's questions and then offered the agent a drink of illegal home-brewed alcohol—from the trunk of his patrol car. Price's story about June 21 was simple: the arrest of the three men, their release, and their taillights disappearing into the night. Agents had discovered, though, that Price could not account for his whereabouts between 10:40 and 11:30 that night. Missing keys added to their suspicions. The Neshoba County jailer said that she normally received the car keys of suspects who were brought into the jail, but Price had given her no keys for the three men. Like the sheriff, the deputy refused to be questioned without a lawyer present.

The Civil Rights Act

On the evening of July 2, television shows were interrupted by a national news event. President Johnson urged Americans to "close the springs of racial poison." Then, on camera, he signed the Civil Rights Act. It was the first major civil rights bill since the Reconstruction period after the Civil War.

President John F. Kennedy had introduced the Civil Rights Act before he was assassinated. It met massive resistance from Southern senators. When Vice President Johnson became president, he threw his powers of persuasion behind the bill and managed to twist enough arms to get it passed. Now it was law, and now came what Johnson called the "time of testing." He had barely finished signing the act when a blazing Klan cross lit the sky in the central Mississippi town of Harmony.

The testing continued all weekend. There were beatings and shootings across the South. Demonstrators in New York City marched with black-bordered signs in memory of Chaney,

Goodman, and Schwerner. Across Mississippi, whites swore "Never!" and blacks tried to be hopeful. The summer project volunteers saw it all.

Volunteers celebrated the Fourth of July with local heroes—people who marched, registered, and risked everything in the name of freedom but who were little known outside Mississippi or even outside their towns. One of them was Vernon Dahmer, a farmer who was light-skinned enough to pass for white but was proud of his black ancestry. Dahmer had hosted the first SNCCs to work in Hattiesburg. Now he hosted a party on his farm. Whites and blacks shared hayrides and an enormous picnic of potato salad, watermelon, and fried catfish. Everyone had a great time until a pickup truck with a rifle rack passed. Dahmer and his sons, who were home on leave from the Marines, went into their house and came out with rifles of their own. The pickup passed again but drove on. The picnic continued until dusk. Then, before night fell, the volunteers scurried to wherever they were staying.

In Clarksdale, volunteers ate hot dogs and strummed guitars at "Doc" Henry's place. After the 1963 murder of his friend Medgar

At local civil rights leader Vernon Dahmer's fish fry for the volunteers on his property at the Kelly Settlement on July 4.

Evers, a slain civil rights activist, Aaron Henry had become the leading spokesman for black Mississippi. His home and pharmacy had been bombed. He had been arrested on trumped-up charges and had worked on a chain gang in a prison farm. Finally back at his home and business, Henry had supported Freedom Summer from the first day.

Women were also among the local heroes. From SNCC's first days in Mississippi, they had marched to courthouses, rallied their neighbors, and sung at mass meetings. One of them, Laura McGhee of Greenwood, had become a legend in 1963 when a cop knocked her down and she yanked away his nightstick. At the Dahmer picnic in Hattiesburg, volunteers met Victoria Gray, who had felt her life change when she took the step of registering to vote. A year later she was a field secretary for SNCC, running for Congress as the candidate of the Mississippi Freedom Democratic Party, which was organized by civil rights activists to challenge the power of the state's Democratic Party.

And then there was Fannie Lou Hamer, who hosted a Fourth of July picnic in Ruleville. The twentieth child of sharecroppers, she had

Victoria Gray at the Dahmer picnic on July 4, 1964.

worked in the cotton fields since the 1920s, growing up barefoot and hungry, wishing she were white. She had watched her father save to buy wagons and farm tools, only to have an envious white man poison his mules. When she went into the hospital for stomach pain, Hamer was sterilized—operated on so that she could not have children—without her consent. Something had to change.

In 1962 Hamer went to her first SNCC meeting. She heard a speaker say that if enough black people registered, they could vote racist politicians and sheriffs out of office. When he asked for volunteers, her hand shot up first. "Had it up as high as I could get it," she later said. She failed her first attempt to register because the registration test asked her to explain de facto laws. "I knowed as much about a facto law as a horse knows about Christmas Day," she later said. When the "boss man" who owned the property where Hamer worked heard that she had tried to register, she lost her job and was kicked out of her shack. She moved to a neighbor's place. One night her bedroom there was riddled with sixteen shots.

Fannie Lou Hamer, Mississippi Freedom Party delegate, at the Democratic National Convention, Atlantic City, New Jersey, August 1964.

MURIEL FACES HER FEARS

ANOTHER WEEK OF HOPE AND HATRED PASSED
in Mississippi, but the second week of the
summer project saw half as much violence of
the first. No one believed the terror had ended,
but fearful volunteers began to feel a little
confidence—at least during the day.

Muriel Tillinghast had spent two weeks
upstairs in the project office in Greenville. Other
volunteers came in early each morning and left
late each evening. The office had no refrigerator,
so Muriel lived on whatever food the others
brought her. No matter how they tried to get her
outside, she refused to leave. She was convinced
that her black skin and natural African hair made

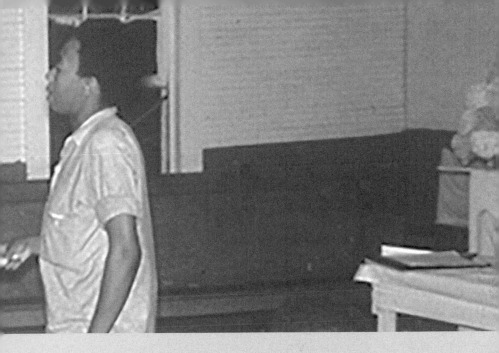

her a target. All her skills, her years of protests and picket lines, were overwhelmed by fear. Nightly anonymous phone threats fed those fears.

Meanwhile, volunteers marched around the Greenville courthouse, protesting the president's refusal to send federal marshals to Mississippi. The police watched, but they made no arrests. Even more startling, a Greenville jury gave a "not guilty" verdict in the trial of a black man accused by a white woman of sexual assault. No one could remember that ever happening in Mississippi. Several local high-school students led sit-ins at their school and started hanging around the project office.

Muriel Tillinghast addressing Precincts 4 and 5 regarding the Freedom Democratic Party in Greenville, Mississippi, August 4, 1964.

MEMO TO ALL STAFF
RE: JACKSON OFFICE SITUATION
FROM: MURIEL TILLINGHAST, JACKSON OFFICE MANAGER

As of my arrival in Jackson, the office staff and I have attempted the
the reorganization of this office. Undoubtedly, some changes are
slower than others. We are having some difficulty in a) deciding what
functions are vital to the central coordinating office (what persons
and jobs are necessary); b) systematizing the financial structure of
the State; c) getting shipments distributed throughout the State; and
d) handling the problems of personnel. You as the staff should feel
free to make any recommendations you see fit; it would, however,
greatly facilitate matters if these recommendations were in writing and
noted -- Jackson Situation --.

One of the tasks that JACKSON SHOULD NOT HAVE TO DEAL WITH IS THAT OF
ACCOMMODATING MEMBERS OF THE STAFF WHO DRIFT INTO JACKSON for one

Finally, Muriel realized: "I couldn't register people to vote on the second floor of the office. I had to come out." Sometime that Fourth of July weekend, she edged her way down the stairs and into the blinding glare of the Mississippi sun. Step by step, she learned to walk alongside her fears. She visited the mom-and-pop store she had seen from the second-story window and the juke joints farther down the street. No one drove by, shouting. No one noticed at all.

reason or another. All appointments (for the sake of having griev-
ances satisfied) should be made over the WATS line; and time to check
appointments with the persons necessarily involved in Jackson. Moreover,
appointments should be made early enough so to allow YOUR RETURN TO
YOUR PROJECTS BEFORE DARK. Anyone who wishes to remain in Jackson over-
night and who has intentions of staying at one of the Freedom Houses
must see me. It must be remembered that the Jackson Office Staff resides
at the Freedom Houses and therefore, can only take in a few "extra"
people at a time.
It may be important that you start thinking of your District Offices
as the centers to which you take unique problems. That is, with
respect to the five district offices, there would swiftly come about the
decentralization of the Jackson Office. Then whatever tasks can not be

By the time she began her third week in Mississippi, Muriel was herself again. She was still shaken, but she was ready to be the take-charge activist with the degree from Howard University and the street credentials from its Non-Violent Action Group. She thought she was ready for whatever Mississippi could throw at her. She didn't know that two weeks later she would be put in charge of the Greenville project.

Muriel Tillinghast's memo about the use of Freedom House in Jackson, Mississippi by volunteers. Council of Federated Organizations (COFO), 1964.

Hamer dug in and became a strong pillar of SNCC. She was not afraid of the risks. "The only thing they could do to me was kill me," she said, "and it seemed like they'd been trying to do that just a little bit at a time since I could remember." Hamer was deeply religious. She saw the movement in biblical terms. Beatings and jail were crosses to bear. The summer volunteers were Good Samaritans. Freedom was her own Promised Land. By 1964 her signature phrase— "I'm sick and tired of bein' sick and tired"—was widely known among black people in the Delta. Her favorite song—"This Little Light of Mine"— kicked off every mass meeting she attended.

Throughout Freedom Summer, Hamer's home would be a refuge and a headquarters for volunteers and for reporters looking for stories. When a cop asked her husband how he liked having "white boys" sleep in his house, Pap Hamer said, "I feel like a man because they treat me like a man." At Hamer's Fourth of July picnic, a local black woman said, "These young white folks who are already free, they come here only to help us. They is proving to us that black and white can do it together. . . ."

Barbara Schwartzbaum
and others singing, 1964.

Impossible to Imagine

At the end of the second week, leaders of the NAACP flew to Jackson, Mississippi. They came to put the new Civil Rights Act to the test. They expected to be arrested, maybe beaten.

Police met them at the airport and escorted them downtown to the Heidelberg hotel. There the local heroes of Jackson's civil rights movement joined them. The black men walked into the hotel, up to the desk—and checked in. A white bellboy took their bags. They ate lunch in the hotel restaurant. "The food was good, the service was good, and the attitude was good," said a Jackson minister. Just twelve days earlier, shots had been fired into his home. Tests at another hotel and a motel also went smoothly. The minister called these "helpful signs that Mississippi will get in step with the nation." The motel manager said, "We are just going to abide by the law."

On Monday morning, the NAACP leaders set out to tour Mississippi, making more tests of the law. SNCC prepared staffers to work in the "tough town" of McComb, a Klan hotbed.

Volunteers prepared to canvass and open Freedom Schools across the state. None of them knew that the holiday of progress and good feelings would end that night.

CHAPTER 6

THE SICKNESS
AND THE SCARS

MOSS POINT, A SMALL TOWN IN SOUTHERN Mississippi near the Gulf of Mexico, had already seen trouble that summer. Volunteers had been there only a few days when a meeting hall was firebombed. Tensions rose. Black and white people alike were buying guns. The town was a racial landmine, waiting to explode.

On Monday evening, July 6, three hundred people packed into the meeting hall that still had black scorch marks from the firebombing. Lawrence Guyot spoke to the crowd. He was angry and disappointed that only a few people had shown up to register in spite of much canvassing. "What will it take to make you people move?" Guyot shouted. Other speeches

The Society Hill Missionary Baptist Church in McComb, Mississippi, after a September 20, 1964, attack. It had been used as a Freedom School.

followed, and then Freedom Songs lowered the tension in the hall.

Meanwhile, in the nearby town of Pascagoula, three men crammed into a small car. They barely had room for the rifle.

Back at the meeting hall, the crowd had reached the song that ended many meetings: "We Shall Overcome." Their faces glowed as they sang together, arms clasped, swaying to the music. The cop who was there to prevent violence decided that the meeting was over. He drove away.

As the final "We Shall Overcome" filled the hall, a car sped past. Three sharp cracks rang out. A black woman near the window crumpled and fell. Chaos erupted. One volunteer saw the shot woman "lying on the ground and clutching her stomach." Several men ran out of the meeting hall, hopped into a car, and chased the attackers to a gas station. They fled when one of the white attackers raised the rifle. The police arrived, arrested the black men, and let everyone else go.

Reports said that the wounded woman was in good condition at a hospital. But the sudden, shocking outburst had shown that in spite of all the hopeful singing and the new Civil Rights Act, this was still Mississippi. The "long, hot summer" that had been predicted was under way—and it was only July. That night a volunteer wrote home from Moss Point, "Tonight the sickness struck."

Heat and Fire

July was an oven. The sky blazed, and thunderstorms sent marble-sized raindrops splattering onto dusty roads. The volunteers were still getting used to the weather, along with everything else. Only the richest homes had air-conditioning. There was no relief to be had by swimming. Rivers were muddy or full of snakes. Public pools were off-limits to the northern "invaders."

A Confederate flag flew outside the elegant Robert E. Lee hotel in Jackson. A sign read "Closed in Despair—Civil Rights Act Unconstitutional." A few days later, the hotel reopened as a club. It was private, which meant that it did not have to desegregate under the Civil Rights Act. Across town, city officials fenced off a park after white people complained about black kids running through it shouting, "I'm free!"

Pools and libraries closed in other parts of Mississippi. Restaurant owners drove black people off at gunpoint. Governor Paul Johnson predicted more violence "unless these people get out of the state"—meaning the summer project volunteers and SNCC staff. And just a few hours after the Moss Point shooting, flames torched three more black churches. The pattern was set: heat and fire.

By the second week of July, everyone was sure that James Chaney, Andrew Goodman, and Michael Schwerner were dead. Everyone except their mothers, that is. In her New York apartment, Carolyn Goodman was drawn to her son's room. Silent and sad, she sat staring at his books and folk music albums. She wondered what he had thought of each of them. She fought the fear that she might never be able to ask him. The Goodmans received many letters, but they were especially comforted by one from a mother in Meridian, Mississippi. She apologized for her state, saying, "Who are these fiends and where do they live who would come out of the darkness and kill?"

Meridian was home to James Chaney's mother, Fannie Lee Chaney. She paced outside her house each night until the sky grew light, wearing a new path in the grass. She refused to let twelve-year-old Ben go down the street to play ball. One evening she got a call from a young woman who said she had recently given birth to James's daughter. Fannie Lee did not believe her at first, but with just one look at the baby, she knew she was a grandmother. She took her granddaughter in her arms and wished she could do the same with her son.

Still there was no trace of the men. One new lead appeared—a grave along a river south of Neshoba County. It turned out to contain a dead horse. As hope faded, America's attention shifted away from Mississippi. Some whites in the state welcomed this as a return to "the good ol' days," when what happened in Mississippi stayed there and did not make national news. They stepped up their fight against Freedom Summer.

Cops continued to arrest volunteers on any excuse, but now they raised the bail. Instead of $100, volunteers had to pay $250 or even $400 to be released. Arrested for trespassing—$500. Trespassing with public swearing—$1,000 (equal to $8,280 in 2019). Ordinary citizens lashed out, too. In Hattiesburg, several black kids went to an inn where the "Whites Only" sign had been taken down. The owner's wife pulled a gun on them. In the Delta, a volunteer was physically thrown out of a courthouse. In Jackson, a white man parked his pickup truck, got out, decked an African American, and drove off. Encounters like these happened all over the state.

In Pike County in southern Mississippi, McComb was the toughest of the state's "tough towns." But Bob Moses felt that SNCC should "share the terror" of the African Americans who lived there, so they planned to open a Freedom House on the black side of McComb. Five volunteers and two SNCC staffers drove south from Jackson. A highway patrol car followed them into McComb and pulled them over. To their surprise, they were not beaten or arrested. No angry whites waited at the tumbledown building that was the new Freedom House. No pickups circled it. The next day, the SNCC staff and one of the touring members of Congress met with the mayor of McComb and the sheriff of Pike County. The sheriff promised police protection for the Freedom House. SNCC sent word to Jackson: "Morale is building."

But Bob Moses was not fooled. He visited the

Freedom House and begged the people he had just sent there to leave. Something was going to happen, he said. One SNCC staffer, Curtis Hayes, was from McComb. He had convinced Moses to open the Freedom House there, and he refused to leave. The others said they would leave in the morning. Moses left, and everyone went to sleep.

Later that night, with a blast heard all over McComb, eight sticks of dynamite blew open the front of the Freedom House. Curtis Hayes had been sleeping by the front window. The explosion knocked him across the room, unconscious. He woke with his ears ringing and cuts on his arms, legs, and face. A volunteer from Oregon had suffered a concussion. The others were unhurt, although the house was badly damaged. The team reported to COFO headquarters in Jackson that the bomb would not drive them out: "We are going ahead in the community. Everyone determined. Mass meeting tonight."

Mississippi's Freedom Schools Open

Three dozen Freedom Schools opened across Mississippi in the second week of July. Classes met in fixed-up shacks, in church basements, and on lawns in the shade of trees. No one *had* to attend—people came because they wanted to. There were no lectures, no tests, and no homework. The young volunteer teachers had few textbooks and only a little training. What they *did* have was eagerness and enthusiasm. The lessons of these Freedom Schools would change the lives of nearly every student and every teacher.

It was 1964, ten years after the Supreme Court's ruling in *Brown v. Board of Education*. That ruling had officially ended racial segregation in public schools—yet Mississippi had defied the law. Its schools remained completely segregated. The state spent much more money on white schools than on black ones. Only 42 percent of white Mississippians had graduated from high school. For blacks, though, that figure was just 7 percent. SNCC's "Notes on Teaching in Mississippi" told the volunteers of the Freedom Schools what to expect:

> You will be teaching young people who have lived in Mississippi all their lives. That means that they have been deprived of decent education from first

grade through high school. It means that
they have been denied free expression
and free thought. Most of all it means
that they have been denied the right to
question. The purpose of the Freedom
Schools is to help them begin to
question.

The volunteers would meet students bearing
"the scars of the system. . . . [A]ll of them will
have a knowledge beyond their years. This
knowledge is the knowledge of how to survive in
a society that is out to destroy you."

The teachers' main responsibility was to
be honest. "Honesty means that you will *ask*
questions as well as answer them," the SNCC
teaching guide said. "It means that if you don't
know something you will say so."

It hadn't been easy to plan three dozen schools
for a thousand students. Teachers and college
professors had helped SNCC create a program of
study. In addition to classes in reading, writing,
and math for all levels, the schools would teach
students about the Civil Rights movement and
black history. Teachers were also encouraged to
offer the kinds of classes that only white children
enjoyed in Mississippi: art, dance, theater, and

FRAN AND THE CHILDREN OF VICKSBURG

WHEN VOLUNTEER FRAN O'BRIEN ARRIVED in Mississippi, she stepped off the Greyhound bus into warm, soft rain on the bluffs above Vicksburg. This was very different from her home in southern California, where it never rains in the summer. Yet as soon as she stepped into COFO's Freedom House in Vicksburg, Fran felt right at home among her lifelong friends—children.

A guest in the Freedom House was a black woman whose husband had been killed by the Klan. Her house had been bombed, so she was staying in the Freedom House with her six children. At once the children gathered around Fran, a young woman with curly hair and a sweet smile. They begged her to do something with them on this rainy day. So she sat at a broken-down piano and played every song the

kids knew. While other volunteers explored the neighborhood, Fran spent all afternoon singing, inventing games, and telling stories.

Twenty-one-year-old Fran O'Brien did not care much about the politics of Freedom Summer. She saw the project as a chance to test her Christian values, and to teach. Fran was shy around adults, but she came alive with children. In the seven weeks that followed that first day in Vicksburg, Fran would meet Martin Luther King, Jr. She would have a terrifying run-in with the Ku Klux Klan. But always she would focus on the children.

On the evening when President Johnson signed the Civil Rights Act, Fran was at the Freedom House. It was crammed with volunteers and neighbors who didn't have televisions. Everyone cheered when Johnson signed the bill. They sang

Teachers at the Freedom School convention during Freedom Summer, August 8, 1964. The woman in the center is Liz Fusco, one of the coordinators of the Freedom School project.

"We Shall Overcome." Then, for fun, they sang a
new version: "We Have Overcome."

Four days later, Fran began teaching at the
community center. She helped kids weave on
looms made of cardboard. She read stories.
That afternoon, while a mob in Neshoba County
menaced the visiting NAACP leaders, Fran led
the children in outdoor games. And that night,
while shots rang out in Moss Point, she and other
teachers planned the next week. Just before going
to bed, Fran wrote to her mother:

> Please try not to worry too much.
> Vicksburg is the best place to work in
> Mississippi so far as staying out of trouble
> is concerned. . . . I'm very grateful to you
> for standing behind me in this.
> Good Night and Love,
> Fran

Fran O'Brien
teaching at a
Freedom School in
Mississippi, 1964.

foreign languages. Above all, the teachers were told to "be creative. Experiment. The kids will love it."

But would anyone come to classes taught by strangers? In the middle of the summer?

Three Freedom Schools were planned for the town of Canton, half an hour from the capital of Jackson. Before they opened, one man threatened to bomb the homes of any students who came to the schools. Another broke into the new library and vandalized the books. No one signed up for classes at one of the schools. Just a handful came to the other two.

The volunteers in Canton fought back—in their nonviolent way. They went door to door to talk to families. They hosted a Fourth of July picnic. Students started coming to the schools. Before long, more than seventy-five young people had enrolled in Canton's Freedom Schools. In Ruleville, where Fred Winn and other volunteers had turned an old outhouse into a school, the public schools had not yet let out for the summer, so the Freedom School offered morning classes for adults. Some of them brought their preschool-age children with them. While adults studied citizenship, health,

"Notes on Teaching in Mississippi."

NOTES ON TEACHING IN MISSISSIPPI

INTRODUCTION TO THE SUMMER - - - Jane Stembridge

This is the situation: You will be teaching young people who have lived in Mississippi all their lives. That means that they have been deprived of decent education, from the first grade through high school. It means that they have been denied free expression and free thought. Most of all -- it means that they have been denied the right to question.

The purpose of the Freedom Schools is to help them begin to question.

What will they be like? They will all be different - but they will have in common the scars of the system. Some will be cynical. Some will be distrustful. All of them will have a serious lack of preparation both with regard to academic subjects and contemporary issues - but all of them will have a knowledge far beyond their years. This knowledge is the knowledge of how to survive in a society that is out to destroy you . . . and the knowledge of the extent of evil in the world.

Because these young people possess such knowledge, they will be ahead of you in many ways. But this knowledge is purely negative; it is only **half** of the picture and, so far as the Negro is concerned, it is the first half. It has, in a sense, already been lived through. The old institutions are crumbling and there is great reason to hope for the first time. You will help them to see this hope and inspire them to go after it.

What will they demand of you? They will demand that you be honest. Honesty is an attitude toward life which is communicated by everything you do. Since you, too, will be in a learning situation - honesty means that you will **ask** questions as well as answer them. It means that if you don't know something you will say so. It means that you will not "act" a part in the attempt to compensate for all they've endured in Mississippi. You can't compensate for that, and they don't want you to try. It would not be **real,** and the greatest contribution that you can make to them is to be real.

Remember this: These young people have been taught by the system not to trust. You have to be trust-**worthy.** It's that simple. Secondly, there is very little if anything that you can teach them about prejudice and segregation. They know. What you can and must do is help them develop ideas and associations and tools with which they can do something **about** segregation and prejudice.

How? We can say that the key to your teaching will be honesty and creativity. We can prepare materials for you and suggest teaching methods. Beyond that, it is your classroom. We will be happy to assist whenever we can.

How? You will discover the way - because that is why you have come.

reading, writing, and math, children raced in and out as they played. High-school students took over the school in the afternoons. They explored literature, African culture, art, and biology.

Mickey and Rita Schwerner's Freedom House in Meridian had paved the way for the Freedom Schools there. SNCC expected fifty students in Meridian. One hundred and twenty showed up. Other schools opened up that week in Greenwood, Vicksburg, Greenville, and Moss Point. But the most successful schools were in Hattiesburg. Black people there still talked about "Freedom Day" six months earlier, when two hundred people marched outside the courthouse in the rain. Since then, more than a thousand people in Hattiesburg had tried to register to vote. Some had tried eight times.

Why was Hattiesburg so fired up? The answer: Clyde Kennard. He was a black Army veteran who had tried to enroll at the all-white Mississippi Southern College. The State Sovereignty Commission refused to let Kennard integrate the college. Instead, it helped frame him for a crime he didn't commit—stealing chicken feed. Kennard was sent to Parchman,

the state's high-security prison. He became
ill with cancer, but the state did not release
him until a few months before he died. (In
2005, evidence was published that showed
that Kennard was innocent. The next year his
conviction was overturned, more than forty
years after his death.)

Outrage over Kennard's treatment had
united the black people of Hattiesburg. The
town welcomed SNCC. As Freedom Summer
approached, SNCC planned seven Freedom
Schools for the town. The organizers expected
150 students—and 575 showed up. The first
person to sign up was an eighty-two-year-old
man. He had taught himself to read, but he
needed help with the voter registration form. All
seven of Hattiesburg's Freedom Schools were
full when classes started. The organizers had to
promise a second set of classes in August.

One Freedom School teacher, Pamela Parker,
wrote to her parents back home in Pennsylvania:

> The atmosphere in class is unbelievable.
> It is what every teacher dreams about—
> real, honest enthusiasm and desire to
> learn anything and everything. The girls
> come to class of their own free will. They

respond to everything that is said. They are excited about learning. They drain me of everything I have to offer so that I go home at night completely exhausted but very happy. . . .

Kids who came to the Freedom Schools were amazed to learn that African Americans had a proud history. Smiles spread across their faces when they heard the story of the African captives who had rebelled on the slave ship *Amistad* in 1839. They were stunned to hear that a black man, Matthew Henson, had been one of the first people to reach the North Pole. They ate up the poems of African American writer Langston Hughes. Endesha Ida Mae Holland, who later became a scholar and playwright, was a student at the Greenwood Freedom School when she read the book *Black Boy* by Richard Wright. "I kept thinking, 'Well, you mean black folk can actually write *books*?'" she later said. "Because I'd always been told blacks had done no great things . . . We had *nothing* that we could be proud of."

A few Freedom Schools, however, were almost silent. The town of Moss Point was still shaken by the drive-by shooting that had happened there. Fewer than a dozen students came to its

Freedom School every day. In several towns, ministers refused to turn church halls into classrooms for fear of firebombings. And in the deeply poor town of Shaw, in the Delta, the number of students fell from forty on the first day to ten on the second. Overall, the Freedom Schools were a success, but pockets of despair remained.

The KKK and the FBI

Two forces would shape that summer in Mississippi. One was the Ku Klux Klan, doing what it had always done—using fear to terrorize black people. The other was the FBI, which had delayed its arrival in Mississippi but, once there, went quickly to work. The key to finding the three missing men, FBI agents soon realized, lay with the Klan.

The Ku Klux Klan was a "secret" organization. Its members used handshakes and code words to communicate with each other in public. When racial violence took place, the KKK almost never claimed to be responsible.

It had been ninety years since KKK violence had "redeemed" Mississippi—that is, returned whites to total power after the Civil War. Since that time, although the Klan surfaced in other states, it had rarely been strong in Mississippi. Whites there saw little need for it. Black people "knew their place," and ordinary white people knew enough about terrorism to keep them in it. The state's long history of lynching was proof of that.

Then, during the Civil Rights movement, the Klan rose again, and not just in Mississippi. By 1964, North Carolina's Klan had seven thousand members. A "Razorback Klan" raged across Arkansas. Fiery Klan rallies sparked violence in Florida. In Mississippi, most beatings, threats, bombings, and other mayhem were carried out by people who were not Klansmen. But several months before Freedom Summer, a new Klan offshoot began infecting the state.

The White Knights of the Ku Klux Klan of Mississippi had a mission. They explained it in *The Klan Ledger*, a pamphlet that was handed out on the Fourth of July. The group's mission was to fight the "savage blacks and their communist masters" who were bringing agitation to "the Innocent People of Mississippi." The *Ledger* claimed that Klansmen were not involved in the disappearance of Chaney, Goodman, and

Schwerner. Klansmen said that the three men hadn't really disappeared—it was all a hoax. But, the *Ledger* warned, "We are not going to sit back and permit our rights and the rights of our posterity to be negotiated away by . . . brainwashed black savages . . . meeting with some stupid or cowardly politician."

No matter what the *Ledger* said, many people thought the Klan was responsible for the disappearance of the three civil rights workers. Locals in Philadelphia, in Neshoba County, tried to guess which tight-lipped farmers, or hot-tempered businessmen, or brutal cops had joined the Klan. A group of white men called "the goon squad" was often seen entering the Steak House Cafe, which soon became a private club. Its windows were covered with white sheets—not so different from the white robes worn by the Klan. On the other side of the railroad tracks, in the African American neighborhoods, people heard whenever a black maid found white robes in her white boss's closet.

The Klan's main targets were black, but it also terrorized whites who got in its way. Before Freedom Summer was over, crosses would burn on the lawns of two mayors, a newspaper editor, a doctor who gave money to rebuild a burned church, a grocer who refused to fire his black employees, and a judge. The message was clear.

The head of the Mississippi Klan—known as the Imperial Wizard—was a businessman named Sam Bowers. He was the only Klansman who could order the most drastic act of terror: "extermination," or murder. No one outside the Klan knew the identity of the Imperial Wizard. No one knew whether he had ordered the extermination of Chaney, Goodman, and Schwerner. But as the summer heated up, Klansmen stockpiled gasoline and dynamite, knowing they would carry on with their "sacred mission."

Attorney General Robert Kennedy had warned President Johnson that the Klan was on the rise. "I have little doubt that this will increase," Kennedy said. In July, after the disappearance of the three men, Johnson ordered FBI director J. Edgar Hoover to assign a large number of agents to watch the Klan. "I don't want the Klansmen to open their mouth without you knowing what they're saying," Johnson told Hoover. On July 9, Hoover stunned Mississippi by announcing that he would visit Jackson the next day.

The FBI director had never come to Mississippi before. His announcement set off a frenzy of guesswork about the case of the missing men. One newspaper ran a headline saying that there would soon be arrests. The truth was that the FBI was nowhere near arresting anyone. Agents got no information from locals. Instead, people shouldered them off sidewalks, spat at them, and even planted rattlesnakes in one agent's car.

FBI agent Joseph Sullivan was in charge of the investigation. He had found just one good witness: the highway patrolman who had handed over the list of suspects. This informant talked with Sullivan about which citizens might be Klansmen. But whenever Sullivan asked about the three missing men, the patrolman fell silent. One FBI agent said, "We haven't even started leaning on suspects yet. When we do, we're going to lean real hard. I feel like somebody will break."

The governor and mayor greeted FBI director Hoover when he arrived in Jackson. "This is truly a great day!" exclaimed the mayor as he pumped Hoover's hand. The FBI director did not seem to agree. His usual scowl did not change.

Rabbi Arthur J. Lelyveld shortly after he and fellow voter registration volunteers Lawrence Spears and David Owen were attacked
by two white men from Collins, Mississippi. The assault took place
at 11:30 a.m. on July 10, 1964, as they were walking to Morning
Star Baptist Church with Hattiesburg resident Janet Crosby and
another young African American woman after a morning of voter
registration canvassing. This photograph was published the following day on the front page of the *New York Journal-American* under
the banner headline "The Beaten Rabbi / Racists Did This."

When reporters asked Hoover about Chaney, Goodman, and Schwerner, he paused. Then he said, "I don't close it as an absolute certainty, but I consider that they are dead." He hinted that he might visit Neshoba County. (Death threats later made him cancel that plan.) Hoover also insisted that the fifty new agents who had come to Mississippi were there only to investigate the case, not to serve as bodyguards. "We most certainly do not and will not give protection to civil rights workers," he said. A state senator, however, called it an "insult" that there were two hundred FBI agents in Mississippi.

The Sickness Strikes Again

While Hoover spoke that morning in Jackson, the sickness struck again in the glare of daylight.

In Hattiesburg, a middle-aged man and his nephew tossed a tire iron into a pickup truck and set out to beat up the first white people they saw showing friendship or kindness toward African Americans. When they spotted three white men walking with a couple of black girls, they leaped from their truck and attacked the men. A Jewish religious leader named Arthur Lelyveld got the worst of the attack. The tire iron smashed him in the head. The attackers fled while he slumped to the ground, badly injured. The next day, photos of the bloodstained rabbi were seen around the country. He spoke of his "deep sorrow for Mississippi."

More reasons for "deep sorrow" soon appeared. Another Freedom House was firebombed. A twelve-year-old boy was beaten with baseball bats while cops looked on. Churches were doused with kerosene and set afire. An elderly white man beat a black woman in a coffee shop. Then news broke that a fisherman in Louisiana, down the Mississippi River, had found half a body—just the legs— snagged on a log in the river. The following day, agents found another half body on a sandbar.

Both corpses were black. Papers in their pockets identified them as students from Alcorn, an African American college in Mississippi. They had been kidnapped in May, murdered, tied to an old engine, and thrown into the river. One volunteer wrote to his parents, "Mississippi is the only state where you can drag a river any time and find bodies you were not expecting. Negroes disappear down here every week and are never heard about. . . ."

Local law cracked down on Freedom Summer volunteers. On July 15, thirty-four of them were arrested. In the "tough town" of Drew, two dozen were crammed into a stinking cement jail. They sweated, swatted mosquitoes, and sang until they were hoarse. Across Mississippi, volunteers struggled to keep up their spirits. They had seen disappearances, bombings, beatings, and arrests. Some must have wondered whether coming to Mississippi had been a mistake. But the volunteers soldiered on.

Parents Take Action

Church burnings. Attacks with tire irons. Corpses floating in rivers. What could volunteers' parents think when reading of such horrors in the state where their children were spending the summer? Friends kept asking parents how they could let their children go "down there." Some parents were now calling their children every day, begging them to come home. But most parents only called each other.

Even before the volunteers went to Mississippi, their parents had been sharing their worries with one another. In late April, parents in Pennsylvania had written to President

FRED AND THE NIGHT OF TERROR

IN THE THIRD WEEK OF JULY, FRED WINN'S FATHER
came home to find a letter from his son. Fred had
been sent to the bone-poor Delta town of Shaw,
where his handyman skills were needed. Fred was
"running [his] rear end off," the letter said. And he
was shocked by the suffering and poverty he saw
in the black community.

Charlie Capps, the county sheriff, considered
volunteers like Fred to be "dirty" and "unclean."
Still, the sheriff did not want the FBI to "invade"
his county as it had in Neshoba County. He called
Fred and other volunteers into his office and
advised them to go home where they belonged.
He warned them that local whites hated them

with a fury that no sheriff could contain. Then, seeing that the volunteers would not leave, Capps said that he and his deputies would do their best "to keep a lid on things." Reading the letter, Fred's father felt that the lid was about to blow off.

On July 11, the volunteers in Shaw were relaxing in the community center that was about to open. Blacks and whites talked together, sang, and shared a watermelon. Then a panicked African American boy ran in and said he'd just been offered $400 to blow up the building. At once the volunteers turned off all lights and fled to the back office. Several made long-distance phone calls. Fred called the *San Francisco Chronicle*, but got no interest in the story.

The minutes crept by. Every time headlights slid across the walls, the volunteers wondered if Shaw was going to be the next McComb, with bombs blasting in the night. From the roof, a volunteer spotted two police cars and six helmeted cops standing guard. As lightning lit the horizon, the cops joked and talked while cars drove past, headed for the Freedom House. A shotgun blast, bomb, or flaming bottle could come flying from any one of those cars.

Around midnight, the storm broke out, lashing the trees and spattering the dusty earth. Cops and cars headed home. So did the weary volunteers. The FBI showed up at 1:30 in the morning.

In his home in San Francisco, Fred's father read another volunteer's angry account of "our night of terror," which Fred had included in his letter:

> I was and am furious. Here are youths
> who would be the glory of any nation,
> and they waited for a bomb to blow
> them out of this hostile land. . . . And
> this is in the land of the free. Here where
> millions have come seeking streets paved
> with gold, there have lived millions on
> streets drowning in mud. . . . Here in the
> beautiful land of the purple mountain's
> majesty, we sat and waited for the
> bombers.

Johnson, asking for federal protection for the volunteers. A month later, Massachusetts parents did the same.

Two weeks before Chaney, Goodman, and Schwerner disappeared, a "Parents Emergency Committee" in New York City had sent a telegram to the president. They urged him to do something "before a tragic incident takes place." Three days after the tragic incident, two dozen parents flew to the nation's capital to talk with senators, the deputy attorney general, and a White House staff member.

In California, Fran O'Brien's mother subscribed to the Vicksburg newspaper and worried about her daughter. In Massachusetts, Chris Williams's mother saved his letters and hoped for the best. In Washington, D.C., Muriel Tillinghast's mother feared the worst. The parents who could only sit and wait refused to do so alone. They formed parent support groups across the country. "Sometimes when I lie awake at night," a woman said at one meeting, "I can't get the picture of my child, mutilated or dead, out of my mind."

In Los Angeles, parents held their first meeting beside a pool at a house in Beverly Hills.

The group included a movie director, a janitor's wife, and a high-school teacher. They were from different walks of life, but they shared the same fear. A woman talked about her son David, a Hattiesburg volunteer who had been beaten along with Rabbi Lelyveld. David now had seven stitches in his scalp. He was saving his bloody shirt as a souvenir. Other grim-faced parents shared letters from their children. One volunteer had written, "I'm hot, I'm miserable and I can't get my clothes washed. Would you please let me stay another month?"

The Los Angeles group also heard from a group that had formed in the San Francisco area. Those parents had talked to people from Mississippi who had come to San Francisco for the national convention of the Republican party. The Mississippians had given the parents two pieces of advice to pass on to their children. The first was "leave." The second was "pray."

JULY 16, 1964

ANOTHER SO-CALLED "FREEDOM DAY"

SNCC HAD DECLARED THAT JULY 16 WOULD BE a statewide Freedom Day in Mississippi—a time for African Americans to march on their county courthouses, making their voices heard and registering to vote. Summer project volunteers and staffers would help them get there.

In Greenville, where Muriel Tillinghast was stationed, several COFO cars broke down. Trips to the Washington County courthouse were delayed, but by noon the line of people waiting to register stretched to the street. Police watched, but they didn't arrest anyone. By the end of the day, a hundred people had filled out voter registration forms.

An impromptu concert held outside the Freedom School, Priest Creek Baptist Church, 1964.

To the north, in Bolivar County, dozens of volunteers had come from all over the Delta to the county capital of Cleveland. Many of them came from Shaw, with memories of the recent bomb threat. The Shaw volunteers had feared there would be trouble, so they gave lessons in nonviolence to the local people. As it turned out, the lessons weren't needed. Volunteers lined the sidewalk, chanting "Jim Crow must GO!" Three dozen sheriff's deputies with shotguns stood on guard, keeping angry whites at a safe distance. When the courthouse closed for lunch, blacks and whites shared sandwiches beneath the trees. Three cars filled with young white men circled the integrated picnic. After the volunteers asked the deputies to keep them away, the cars were not seen again. More than two dozen people registered to vote in Cleveland that day. Bolivar County Sheriff Charlie Capps had kept his word to "keep a lid on things."

Freedom Day was uneventful in Greenville and Cleveland. But Greenwood, the capital of Leflore County on the other side of the Delta, was a different story.

Trouble in Greenwood

On its front page, the *Greenwood Chronicle* had warned of "another so-called 'Freedom Day.'" Ever since SNCC first came into the Mississippi Delta, Greenwood had been its biggest battle. Like many other towns in the state, Greenwood was part of the cotton empire. It depended on the cheap labor of sharecroppers. The threat of black people voting put that empire at risk.

The slightest push toward full democracy had already sparked violence in Greenwood. Two years earlier, in the summer of 1962, SNCC staffers had fled out the back window when a white mob ransacked their office. Bullets and firebombs hit the office the following spring. Shots fired at Bob Moses' car had hit driver Jimmie Travis in the shoulder, neck, and head. Travis survived, after a frantic rush to the hospital. He had shown his scars to the volunteers during their training week in Ohio.

By July 1964, Greenwood's anti-black terrorism was backfiring. Hundreds of people were coming to meetings to sing, shout, and chant "Freedom Now!" SNCC had just moved its national headquarters from Atlanta, Georgia, to Greenwood. Excitement rose as Freedom Day approached. Students at the Greenwood Freedom School could talk of little else. Signs in storefront windows urged everyone to come to the courthouse on July 16. SNCC expected five hundred people to show up. In the office, volunteers drew lots to see who would test the state's new law against picketing—that is, standing or marching slowly outside a building, often with protest signs. "I want to go to jail," said one volunteer from California. "I'm honest. I've never been."

Finally the day arrived. Black women in flowered dresses and men in weathered suits made their way up the courthouse steps. Volunteers and SNCC staffers took up their picket signs on the sidewalk. A row of helmeted cops hefted their nightsticks. Across the street, a bus waited to take arrested picketers to jail. The police chief announced, "No one will interfere with you if you want to stand here to register but we will not allow any picketing." The chief gave the picketers two minutes to stand down. They kept marching.

The *Student Voice* covers Freedom Day in Greenwood, Mississippi. July 22, 1964.

SELMA, ALABAMA
PROGRESSIVE & FRIENDLY
Coca-Cola

INTIMIDATION

IN ALABAMA

ON PAGE TWO

THE STUDENT VOICE

VOL. 5 NO. 17   STUDENT VOICE, INC.   6 Raymond Street, N. W.   Atlanta, Georgia 30314   JULY 22, 1964

IN GREENWOOD

111 ARRESTS MARK MISS. FREEDOM DAY

FORMAN CALLS FOR FEDERAL PROTECTION

GREENWOOD, MISS. - In what SNCC Executive Secretary James Forman described as "flagrant violations of the 1960 and 1964 Civil Rights Acts and the First Amendment," 111 local Negroes, SNCC workers, and Mississippi Summer Project volunteers were arrested here after a Freedom Day on July 16.

On July 17, the cases were removed to Federal court.

SNCC has been working in Greenwood since 1962. Greenwood's first "Freedom Day" was held March 25, and resulted in the arrests of 14 workers and local residents. A second "Freedom Day" was held April 9; 46 persons were arrested.

The jailings were made as integrated groups picketed the Leflore County Courthouse, carrying signs urging Negroes to reg-

CONTINUED ON PAGE 4

GREENWOOD POLICE drag pregnant rights worker during Freedom Day to increase Negro voter registration.

RUINS OF JERUSALEM BAPTIST AND BETHEL METHODIST CHURCHES in Kingston, near Natchez. The two churches are among 10 burned or bombed in Mississippi since the Mississippi Summer Project began.

CHURCH BURNINGS STILL UNCHECKED

FLASH! At press time STUDENT VOICE learned that three more churches have been bombed in Mississippi. Details and pictures next week.

GREENWOOD, MISS - Another church burning in Mississippi on July 17 raises the total burned or bombed to 10. SNCC re-

ported this week.

The most recent burning occured in McComb, July 17 when the Zion Hill Baptist Church burned to the ground. The church, located west of McComb on Route 44, had not been used for civil rights activity.

Two other burnings occurred

CONTINUED ON PAGE 3

Then the roundup began. Cops yanked people to the bus. A few went limp and had to be dragged. Some were cracked with nightsticks. Soon the bus was full of black and white protestors, singing. A second wave of picketers began to march. Inside the courthouse, black people patiently waited in line to fill out forms for the county registrar.

A Nation of Change and Fear

By July 1964, years of violence and civil rights marches across the South had widened the gap between black and white in America. Today, when Martin Luther King is a national hero and his birthday is a national holiday, we assume he was always admired. But during the 1960s, many white people questioned his motives. And in the summer of 1964, with the Civil Rights Act just passed, a white backlash was brewing. A man in Chicago said, "When are they going to do something for white people?" A poll showed that 60 percent of Americans thought black people wanted to take their jobs. And while most white people *said* they supported integration, three out of five also said that neighborhoods and social clubs should be able to keep out black people.

Racial resentment was just part of the nation's uneasy mood. The assassination of President Kennedy and other highly visible murders had shaken the image of the United States as a peaceful country. The Supreme Court had banned prayer in public schools. There was talk of bombing Vietnam. In some ways, the country still looked the way it had in the 1950s. Behind that appearance, though, many people feared things were changing too quickly.

Yet most Americans had never had it so good. The median family income (meaning that half of all families earned more money, and half less) had gone up a staggering 53 percent since 1950. The country was more productive than it had ever been. There were more things to buy than ever, and many people had more money than ever with which to buy them. A lot of well-off people disapproved of anything that might rock America's smooth-sailing boat.

Two-thirds of all Americans, according to one poll, were against the Mississippi summer project. "It's too much like taking the law in their own hands," said a worker in Detroit. The nation's newspapers showed little sympathy for the project. *The Wall Street Journal*, for example, said, "Without condoning racist attitudes, we think it understandable that the people of Mississippi should resent such an invasion. The outsiders are said to regard themselves as some sort of heroic freedom fighters but in truth, they are asking for trouble."

Readers shared their opinions in letters to newspaper editors. A woman in Oklahoma called the three missing civil rights workers "no-good rabblerousers." Someone in Louisiana asked, "By what stretch of the imagination does anyone consider that these kids have any right in Mississippi in the first place?"

Freedom Summer had opened wounds between North and South—wounds that dated back to the Civil War. Suddenly the South seemed fair game for insults. A California man wrote that Lincoln had made a mistake in fighting to keep the Southern states in the Union. He said, "Isn't there a way to 'secede' them NOW?" Southerners rose up in defense. In the crossfire, only a few Americans praised the summer project volunteers. Many suspected that "the whole scheme," as an Indiana man called it, was "not to help the Negro people but to agitate and create unrest and strife in the hope of more votes" for Democrats.

Mississippi's Freedom Day took place during the week of the national convention of the Republican party in San Francisco. Republicans competed to be their party's nominee for president, hoping to defeat Johnson. Barry Goldwater, a conservative Republican who had been against the new civil rights law, won the nomination. In Goldwater's view, Johnson's support for civil rights made him "the biggest faker in the United States." Goldwater would lose badly to Johnson in the November presidential election, but he had started the Republicans on a sharp shift to more conservative positions. That shift would grow stronger in the years ahead.

The Day Ends in Mississippi
As Freedom Day continued in Mississippi, word spread of arrests in Greenwood. Volunteers and SNCC staff poured into town. A third wave of picketers hit the sidewalk just after lunch. Like the first two groups, they were arrested and hauled off to jail, sometimes violently. One volunteer would never forget seeing an electric

cattle prod used on SNCC member Stokely
Carmichael.

Once under arrest, picketers came face-to-
face with the terror of a Mississippi jail. Cops
smirked at them. On the wall hung a plaque
awarded to the same police dog that had attacked
civil rights marchers a year before. The FBI
poster of Chaney, Schwerner, and Goodman
hung there, too—with a mustache drawn on
Goodman. Down a dark hallway were the cells
where a cop could beat a black inmate.

On Greenwood's courthouse steps, African
Americans kept filing into the registrar's
office. The jail, though, was filling up. That day
Greenwood had the summer's largest total of
arrests: 111 men and women, black and white.
Men were kept in segregated cells on one floor,
women in segregated cells on another. Packed
together, breathing stinking, muggy air, they
sang, talked, and refused to eat. Their hunger
strike started after one woman spit out her
food—rice and beans, heavily laced with pepper.
The prisoners wondered: When would they hear
from their lawyers? When would SNCC get them
out?

Freedom Day had been a sign of change coming to America. In Mississippi, it had been a day of victories and defeats. Cops harassed volunteers. Project offices received phone threats. Rumors flew that whites would soon bomb McComb's Freedom House. But black citizens had registered to vote, and in Natchez, a white minister had collected money to help rebuild black churches. And in the Greenwood jail late that evening, a tap came on the wall of the white women's cell. A small, flat panel opened, and a face appeared. A black face. Identifying himself as a "trusty," the man passed in candy bars and a note from the black women: "We will sing loud about daybreak. Freedom."

CHAPTER 7

"WALK TOGETHER, CHILDREN"

TREMBLING, NAUSEATED, AND TERRIFIED, IRA Landess rode the bus toward McComb. After the McComb Freedom House was bombed, SNCC had called for more volunteers to come "share the terror." Landess, a reading teacher from New York, had answered the call. Even before he got to Mississippi, he had seen what some people in the South thought of his mission. On his way South, Ira had stopped in Memphis, Tennessee. There a cabdriver had hurled Ira's bags to the ground after learning he was a volunteer for the summer project.

Ira had entered Mississippi on the Fourth of July. He went to the picnic in Hattiesburg and shared food and a hayride with other volunteers

SNCC field secretary Sandy Leigh, director of the COFO-Hattiesburg Project, lecturing on the Mississippi Freedom Democratic Party (MFDP) to Freedom School students and their teachers at True Light Baptist Church in Hattiesburg, Mississippi, 1964.

and local people. Then he took cover when the truck with the gun rack drove past. His first few nights and days were strange. After dark, sounds startled him awake. By day he realized just how strange a place he had come to when kids asked him if Jewish people like him had tails. And then, terrified, he took a bus to McComb.

By the middle of July, Ira had settled into McComb. Nothing worse than fear had attacked him. He was glad to be teaching. But what made him feel most at home was a greeting he got one afternoon as he walked through a black neighborhood. A bent, gray-haired woman stepped out of her shack and saw him. A big smile broke out across her face. She waved and said, "Hello, Freedom!"

A Game of Chance, Every Day
July crawled toward August. The volunteers wondered—had it only been a month? A month of slow, sweaty afternoons and dark, fearful nights. A month of roof-raising mass meetings and soulful dinners with host families. A month shadowed by the disappearance in the first week of James Chaney, Michael Schwerner, and Andrew Goodman.

Sometimes it felt that the summer had lasted forever. Did their comfortable lives back home still exist? Bob Moses had warned them, "When you're not in Mississippi, it's not real, and when you're there the rest of the world isn't real."

Meeting white people had become a game of chance. Volunteers never knew what might happen when they left the African American quarters and went downtown. Those huge men huddled on the bench might just glare. Those three young toughs hanging around the gas station might settle for threats. But the men on the bench could easily hurl a beer bottle. The young men could throw punches. Most volunteers came home safely. But every day, luck ran out for a few.

A month of Freedom Summer had been enough for a few fearful volunteers, who went home. The rest dug in and focused on their jobs—teaching another class, knocking on another door. They took a defiant new attitude toward Mississippi's "tough towns." Volunteers poured into places like McComb and Drew, filling offices, meeting local heroes, daring police and locals to pounce. In Harmony, Mississippi, volunteers had tried to find a home for a Freedom School. But locals refused to let them use any buildings in the small town. So volunteers in Harmony raised enough money to build their own school. Dozens of people sawed and hammered, while pickups circled menacingly and black women served fried chicken and Kool-Aid.

In late July, COFO sued the Klan, the Citizens' Council, and Sheriff Lawrence Rainey of Neshoba County, who was becoming a suspect in the disappearance of the three men. The lawsuit charged that all three had "engaged in widespread terroristic acts . . . to intimidate, punish and deter the Negro citizens of Mississippi." No one expected COFO to win the lawsuit, but at least the sheriff would have to hire a lawyer and appear in court.

As summer dragged on, volunteers found fresh sources of support. Dozens of doctors, nurses, dentists, and psychiatrists were making two-week tours of Mississippi. They not only tended to the volunteers' health but gave black children their first medical exams. Celebrities also showed up to lend support. Fannie Lou Hamer was surprised to learn that the "little white lady" with red hair who was stirring beans in her kitchen was famous actress Shirley MacLaine. Bill Russell, a star of the Boston Celtics basketball team, gave kids basketball lessons. Soon the biggest name in the civil rights movement, Martin Luther King, Jr., would tour the state.

Into High Gear

While volunteers were getting used to life in Mississippi, SNCC leaders were starting to wonder what Freedom Summer had achieved. Freedom Schools were packed and bursting with enthusiasm. A dozen community centers were offering health classes, day care, story hours, and more. But SNCC's larger purpose in Mississippi was to get African Americans registered to vote—and that was going slowly.

In town after town, in spite of Freedom Days and lessons in how to register, people were either failing the registration test or not even trying. In Canton, twenty-two people took the test. None passed. In Hattiesburg, seventy took the test, and only five passed. One hundred and twenty-three took the test in Greenwood. Two passed.

Just a month remained of Freedom Summer. Leaders realized that there would be nowhere near enough registered black voters to make a difference in the upcoming contest between the Republican and Democratic parties. Even before the summer began, black Mississippians had been locked out of Democratic party conventions where delegates to Atlantic City were chosen. As expected, Mississippi's official delegation would be all white. If blacks, who made up more than a third of the state's population, wanted any voice, they would have to form their own party. Throughout the summer, while volunteers signed up Freedom Democrats, the Mississippi Freedom Democratic Party (MFDP) made plans to issue a challenge at the national convention of the Democratic Party, soon to be held in Atlantic City. There the MFDP delegates would demand that they, the Freedom Democrats, be seated instead of the all-white delegation that had excluded them. With television cameras rolling, the MFDP could demand to be heard.

Bob Moses had hoped that 400,000 blacks would sign up to join the MFDP. So far, he had just 21,431 signatures. He sent word to staff and volunteers throughout the state. No more Freedom Days—they cost too much in time and bail money. Instead, he said, "*everyone* who is not working in Freedom Schools or Community Centers *must* devote all their time to organizing for the convention challenge." The goal was now 200,000 signatures.

Suddenly Freedom Summer shifted into high gear. Mass meetings were held night after night. Freedom School teachers started canvassing on weekends. Standing beside shacks glowing with kerosene lamps, volunteers made their pitch to tired men in overalls and weary women in housedresses and bandannas. The volunteers handed out brochures that explained democracy from the ground up. They promised that the Freedom Democrats wouldn't make anyone pay a poll tax or take a test. The forms would be kept secret. The boss man would never know. Sign your name here.

Many men and women were afraid. "Not me," they would say. "I'm the only one my children's *got.*" Volunteers returned again and again, but fear was not the only obstacle. Politics was a problem, too.

Republicans across America wanted Barry Goldwater to be the country's next president. The job of the Democratic party national convention would be to choose the Democrat who would run against Goldwater. Vice President Lyndon Johnson had become president after John F. Kennedy was killed. The convention was overwhelmingly likely to choose him. But what if the MFDP's challenge splintered the Democratic party?

Johnson had already enraged the South by signing the Civil Rights Act. If the party recognized the black MFDP delegation as the voice of Mississippi, gave them seats on the floor of the convention, and sent the white delegates home, could Johnson win the support of any Southern state? Or would the Democrats fall apart in disunity, making it easy for Goldwater to become the next president?

Major newspapers in Washington, D.C., and Los Angeles used words like "battle royal" and "potentially explosive" to talk about the coming Democratic convention. SNCC and the MDFP, though, just wanted a fair fight. They were careful to follow all party rules and file all the necessary paperwork. They *would* be heard in Atlantic City. They *would* represent Mississippi. It would just take names. Sign here, please.

Photos from
volunteer Thomas
Foner's Freedom
Summer collection.

MURIEL MAKES SNCC HISTORY

FORMING A NEW POLITICAL PARTY IS NO EASY task. Making the Mississippi Freedom Democratic Party strong enough to be recognized at the national convention took organization and leadership. By late July, SNCC had replaced some of its project directors with new leaders they hoped would be more effective.

The new project director at Greenwood, in the Delta, was Stokely Carmichael. In the following years, Carmichael would come to be known across the United States as one of the leaders of the Black Power movement. In Mississippi during Freedom Summer, he was brilliant, fearless, and funny. He called everyone "Sweets." Every week

or so, when a package addressed to FASC arrived at the office, he would gather volunteers to share the latest gifts from the group he called "The Friends and Admirers of Stokely Carmichael." But volunteers who worked with Carmichael knew that, despite his light tone, he would be right there with them on the picket line or in the jail cell.

All of SNCC's project directors in Mississippi were men—except one. When director Charlie Cobb left the Greenville office to make a tour of the Freedom Schools in the state, he recommended Muriel Tillinghast as "a good bet" to replace him. Three weeks earlier Muriel had been afraid to leave the project office. Now she was expected to run it.

Issaquena County was part of the territory served by the Greenville office. It was desperately poor, patrolled by the pickup and the shotgun, and as brutal as any county in Mississippi. More than half the county's population was African American, but no black person was registered to vote. Unita Blackwell, a tall woman who had worked her entire life in the cotton fields, went with SNCC to the courthouse to register. She "failed" the test—and was instantly thrown off the plantation where she worked. The movement became her new job. When Muriel came to Issaquena County, Unita Blackwell became her student and her friend.

Seated in Blackwell's shack, surrounded by fields of tall cotton, Muriel talked about citizenship, voting rights, and black history. "For

someone so young and petite," Blackwell later said, "she had a serene strength about her." She also said, "What Muriel Tillinghast really taught us was to have pride in ourselves." Local people were impressed by Muriel's knowledge, but her hair startled them. Most of them had never seen the kind of natural African American hair that would soon be called an "Afro." Women routinely straightened their hair or wore head coverings. But Muriel let her natural hair grow. Within a year, Blackwell and other African American women were wearing theirs the same way. Black men started wearing natural hair, too.

When Blackwell and other locals in Issaquena County took Muriel and her volunteers into their homes, they ran a risk. Muriel said, "We couldn't have lasted a day without them." Everyone knew

they were being watched. Cars circled houses and black churches. On July 20, whites fired nine shots into a car parked outside a mass meeting. Neighboring Sharkey County, where Muriel also worked, was just as bad. When a black volunteer's car broke down there, cops arrested him and smashed his skull with a blackjack.

But by that time, local people were already talking about opening a Freedom School. More and more blacks were signing up as Freedom Democrats and coming out to meet Muriel and her staff. A meeting of the Mississippi Freedom Democratic Party was scheduled for July 26. Unita Blackwell would be there. So would Muriel, who now knew that she could handle Mississippi.

Martin Luther King Jr. Comes to Mississippi

The last time Martin Luther King Jr. had come to Mississippi was a year earlier, for the funeral of murdered civil rights activist Medgar Evers. Since then, his fame had soared. He had given his "I Have a Dream" speech to a quarter of a million people in the nation's capital. He was about to be nominated for the Nobel Peace Prize. When news broke in July 1964 that he was on his way to Mississippi, many saw the visit as another crisis in a summer full of crises. Attorney General Robert Kennedy told President Johnson, "If he gets killed, it creates all kinds of problems."

The president instantly called FBI director J. Edgar Hoover. Hoover hated King. In fact, he was already bugging King's hotel room, looking for ways to bring down the civil rights leader. Still, he recognized the danger. "There are threats that they're going to kill [King]," Hoover told the president. The president told Hoover to have the FBI guard King while he was in Mississippi. "So that we don't have another burning car," the president said.

President Johnson and his staff weren't the only ones worried about King's trip to Mississippi. People who worked with King were terrified of the state. They had tried to warn SNCC to stay out of it. "We knew better than to take on Mississippi," said Andrew Young of the Southern Christian Leadership Conference, a close colleague. Some pleaded with King not to go, but Bob Moses had invited King, and he accepted. To King, the summer project was "the most creative thing happening today in civil rights." In addition, he wanted to support the Freedom Democrats.

Whites in Mississippi were alarmed. Anti-King billboards calling him a communist had been common in the state for years. One newspaper labeled him "the unspeakable Martin Luther King." But black people were excited—and surprised when they heard that King's first stop after landing in Jackson would be the racially explosive town of Greenwood. The women of the town took to their hot kitchens, preparing chicken, cornbread, pies, and cakes. Preachers argued over whose church the Reverend King should visit. The following morning, reporters swarmed through the town's African American quarters.

Meanwhile, King spoke to reporters at the airport in Jackson. He had come to Mississippi, he said, "to demonstrate the absolute support of the Southern Christian Leadership Conference for this summer project" as well as for the quest for the right to vote "in the midst of bombings, murders, and many other difficult experiences." After meeting with SNCC and COFO leaders, King boarded a flight to Greenwood.

Four FBI agents walked with King past the shacks and along the gravel roads of black Greenwood. Reporters and admirers trailed behind him. He turned heads and astonished everyone who had never heard him in person. As rain started pelting down, his spine-tingling baritone voice rolled across streets lined with pool halls and juke joints.

Standing on a bench outside a cafe, King waved his arms above the crowd. "You must not allow anybody to make you feel you are not significant," he declared. "Every Negro has worth and dignity. Mississippi has treated the Negro as if he is a thing instead of a person." King's followers loved it when he stepped into a pool hall, interrupting a game. Young men stood, pool cues in hand, while he told them it was important for everyone to know that black people want to be free and to be registered voters. Out in the street again, King urged everyone to join the Freedom Democratic Party. Volunteers followed him, handing out flyers.

That evening, King spoke at a small church, then at a mass meeting at the Elks Hall. Volunteer Chris Williams waited in the audience to hear him. So did the volunteers who had been arrested for picketing on Freedom Day. When King arrived, hundreds of people clapped and chanted, "We want free-dom!"

King's speech thrilled the audience that spilled out of the seats, lined the walls, and peered through the windows. He told them that black people in America could "turn this nation upside down in order to turn it right side up." He also talked about the three missing men: James Chaney, Andrew Goodman, and Michael Schwerner. King had seen the FBI's quick work in other cases. He found it hard to believe, he said, "that these same efficient FBI men cannot locate the missing workers." He ended his speech with a chant supporting the political goal of the summer project: a presence at the Democratic national convention. "Seat the Freedom Democratic Party!" The crowd roared along.

King left Greenwood the following morning.

Volunteers were already riding buses out into the cotton fields, finding workers more willing to sign their names to the Freedom Democratic Party list. And back in Jackson, the white-owned newspaper dismissed the previous day's excitement with the headline "Small Crowd Greets King at Greenwood."

Mississippi Fights Back

White Mississippians hoping to end Freedom Summer were growing frustrated. The nation's top civil rights leader was touring their state. Volunteers were refusing to back down in spite of threats, arrests, and violence. Across America, Mississippi's image had sunk so low that Mississippians traveling to the World's Fair in New York had changed their license plates to those from other states. Somebody had to stand up for Mississippi!

The first to do so was Sheriff Lawrence Rainey of Neshoba County. He filed a $1 million lawsuit against NBC. His charge was that an NBC news program made him appear to be involved in the disappearance of the three civil rights workers. (Rainey's lawsuit was later dismissed in court.) Next, Mississippi newspapers reprinted a letter to NBC's *Today* show. Its host had criticized the state. The letter argued that one New York subway was more violent that the whole state of Mississippi.

When riots broke out in Harlem, New York, after police shot and killed a black teenager, whites in Mississippi gloated. A Mississippi congressman complained that "civil rights workers and troublemakers" were in Mississippi, "subjecting innocent, law-abiding people to insult, national scorn, and creating trouble," while "mobs stalk the streets of New York." One Mississippi newspaper headline read: "Latest Wave of Invaders [summer project workers] Badly Needed in New York Area Today."

The strongest weapon Mississippi used against the summer project was talk of communism. This drew on old fears.

Communism was a political theory developed by German thinker Karl Marx in the nineteenth century. It was based on the ideas that the lower classes should resist being ruled by the upper classes, and that all property should be owned by the public and distributed by the state according to people's needs. In 1917 Russian communists had overthrown and executed Russia's ruling family. They established a state called the Soviet Union. From the start, the Soviet Union and communism stood in sharp contrast to the free markets of the United States and Europe.

For decades, fear of Soviets and "commies" played a part in U.S. politics. Membership in the Communist Party of the United States was seen as anti-American. Accusations of being a communist—even false accusations—cost people their jobs. In the 1950s, during a "Red Scare," thousands were accused of being communists or communist sympathizers. Such accusations were made against the civil rights movement. J. Edgar Hoover of the FBI fanned these suspicions. "We do know that Communist influence does exist in the Negro movement," Hoover said.

In the white South, many people believed that anyone who worked for civil rights had to be a communist. All summer long, project volunteers had been taunted about communism. One Batesville volunteer was stopped on the street and asked to say something in Russian because "all communists speak Russian." Now, with their state in disgrace, white Mississippi stepped up the attack and started naming names.

FRAN MAKES AFRICA COUNT

FRAN O'BRIEN HAD BEEN TEACHING ARTS AND crafts to young children in Vicksburg. Then one day, while the children rummaged through the library at the center, they saw a book on American history. They brought it to Fran and said that they wanted to learn history—just like the big kids. Fran smiled and opened the tattered book. She saw that it had been published decades earlier, in 1930. It began, "The history of America really begins in England because all Americans come from England." Looking at the black faces in front of her, Fran closed the book.

She had learned a lot about her students. She had learned that the *Little House on the Prairie* books didn't mean as much to black children in Mississippi as they did to a white girl growing up in California. She had started looking for

other stories. The saddest lesson was how Jim Crow crippled every black child's confidence. The creativity of her students thrilled her—but she was sad to see many of the kids throw their paintings into the wastebasket. She took them out and put them on her classroom wall.

Freedom Summer had bounced Fran around the town. She taught first in the community center, but the city condemned the building. Fran and the other teachers packed up their supplies and moved two blocks to the Freedom House. They could teach there, but they had to share the space with voter registration. Fran also moved to a new host home, because her first host had become terrified she might be attacked for having a volunteer living with her. The second host was a perfect fit for Fran—a retired teacher, with lots of advice for a beginner.

Children play a game outdoors as a part of a Freedom School activity.

Fran's new host talked about what to do
with a history book that was decades old and
whitewashed with lies. "Well," she said, "you just
read the book and then you give them the right
information." The next day, Fran opened that old
book and started teaching history. "The history
of America really begins in England," she said.
"Now, what might be wrong with that sentence?"

A hand went up. "Well, lots of people came
here who weren't from England."

Fran smiled and asked what other countries
people might have come from. Her students
started touring the globe. France? Italy?
Germany? Yes to all. They moved on to Mexico
and South America. Fran was impressed with
their geography, but she noticed something
missing. After the students tried China and India,
Fran asked, "What about Africa?"

The classroom fell silent. Finally a little girl raised her hand and asked, "Does that count?"

Fran had to blink back tears. "Yes," she said. "Yes, that counts."

A few days later, Fran wrote home:

> Sometimes I feel I'm not doing much, but . . . I still feel our real hope of success is in the children. They can't avoid fear, being intelligent, nor resentment, being human. But I hope the stimulation of the Freedom School and the examples of determination set by Negro workers will save them from the apathetic "what's the use?" attitude which oppresses and binds people more than the law ever could.

While Martin Luther King toured the state, Senator James Eastland of Mississippi spoke on the Senate floor for an hour. He called the summer project a communist conspiracy and presented a long list of names—people he said were communists. One volunteer, the senator said, had been thrown out of the Central American county of Costa Rica for handing out communist literature. SNCC was being helped by the National Lawyers Guild, which had defended communists since the 1930s. The lawyer who was representing Andrew Goodman's family was "a long-time Communist legal eagle," Eastland said.

Eastland's charges made headlines across Mississippi. Within days, the state's Sovereignty Commission was trailing some of the people whose names he had given. So was the FBI. The state legislature opened an investigation into communist influence in Freedom Summer.

Investigators would find kernels of truth in Eastland's charges. A handful of summer volunteers did sympathize with Cuba, which had adopted a communist-style government. Many of them were the children of former communists. The National Lawyers Guild and SNCC refused to let the attacks stop them. "If they ain't calling you a Communist," Fannie Lou Hamer said, "you ain't doing your job." The vast majority of volunteers, though, refused to get caught up in the local version of the Cold War between the U.S. and the Soviet Union. They had a job to do.

King on the Ashes

After his visit to Greenwood, Martin Luther King, Jr. went back to Jackson. He shared coffee with COFO workers, canvassed for Freedom Democrats, and gave speech at a mass meeting. The next morning, a death threat was phoned to King's home in Atlanta. It was picked up by the FBI, which had tapped his phone. FBI director Hoover had forbidden his agents to tell King about such threats. He didn't want King to know the agency was eavesdropping on his calls. The FBI said nothing, but it tightened its guard on King.

At a meeting with Bob Moses and other leaders, King talked about plans for the Democratic convention in Atlantic City. The goal of having the Freedom Democrats recognized as speaking for Mississippi was on everyone's minds. King then held a press conference. He called Mississippi "the worst state in the Union." After that, he was off to Vicksburg.

The volunteers at the Freedom House spent the day in high excitement. King was scheduled to have dinner with them that night before speaking at a church. The cars carrying King and his group were supposed to come by the Freedom House to pick up the volunteers. But it was getting late, and King hadn't shown up. Was he coming at all?

Fran O'Brien was straightening her classroom when someone told her to hurry—the last car was leaving! She rushed down the long driveway. There in the front seat was Martin Luther King. Fran could hardly believe it. She just stood and stared until a friend prompted her to get into the car. Fran jumped in the back.

All the way to dinner, other volunteers fell over themselves to tell King about their summer work. Fran sat in silence. Finally King turned around. "And what about you, young lady?" he asked. "What do you do in the project?"

"Nothing," Fran managed to say. "I just work with the kids."

"What do you do with the kids?"

Shyness kept Fran from speaking up, but another volunteer told King what a great teacher she was, and about the activities and lessons she created.

Fran smiled weakly. King studied her, then asked, "Do you call that 'nothing'?"

"No, sir."

"Young lady, don't you ever say you 'just work with the kids," King told Fran. "Our children are the future and you are forming it."

After dinner, King spoke to an enthusiastic crowd. To Fran, nothing he said to the audience was as important as what he had said to her.

Back in Jackson once more, King taped a TV show. Then he headed for Neshoba County, where the Mt. Zion Church had burned and three civil rights workers had disappeared. Bob Moses tried to talk King into staying away from the county capital, Philadelphia. It might be dangerous. A mob there had recently driven off leaders of the National Association for the Advancement of Colored People (NAACP).

But King insisted on going to Neshoba County. No public events were planned. No one knew he was coming. FBI agents met his caravan of cars at the county line and went ahead of them. An hour later, people in the African American part of town were startled when fifteen cars rumbled across the railroad tracks and stopped in a cloud of red dust. King got out and walked through the streets.

He stopped at a pool hall, just as he had done in Greenwood, but this time he took off his jacket and played a game. (He lost.) Then he climbed onto a bench and spoke to the crowd: "Three young men came here to help set you free. They probably lost their lives. I know what you have suffered in this state, the lynchings and the murders. But things are going to get better." Then, in the words of an old spiritual, King told them, "Walk together, children, don't you get weary."

After the pool hall, King moved on beneath the afternoon thunder and rain. He stood on the ashes of Mt. Zion Church and shared the sorrow of those who had worshipped there. At the same time, he rejoiced in the fact that churches could be important and meaningful enough for "people of ill will" to burn them. That evening he spoke in Meridian. The next morning he returned to Atlanta.

Fear Met Its Match

The night after Martin Luther King left Mississippi, Rita Schwerner spoke to an audience of black people in Greenwood. "I know what fear is, but I know that you can risk much more by doing nothing," she said. "It's not unnatural to be afraid but you're cheating your children if your being afraid stops them from having something."

Fear had met its match in Mississippi. There was another weekend of violence. A volunteer's car was burned in Mileston. Another bomb was thrown in McComb. In Batesville, tear gas engulfed the home of Robert and Mona Miles, where Chris Williams and other volunteers had spent their first day in Mississippi. But fear had become like summer thunder. It startled everyone, but it no longer sent them running for cover. All the volunteers' and workers' eyes were on a new prize: the Democratic national convention.

For every bomb and beating, there was a new symbol of hope. Freedom Democrat pamphlets were sent out across the state. Signatures mounted up. Hundreds of people came to mass meetings. In Holly Springs, a crowd surrounded police cars and sang Freedom Songs. In the tiny village of Starkville, two volunteers were dropped off alone. The sheriff confronted them—but they were soon surrounded and protected by black citizens who said, "We've been waiting for you." Almost five hundred people signed the Freedom Democrat forms.

Even shy Fran O'Brien drew strength from the courage around her. Five nights after meeting Martin Luther King, she found herself alone in the Freedom House while everyone else was at a meeting. The phone rang in the silent, dimly lit office. The drawl on the other end asked her where she was from. Whittier, California, she answered. How did she like Mississippi? Oh, she liked it just fine. Then the caller said that everyone in the Freedom House had three days to get out before the place was bombed.

Fran thanked the man for calling. There was a brief silence.

"Listen," the man said. "I said I'm gonna *bomb* y'all. And there ain't gonna be no Freedom School and no freedom there or anyplace else, and no *nothin'!*"

"Yes, sir," Fran replied. "I understood you the first time. Was there anything else?"

"No. . . . No, I don't believe so. But I'll call again."

"Oh, feel free," Fran said. "We'd love to hear from you. Thank you for calling. Good night."

Silence. Then, "G'night."

HELP MAKE
MISSISSIPPI
PART OF THE
U.S.A.
REGISTER TO VOTE ★

CHAPTER 8

"A BLOT ON THE COUNTRY"

EVER SINCE THE FIRST HEADLINE FROM Freedom Summer, three faces had stared down America. In Mississippi and across the South, in stores, banks, police departments, and courthouses the faces of Goodman, Schwerner, and Chaney stared out from posters. Everywhere in America, the three missing civil rights workers looked out from the pages of magazines that were spread out on coffee tables and beach towels.

After five weeks, many white people in Mississippi—maybe most of them—still thought the disappearance was a hoax. "I believe with all my heart they are alive somewhere," said an old woman in Philadelphia. A downtown merchant said what many people were thinking:

Volunteer Jacob Blum hanging a voter registration sign on the front of Mt. Zion Baptist Church in Hattiesburg, Mississippi, prior to a mass meeting during Freedom Summer, 1964.

"I just hope that if they are dead, they won't find the bodies anywhere around here." One man wrote to the *Jackson Clarion-Ledger* to share his suspicions that the three men had either been killed by their Communist masters or were holed up in Cuba, waiting for their next Communist task. "There is no reason to believe them seriously harmed by citizens of the most law-abiding state of the union," he wrote.

Rumors and Rewards

The search for the missing men dragged on. Investigators were no longer looking for bodies in rivers, but they probed remote villages. The basic facts of the case hadn't changed: the Sunday-afternoon arrest, the hours in jail, the late-night release from jail, and the blackened station wagon. Beyond that, searchers had only rumors to guide them. One recent rumor said that the bodies had either been buried in quicksand or thrown into the grinding machine of some backwoods sawmill.

FBI agents had not learned much about the fate of Chaney, Goodman, and Schwerner, but they had learned plenty about Mississippi. They had learned that the Ku Klux Klan membership in Neshoba County had quadrupled since the spring. They had gathered evidence of men selling illegal alcohol that was making some people rich—Sheriff Lawrence Rainey above all. They had also learned how common it was for anyone who went into the county jail to be beaten. Yet the FBI could not find the missing men. They continued to follow every tip or lead.

One tip took agents to a Chicago man named Wilmer Jones. He had come to Philadelphia to visit his mother three weeks before the civil rights workers disappeared. Accused of asking a white girl for a date, Jones was arrested, taken into custody, and beaten by Rainey and Deputy Cecil Price. He was released at midnight. Waiting outside the jail were five men with pistols and shotguns.

While Rainey and Price watched, the men shoved Jones into a car. For hours they drove him along winding roads, a pistol to his neck, shouting questions about the white girl, COFO, and the NAACP. Then they took Jones to "the place." It was an empty well just inside a barbed-wire gate, somewhere in Neshoba County. Finally, the men put Jones on a bus and told him never to show his face in Neshoba County again.

FRED: "THE GREATEST REVOLUTION"

ALL SUMMER, THE ROTTING SHACKS OF SHAW, Mississippi, seemed to drown in despair. Volunteer Fred Winn stopped expecting anything to happen. If paying a kid to plant a bomb did not rouse the black community into action, what would? Each afternoon seemed slower and more depressing than the one before it.

Then a single comment made Shaw wake up. Sheriff Charlie Capps had told the *New York Times* that "95 percent of our blacks are happy." A volunteer posted the *Times* article in the Freedom House and read it aloud at a mass meeting. Word soon spread. African Americans in Shaw fired off furious letters to the newspaper. "Only a fool would be happy in Mississippi down here chopping cotton for 30 cents an hour," said one. Another said, "If Capps thinks that we are happy

why don't he try living like the Negroes. After he
has done that, ask him if he is happy."

Shaw's black high school was also coming to
life. When three volunteers were thrown out of
the cafeteria, students walked out of classes. The
principal closed the school. Kids and parents
protested. Cops had to come to keep order. But
Fred Winn would not be there to see Shaw begin
to stand up. His skills as a carpenter were needed
in the larger town of Indianola, where Freedom
Summer was just getting started.

Indianola was the birthplace of Mississippi's
White Citizens' Council. Blacks outnumbered
whites, but whites controlled everything and were
determined to keep it that way. White Indianola
had watched the "invaders" stir up African
Americans in other towns. They had thought their
town would be spared. Now, in early August,

a summer project office was opening, and a Freedom School was planned. White citizens geared up to resist the troublemakers. Their resistance would end with fires blazing in the night.

But black Indianola was thrilled that the project had arrived. "Where have you people been?" one kid asked. "We've been waitin' and waitin'!" The new project gave Fred Winn the chance to do more than carpentry and handyman work. He also became the communications director for the project in Indianola. Late at night in the Freedom House, he fiddled with a radio that pulled in the scratchy voices of project volunteers and staff from across the Delta.

Fred was starting to think about staying on into the fall. He frequently called the state a "hell hole," but he was coming to like Mississippi—

black Mississippi, at least. Five weeks in the Delta had done away with his fear. He wrote home, "To be quite frank with you all I am quite calm and un-nervous. After a while you get used to the idea of being watched and hated. . . . I am in the midst of a revolution. This is the greatest revolution since the American Revolution."

How was his half-sister, Fred asked his father. Could a black second-grader in San Francisco understand the movement? Did she know how he was spending the summer? Fred's father had hoped his son might come home early, worn down by the disappointment of Shaw. But after Fred moved to Indianola and took on new responsibilities, his father wondered if he would come home at all. He told Fred that he was counting the days until Fred left Mississippi—"counting them like a jail sentence."

FBI agents brought Jones back. They wanted to find "the place," so they drove him all over the county for two days. He was so terrified that he wore a cardboard box over his head, with holes cut out for eyes, until the heat made him groggy. With Jones's help, the FBI did find "the place." Behind a barbed-wire gate were a dozen deep wells. They could have hidden bodies, but they didn't. They held only water.

Another lead came from comedian Dick Gregory, who had announced a $25,000 reward for information about the three men. He had received a three-page letter that claimed the men were buried in "a field not too far from Philadelphia." Gregory turned the letter over to the FBI. They discovered that it had been written by a Mississippian living in Washington, D.C. He was, said the FBI, a mental patient and a nuisance, not a good source of information.

Joseph Sullivan, the director of the FBI investigation, kept meeting his one source, the highway patrolman from Meridian. The patrolman was eager to talk about the Klan, but he refused to talk about murder. Sullivan convinced FBI director Hoover that a reward of $25,000 from the agency might loosen the man's tongue. By the end of July, the reward money had been waiting for a week. No one had claimed it.

The Breakthrough

On the last afternoon of July, the streets of Philadelphia buzzed with rumors. The FBI had grilled Sheriff Rainey! Agents offered him $30,000 to talk! They offered Deputy Price *a million bucks!* As the rumors multiplied and spread, the FBI again invaded downtown. Agents stood outside the courthouse, their sunglasses glinting. Something was about to happen, or already had.

It was true that FBI agents spoke to Rainey and Price that Friday afternoon. The sheriff later boasted of how he had handled them. Yet the agents knew that behind his bluster, Rainey was scared. The agents had laid out their evidence of his dealings in illegal alcohol. He would face fines, jail, and huge back taxes for those crimes alone. If he told what he knew about the missing men, the FBI would cover $30,000 worth of fines and taxes.

Down the hall, FBI agents told Price that the search for the three men's bodies had cost

$3 million. They said they would "pay a million more just to know where they are." The deputy didn't bite at this lure. Like the sheriff, he was quiet.

But someone talked.

Over the years, many people have tried to guess who told the FBI where to find the bodies. Some said a drunk had awakened in the woods to witness a triple burial. Others said a psychic had pointed the way. There were even rumors that the FBI had hired a mobster to scare the truth out of one of the suspects. The real answer may have been much simpler: money.

It is a legend to this day in Neshoba County that someone was paid for the information—but no one knows for sure. Investigator Sullivan always denied making any payoff. But on July 30 he took his informant, the highway patrolman from Meridian, out to a steak dinner. The informant revealed where the bodies were buried. Now the FBI needed the names of the killers.

The next day agents began grilling suspects and talking about rewards. They may have wanted to make the Klan members suspicious of each other once the bodies were found. Someone may have received money, but the highway patrolman never showed a sign of sudden wealth. Because the informant would surely be killed if his identity became known, the FBI called him Mr. X.

On August 1, using Mr. X's information, FBI agents headed into thick woods. They were looking for a large dam made of packed earth. The tangled landscape, though, could hide a big dam as easily as it could hide a body. The agents soon arranged for a helicopter from the Meridian Naval Air Station to fly over the area.

"We've spotted the dam," agents heard on their walkie-talkies. "It's a big one." Following directions from the helicopter, the agents slashed through thickets. They climbed up a rise in the land and saw the dam: twenty feet thick in the middle, nearly twice as long as a football field, making up the edge of a landfill. It had been built in May, but it wasn't yet holding any water. "This is no pick and shovel job," said Sullivan. He filed for a search warrant and asked FBI headquarters for permission to rent heavy digging equipment.

Were the missing men finally going to be found?

CHRIS: "A VERY VIOLENT TOWN"

It was time for Chris Williams to branch out. He had been stationed in Batesville, in Panola County. That county had become Freedom Summer's success story. Thanks to the federal law banning any poll taxes or voter tests for a year, hundreds of African Americans had registered to vote. The local newspaper still listed their names, but now black people pointed to them with pride, not fear. There were too many new black voters for each one's house to become a target.

Now SNCC wanted to broaden its canvassing to all of Panola County. Together with other volunteers, Chris piled into a car and headed down dusty roads past cotton fields toward small, hostile towns such as Sardis and Como.

He passed out material on registering to vote and on the Freedom Democratic Party. He spoke in juke joints and churches, telling people about the important convention coming up in Atlantic City. Once in a while he ventured onto a plantation to speak with workers, but he was usually run off. One planter told Chris that he wasn't going "to turn the government over to a bunch of monkeys."

On the edge of the Delta was Crenshaw. Chris called it "a very violent town." One evening when he was canvassing with Pam Jones, a black volunteer from Maryland, they were cut off by a group of men in a car. The men piled out and started throwing insults. Chris tried to stay calm—but failed. What did they mean, he had

Main Street, Sardis, Mississippi, July 1964.

"no business" here? he shouted. Americans could go where they wanted, couldn't they? Fingers were pointed. Fists were clenched. Faces were jaw to jaw. But after more shouting the men sped away, leaving Chris feeling cocky.

SNCC's Stokely Carmichael warned that an increase in white terrorism was on the way. The summer project had been more successful than whites expected, and they were angry and worried. Beyond that, the challenge of the Freedom Democrats was a serious threat. The Klan and the Citizens' Council would surely rise to meet it.

Carmichael was right. "The whole state is beginning to tighten up," Chris wrote home. "In the last week people have been shot at in

the daytime on the streets of Greenwood and a mob attacked two Civil Rights workers there." A few days later, Chris came home to find a dead rattlesnake nailed to the front door.

By that time Chris was living in the "very violent town" of Crenshaw. He had learned not to challenge whites. Instead, he lived for the friendship of African Americans, who soon knew him by name, greeted him everywhere, and laughed at his jokes. Never lonely, rarely discouraged, Chris was still amazed to be in Mississippi and making history.

White Teenagers Cross the Tracks

From the beginning, the summer project had focused a glimmer of hope on the poor white people of Mississippi. Freedom Summer included a White Community Project, which some called the White Folks Project. The idea was to help poor whites see that "their enemy was not the Negro but poverty." In this way the organizers hoped to bring Freedom Summer to both sides of the railroad tracks—to some white neighborhoods as well as black ones.

For a test location, the White Folks Project chose Biloxi, a town on the coast of the Gulf of Mexico. Like Greenville, Biloxi was known for being tolerant. Eighteen volunteers had gone to Biloxi in June. By July they were speaking every day with white carpenters, barbers, fishermen, and even the high-school principal. Once in a while someone would listen. More often, people were hostile. They asked the volunteers, "Why Mississippi?" Why couldn't the students work in their own states?

The White Folks Project soon ran out of steam. Volunteers spent days arguing about whom they should talk to and what they should say. Two young women decided to "get the feel of the community" by taking jobs at a diner. When they were found to be summer volunteers, they were fired. By August, six volunteers in Biloxi had quit. The rest were going to door to door, trying to find someone who would talk to them. One of them wrote home, "It looks like the pilot phase of our White Community Project is pretty much over."

What about the colleges? Would students and professors be more open-minded than other white people?

Nearly two years had passed since brick-throwing mobs had rioted all night in Oxford, Mississippi, to stop James Meredith, a black man, from enrolling in the state university. Not much seemed to have changed at Ole Miss. Professors were still leaving for other universities. Students and locals still blamed the federal marshals for the riot. Meredith had quickly finished his degree and left Mississippi, but now more "outsiders" were coming to campus to preach integration and stir up trouble. When two volunteers visited the university, city and campus police trailed them.

The students met with Meredith's former advisor and with the editor of the campus paper. The editor complained that the press had made Mississippi look bad. The next week, the volunteers spoke to a class, explaining their work. They were asked questions such as "Would you marry a Negro?" "Is your organization Communist?" and "Why are Negroes so immoral?" The volunteers didn't change anyone's mind, but they thought that the students at least seemed to listen.

The volunteers kept searching for tolerance— or at least someone who might listen. They finally turned to the only white people in Mississippi who had little to lose: teenagers who already felt alienated, or apart, from their society. It started with an outdoor concert behind the Freedom House in McComb.

Folksinger Pete Seeger had come to Mississippi to perform for the cause. The audience of black kids and volunteers sang along. Toward the end of the show, volunteer Ira Landess noticed two white teenage boys standing by themselves. They weren't singing, but they didn't look dangerous. Landess went to talk to them. Gary and Jack said they just wanted to hear Seeger. But as they talked, Landess discovered that not every white young person in Mississippi was content to live in a closed society.

Gary Brooks had recently taken up the dangerous habit of asking questions. He had read *Black Like Me*, a startling bestseller by a white journalist who darkened his skin to roam the South and see what black life was really like. Now Brooks had begun daring himself to cross the tracks and walk through the black side of McComb. He wondered why there were so few businesses, so few decent homes, so much poverty. And who were these "invaders" coming to Mississippi?

After the concert, Gary and Jack agreed to meet Landess again. Gary called the Freedom House and said he had some friends who wanted to reach out. They arranged a meeting at a hotel. Others at the Freedom House suspected it was a trap, but Landess trusted the two young men. He went to the hotel to meet them. Only Gary and Jack showed up—the friends had chickened out. But the New York teacher and the Mississippi teens talked for a few hours. Throughout August, Gary and Jack would drop by the Freedom House. Ira Landess saw them as the beginning of a new Mississippi.

A NATIVE SON FORCED TO FLEE

FOR A WHITE PERSON IN MISSISSIPPI, SPEAKING out against segregation and racism was risky. Doctors and ministers who visited the state were sometimes pulled aside by whites. Looking nervously over their shoulders, these white citizens confessed that they supported integration of the races. But they dared not say so. Journalists met locals who admitted that their state needed help, but these people would not let their names appear in newspapers. "If you print my name next to what I'm going to tell you," said one Mississippian to the *Washington Post*, "I'll be ruined. I'll lose my business, my friends, I'll be run out of this state."

It had already happened to some. Albert "Red" Heffner was a loyal son of Mississippi. He grew

up on a plantation in Greenwood. He went to
college at Old Miss, where he met his wife. She
was also Mississippi-born. One of their daughters
had been crowned Miss Mississippi in the
statewide beauty pageant.

The Heffners lived in McComb. When the
bombings started in town, Heffner wrote to
the Sovereignty Commission. He suggested
that "responsible citizens" should stand up
to the Klan. He added that he wasn't trying to
push integration *or* segregation. He was just a
community member and a businessman, "an
insurance man in debt up to my ears." But in the
middle of July, Heffner went too far for McComb.
He invited two "mixers"—white volunteers who
worked with African Americans—to his home for
dinner.

Heffner had only wanted "to let the Civil Rights workers hear the Mississippi point of view," he later explained. But with bombings on the increase, and sales of guns and dynamite soaring, he became the target of his town's feverish fear. Word of his dinner guests inflamed his neighborhood. When Heffner opened his front door after dinner, he was blinded by the headlights of ten cars parked in his front yard.

The volunteers slowly slipped past the blockade. They made it safely back to the project office, but the Heffner family's ordeal had just begun.

First came the phone threats. "You're gonna get your teeth kicked in." "If you want to live, get out of town." Next, Heffner was forced to leave his insurance office. There were rumors that the

Heffner house would be bombed. Driven out
by fear, Heffner's wife and daughter moved to a
hotel. That wasn't the only rumor. The Heffners
heard vile lies being spread about members of
the family. Old friends refused to talk to them. No
one from their church or their community came
to their defense.

By August the Heffners were thinking about
something they could not have imagined at the
beginning of summer—leaving Mississippi. And
by September, after more than three hundred
phone threats and their poisoned dog dead on
their doorstep, they were gone. They would never
live in Mississippi again. Decades later, they still
cried when they talked about how they had been
driven out of their home state.

The Hour of Reckoning

FBI agents showed up at the landfill site on the morning of August 4. Standing atop the huge earthen dam were a steam shovel and a bulldozer, trucked in from Jackson. Agents also had a ten-day search warrant and sleeping bags, food, and supplies to last as long as the search might take.

The agents had been told that the three bodies were buried near the middle of the dam. That's where the digging started at 9:00 a.m. Skinny pine trees framed the death scene against a cloudless sky. The temperature was already almost 90. Before long, the agents and the equipment operators were soaked with sweat. As the steam shovel bit into the dam, agents scurried like insects. They scribbled notes, took photos, and gathered samples of the dirt. Beyond the people at the site, the president, and top FBI officials, no one in America knew about the digging.

Two hours after digging started, agents noticed a faint smell of decay. Those who had fought in World War II knew that smell. It was not faint for long. Agents halted the steam shovel and started digging with hand tools. Still they found nothing. By noon the steam shovel was plunging deeper.

By 3:00 p.m., the temperature was above 100. The steam shovel had gouged out a V-shaped gash in the dam, almost down to ground level. Flies swarmed around the gash. Vultures circled above. Then an agent spotted a boot sticking out of the earth.

Once again agents started digging with hand tools—or just their hands. One of them stumbled away, vomiting. Others put on masks or lit cigars to mask the stench of death. For two hours they clawed at the Mississippi earth. Slowly they uncovered legs wearing jeans, then a hand with a wedding ring, and finally the upper body of a white man. He wore no shirt. He had a bullet hole in one armpit. It was Michael Schwerner.

Soon agents unearthed another body. Andrew Goodman had been buried facedown under Schwerner. He had taken a bullet through the chest. His arms were outstretched, and one hand was clenched around a fistful of earth. Some of those who were there wondered if Goodman had been alive when he was buried, and had struggled.

Seven minutes later the third body came to light. James Chaney lay on his back, barefoot, beside the other two. A Freedom House worker had once said, "Mickey could count on Jim to walk through hell with him." Now Mickey and Jim, and the new friend they had brought from Ohio, had been through hell and reached the other side.

Someone called the county coroner. Soon the news was rippling across Mississippi and across America.

Freedom Summer volunteers would always remember where they were when they heard the news. In Meridian, many of them were singing along with Pete Seeger. Someone came onstage and handed Seeger a note. He lowered his eyes before standing to his full height to tell the crowd, who gasped and cried. Seeger then led the audience in a slow, haunting song that pleaded with a "healing river" to wash the land.

President Lyndon Johnson had spent the day wrestling with a crisis in Southeast Asia. It seemed that two U.S. Navy boats had been shot at in the Gulf of Tonkin, off North Vietnam. Should the United States strike back? In the end, the president authorized air strikes against

North Vietnam. An hour later, Johnson heard the news from Mississippi. He asked that the public announcement be held back for a few minutes so that the families could be told before they heard it on the news.

By the time darkness fell on the burial site, the faces of Schwerner, Goodman, and Chaney were once again staring at America from television screens. The news bulletin broke into programs on all three networks. Meanwhile, floodlights lit up the dam site. The coroner arrived. With him came Deputy Cecil Price, one of the FBI's chief suspects. Sheriff Rainey, also a suspect, was on vacation in Biloxi. Agents watched Price closely for any hint of guilt. The deputy was stone-faced beneath his cowboy hat as he helped load three black body bags into a hearse.

After forty-four days of fearing the worst, the worst had been dug out of Mississippi clay.

The media asked family members of the three men for their thoughts. Andrew Goodman's parents shared a statement they had written. It said that the tragedy of the men's deaths "is not private, it is part of the public conscience of our country." Rita Schwerner told reporters that her husband was "a very gentle man . . . totally committed to the goodness in human beings." When asked what her husband had died for, she said, "That, I would imagine, is up to the people of the United States. For me, I think three very good men were killed, men who could have made unbelievable contributions to American life." James Chaney's mother said, "My boy died a martyr for something he believed in—I believe in—and as soon as his little brother Ben gets old enough he'll take James's place as a civil rights worker."

Newspaper reporters also offered their own thoughts, which did not make Mississippi look good. The *Hartford Courier* said, "The closed society that is Mississippi is a blot on the country." The *New York Times* called the men's deaths "a horrendous example of an unthinking and inhuman reaction" when mobs take the law into their own hands. The *Washington Post* said that the three bodies were "witnesses to a way of life that is indifferent to life." The discovery of the bodies had ended the parents' long ordeal, the *Post* said. But, the newspaper added, "The ordeal for Mississippi is just beginning."

"If They Had Stayed Home"

Back in Mississippi, a few voices called for justice, even for change. "We must track down the murderers of these men and bring them to justice," said the *Vicksburg Post*. The honor of our state is at stake." The *Delta Democrat-Times* said, "Many of us in Mississippi need to take a long hard look at ourselves. We could begin by altering the sorry record of interracial justice we have made over the past decade."

Others were defensive or defiant. They predicted "a new hate campaign against Mississippi." A farmer in Meridian blamed it all on the "integrationists," as he called the civil rights workers. "It was those integration groups that got rid of them," he said, referring to the three dead men. "They couldn't let them live after they disappeared for fear everyone would find out it was a hoax." Someone else said what many were thinking: "If they had stayed home where they belonged nothing would have happened to them."

On the day the bodies were found, dozens of volunteers had been arrested for passing out Freedom Democrat leaflets. But once the news of the bodies' discovery spread from Neshoba County, the violence ended—for a few days. Mississippi was again in the national spotlight, in shame. Things were tense, but calm.

The Schwerners had sent Dr. David Spain, their own physician, to Mississippi to examine the three bodies. They did not trust Mississippi doctors. As Spain performed autopsies, details of the murders began to come out. Both Schwerner and Goodman had been shot once, at point-blank range. Their bodies showed no signs of having been beaten. James Chaney, the only African American among the three, was a different story. He had been shot three times, but he had also been horribly beaten.

Speaking from his ranch in Texas, President Johnson predicted "results" in the Neshoba murder case. Reporters flocked to Philadelphia, expecting arrests. They found the town swarming with activity, but it had nothing to do with the case. The Neshoba County Fair was just days away, and that was all anyone would talk about. Philadelphia lived for its famous fair, and not even the stench of death would get in the way. Thousands of people from all over the state were expected to come to the fairgrounds, just two miles from where the bodies had been found.

But although the people of Philadelphia wouldn't talk to reporters, behind closed doors they were asking how the bodies had suddenly turned up. Who had told the FBI where to find them? People who were still enraged by the FBI's "invasion" of their state said that agents had planted bodies in the dam.

Talk of a payoff was also spreading. Anyone who had a new car, barbecue grill, or hunting rifle was suspected. Many people said they would "hate to be in [the informant's] shoes" if his identity ever became known. Suspicion and guesses swirled, but the identity of the FBI's Mr. X—the highway patrolman from Meridian, who died two years after the bodies were found— would not be revealed until 2005. It is still not known which member of the Ku Klux Klan told Mr. X where the burial site was located.

At the site, meanwhile, state troopers kept sightseers away. FBI agents sifted dirt and studied the roads leading to the site, looking for clues. They found none. The owner of the land denied that he was involved. "I want people to know I'm sorry it happened," he said. The bodies had been found, but the burning question remained: Who had killed the three men?

The bodies that had lain together in the earth were soon separated. James Chaney was buried on a hilltop outside Meridian. Rita Schwerner had hoped that her husband could be buried beside his friend, but no undertaker in Mississippi would perform an integrated burial. So Schwerner's body, like Andrew Goodman's, was flown back to New York.

The End of Nonviolence?

On the night of August 4, African Americans gathered for a rally in Greenwood. They raged against black neighbors who still refused to join the movement, telling them to "have some race pride!" Stokely Carmichael said, "We're not goin' to stick with this non-violence forever. We don't go shooting up *their* houses. It's not *us* who does that."

Later that night at SNCC headquarters, Carmichael and others debated bringing guns back into the office. They agreed it was time. Then Carmichael left the room to call COFO headquarters. He wanted Bob Moses to give his okay to the decision about guns. No one knows what Moses said, but when Carmichael returned to the room, he was quiet. He said, "What I think we ought to do is work harder on freedom registration forms." The gun debate was set aside. Later that week, Bob Zellner of SNCC privately asked others if they were interested in his plan to kill Sheriff Rainey and Deputy Price, but they all said no. But how much longer could Bob Moses keep the Student Nonviolent Coordinating Committee nonviolent?

James Chaney was buried on Friday, August 7. The burial was private, but a memorial march through Meridian drew streams of silent mourners. At dusk, hundreds gathered inside a church. TV lights lit the scene. Sobs, shouts, and a chorus of "We Shall Overcome" filled the air. Fannie Lee Chaney stood in a black veil, hugging twelve-year-old Ben. The boy had lost his brother and best friend, and he wavered between sorrow and rage. Watching Ben Chaney weep, a black man named David Dennis abandoned the speech he had planned to give.

Dennis was chairman of COFO. He had taught classes in nonviolence, and he had helped prevent a riot at the wake for murdered civil rights activist Medgar Evers. It was

Dennis who had suggested to Michael and Rita Schwerner that they should work in Meridian. He was supposed to have been with Schwerner, Goodman, and Chaney when they disappeared in Neshoba County. He'd come close to sharing the three men's fate, but he'd been sick, so he stayed home.

Now Chaney's mother had asked Dennis to give Chaney's eulogy—a speech in honor of the dead. She expected something calm and inspiring. But the sight of Ben Chaney's rage and grief changed Dave Dennis. Suddenly he saw nonviolence as "a mistake." Speaking from the anger of an entire race, he said:

> Sorry, but I'm not here to do the traditional thing most of us do at such a gathering. What I want to talk about right now is the living dead that we have right among our midst, not only in Mississippi but throughout the nation. These are the people who *don't care*. . . .

Mourners rose to meet his words. They called out "Amen!" and "All right!" Dennis went on to place James Chaney in the growing list of martyrs: Emmett Till, Medgar Evers, Herbert Lee, and the countless others in Mississippi

Ben Chaney, younger brother of James Chaney, comforted by his mother during funeral service.

whose murderers had not been punished. "I'm sick and *tired* of going to memorials," he cried. "I'm sick and *tired* of going to funerals."

"*Yes!*" from the crowd.

"I've got a bitter vengeance in my heart tonight," Dennis said.

"*So have I!*"

"And I'm *not* going to stand here and ask anybody here not to be *angry* tonight!"

"*YES!*"

Dennis spoke of the African Americans who had fought in World War II, only to come home to Mississippi "to live as slaves." He said that when the killers of the three civil rights workers were found, there would be a trial—and "a jury of their cousins, their aunts, and their uncles." He knew the verdict would be "not guilty. Because no one saw them pull the trigger. I'm *tired* of that!"

The best way to honor the three fallen men, Dennis said, was to "stand up and DEMAND our rights!" After pleas to stop bowing down, to stand up, because "I don't want to go to another memorial," Dennis's voice broke. In tears, he left the stage.

Two days later, separate memorials were held for Goodman and Schwerner in New York. Nearly two thousand people came to each of them. Rabbi Arthur Lelyveld gave one of the many eulogies at Goodman's memorial. Still scarred from his severe beating in Hattiesburg a month earlier, Lelyveld said, "The tragedy of Andy Goodman cannot be separated from the tragedy of mankind." When the service ended, someone took the yellow rose atop the coffin and handed it to Carolyn Goodman. She came to the center aisle, turned back, and took the arm of Fannie Lee Chaney, just flown in from Mississippi. The two were joined by Anne Schwerner. Three mothers, heads bowed, dressed in black, weeping as one, walked slowly from the chapel.

CHAPTER 9

THE FLOWERING OF
FREEDOM SUMMER

AS THE NATION REELED FROM THE DISCOVERY
of three bodies in Mississippi, Bob Moses
rediscovered his hope for the future.

The Mississippi Summer Project had so far
claimed four lives. (A black volunteer, Wayne
Yancy, had been killed in a car crash.) And no
one knew what further mayhem might break out
during the hot nights of summer.

"Success?" Moses told the press. "I have
trouble with that word. When we started we
hoped no one would be killed." Yet on the same
weekend that Chaney, Goodman, and Schwerner
were laid to rest, more than a hundred Freedom
School students met at a convention in Meridian.
What Moses saw there lifted his troubled spirits

Dancing to the juke-
box in Milestone,
Mississippi, 1964.

The students had not come to mourn. They were there to show the world the joy of their Freedom Schools and their hunger for learning. They were there to claim their rights as Americans. Under a banner that read "Freedom Is a Struggle," the convention lasted for three days. The students ran it. They formed eight committees that hammered out a platform of demands, policies, and goals, including slum clearance and an end to the poll tax. They supported a revised version of the Declaration of Independence, declaring independence from "the unjust laws of Mississippi." They cheered a student play about Medgar Evers, the Mississippian who had been killed in 1963 for his civil rights work.

Throughout the weekend, Bob Moses wandered shyly from group to group. He didn't smile often, but it was clear that he was content. A friend there with him said, "It was the single time in my life that I have seen Bob the happiest. He just ate it up. . . . He just thought this was what it was all about."

MURIEL: NERVE TO SPARE

Since the beginning of August, Muriel Tillinghast had moved deep into the plantations of Issaquena and Sharkey counties, canvassing people to register as voters. Through her work, she was learning Mississippi inside and out. She slept on the floors of shacks and woke early to talk to sharecroppers as they trudged to work in the field. She met with black maids and cooks in the mornings before they crossed the tracks to work in white homes.

Being responsible for the Greenville summer project had given Muriel back all her nerve, with some to spare. Beyond that, the courage of local African Americans made Muriel more daring than

she had thought possible. She learned to drive, for one thing. Her ancient SNCC car would not go faster than fifty miles an hour, but she bounced over rutted roads and along cotton fields.

Once Muriel got into a minor accident with a police car. The cop ranted and cursed, but some smooth talking got her back on the road with just a warning to get out of the county. She didn't. Instead, she covered fifty miles or more each day, spreading the word. Sharkey County was going to have a Freedom Day on August 14. Come to the courthouse and register to vote!

A Freedom Day in nearby Tallahatchie County had not gone well. A white mob and the sheriff had ordered blacks away from the courthouse. Every night since, cars had roared past black

people's homes. The drivers waved guns. In Sharkey County, Muriel had already rescued one volunteer. He was a fellow student she remembered from her geology class at Howard University. One day he had phoned Muriel's project office. Hurry, he shouted. He was being chased by men with shotguns and dogs. Muriel heard the baying of the dogs over the line. She and a friend drove the back roads among the plantations until they found the volunteer hiding in a ditch.

As Sharkey County's Freedom Day drew near, two volunteers were arrested for passing out leaflets. By the time the day arrived, though, leaflets had been spread across the county. The volunteers had taught classes in voter registration. Freedom Day was on. Now it was up to the people to show up. Everyone feared the worst. But as Muriel had seen all summer, "courage overcame fear."

All morning and into the afternoon, black men and women walked up to the small brick courthouse in the county seat of Rolling Fork. Blacks smiled at the registrar, filled out the papers, and walked out. No one was arrested. No one was threatened or chased out of town. In the end, not one of the registration forms that was filled out on Sharkey County's Freedom Day was accepted—but the day was a success. Just by mastering their terror and showing up at the courthouse, black people who had spent their

lives under oppression and the threat of violence showed that they would not be intimidated any longer.

In less than a week, the Freedom Democrats would go to the convention in Atlantic City, hoping to take their place on the stage of politics. Muriel turned her attention to their challenge. She kept driving the back roads, signing up members for the Freedom Democratic Party. One day she took actress Shirley MacLaine to meet her friend Unita Blackwell. The sharecropper and the movie star spent hours on a porch overlooking the fields. They drank beer and talked about how women were held down and kept back, black and white alike.

August Surprises

July had been an oven in Mississippi. August was a furnace. Heat and humidity made the slightest motion feel like drowning in quicksand. The hours dragged, especially on Sundays, when volunteers had little to do. In sizzling small towns, in baking backwaters, a turtle plodding across a road was a huge event. A letter from a friend was a lifeboat. August was the month when only a fool or a Northerner went out in the noonday sun.

A few volunteers were pleading with their parents to let them stay on into fall. Most, though, were ready for summer to end. One wrote home, "I am tired. I want very much to go to a movie or to watch TV even. . . . I want to look at a white man and not hate his guts, and know that he doesn't hate me either."

Clarksdale volunteers held a "depression session" to gripe about how little they had accomplished. A volunteer in another town confessed, "If I stay here much longer, I'll become hard. That's what happens. . . . You lose patience with anyone that's not right square on your side, the liberals and the moderates and 'the good people' caught in the middle, and the

Negroes who won't cooperate or are indifferent. They all become enemies."

Yet August also brought the flowering of Freedom Summer. Volunteers defied the heat to knock on doors and sign up names. It was their final surge of canvassing for new members of the Freedom Democratic Party.

The month brought a few surprises. One of them happened in Greenwood, when two of Hollywood's biggest celebrities sneaked into town. SNCC did not have enough money to send Freedom Democrats to the national convention in Atlantic City. The group had put out a call for help. It was answered by Harry Belafonte.

In addition to being a world-famous black singer and actor, Belafonte was an activist. In the past, he had raised money for the Freedom Rides and the March on Washington. During the first week of August, he hosted dinners in five East Coast cities to raise money for SNCC— and money had poured in after the discovery of the three bodies. Now Belafonte had $60,000 in cash to deliver to SNCC in Mississippi. He invited a friend to come with him: Sidney Poitier, another world-famous black actor.

Belafonte had asked that no reporters be on

hand when their small plane landed, but word of the visit got out. The Elks Hall in Greenwood, where Belafonte and Poitier would appear, started rocking with song at dusk. Shortly after sunset, the plane touched down. Three SNCC cars were on hand. Belafonte and Poitier took seats in the middle car. As they drove off, headlights flashed in the distance. Holding a bag full of cash, Belafonte said how comforting it was to see SNCC support out there in the night. The headlights, he was told, belonged to Klansmen.

For twenty minutes, the convoy of three SNCC cars wove through cotton fields like hunted rabbits, with the Klansmen's trucks chasing them. Again and again the Klansmen rammed the rear car of the convoy. The lead car sometimes had to fall back to keep the Klansmen from pulling alongside the middle car, carrying the two visitors. Poitier remembered the chase as "a ballet, although a nerve-wracking one." Only when the convoy got close to the black part of Greenwood did the pursuing Klan turn back.

The crowd exploded when the two stars entered the Elks hall. Freedom Songs were sung, and Belafonte sang one of his own hits.

He held up the bag of money and handed it over. Poitier stepped to the microphone to say, "I have been a lonely man all my life until I came to Greenwood, Mississippi." He choked up as he spoke of the "overflowing" love in the room.

The celebrities spent that night in a house guarded by shotguns. They kept themselves calm by exercising and telling ghost stories. The next morning they flew back to New York.

Other famous voices visited as part of the Mississippi Caravan of Music, which brought folksingers to the state in support of Freedom Summer. Folk music was at the height of its popularity, and white audiences and singers had recently "discovered" old Mississippi blues singers such as Muddy Waters and Mississippi John Hurt. Both of those bluesmen had played at the big Newport Folk Festival on the East Coast. Now folksingers came south to share their music. They introduced black kids not just to English ballads and American folk songs, but to the blues music born in their own part of the country.

Some of the singers who came to Mississippi were little-known acts. Others were stars like Pete Seeger, who cut short a world tour to lend his voice to Freedom Summer.

Seeger took Mississippi in stride. It was just another country. Some of the visiting singers, though, felt terror. Phil Ochs was a folksinger whose songs were often political. "Too Many Martyrs," for example, was about Emmett Till and Medgar Evers. In Mississippi, Ochs was convinced he would be shot onstage. Black folksinger Julius Lester felt death all around him. "Each morning I wake thinking, today I die," he wrote in his journal. Every time a car backfired or a door slammed, Lester jumped. But once he was back in New York's Greenwich Village, he talked other singers into coming to Mississippi.

A Human Firestorm

Violence in Mississippi had died down after the discovery of the three buried bodies. But by the middle of August, the short period of quiet was over. That weekend, a human firestorm swept the state. At midnight on Friday, a bomb shattered windows in McComb, and the weekend spiraled into chaos. Shots echoed down the streets of Natchez and Canton. A bomb meant for the Natchez Freedom House set fire to a tavern next door. A mob in Laurel waved baseball bats.

In Greenwood, volunteers were closing the office when someone shouted, "They've shot Silas in the head!" Silas McGhee, a twenty-one-year-old Greenwood native, had spent the summer trying to integrate the local movie theater. Despite arrests and beatings, he had seated himself in the theater's white section again and again. Then on August 15, McGhee was sleeping in a car outside a restaurant. He awoke just in time to see a pistol aimed and the flash of fire. When the car door was opened, McGhee tumbled into the gutter, shot in the face. Frantic SNCC staffers tore off their shirts to soak up the blood. They plugged the hole in Silas's jaw with their fingers and rushed him to a hospital—where he had to wait for the "colored doctor." Silas's jaw was shattered, but after surgery, he survived.

Elsewhere in Mississippi, a pickup rammed a SNCC car. There were arrests for no good reason and a mindless beating or two. Four random shootings missed their targets. To cap the madness, at precisely 10:00 p.m. Saturday night, a hundred burning crosses blazed across southern Mississippi and into Louisiana. Six crosses burned in Jackson. One of them was a mile from the COFO office. Volunteers went out to study this century-old symbol of hate.

Before the chaos ended, two dozen cops had raided the Freedom House in McComb. They said they were looking for liquor, but they went through papers and read letters. The enraged SNCCs responded by scheduling the county's first Freedom Day.

One cop summed up the weekend. The cop was standing on a street corner in Greenwood when a white man rushed up, rubbing his knuckles. "I got me one," said the man, who had just pounded a volunteer. Then the man asked the cop whether he was "the law." The officer said, "We don't have any law in Mississippi."

The President and the Ticking Time Bomb
The national convention of the Democratic Party loomed in the coming week. Preparations were under way in Atlantic City, New Jersey. Democratic delegates from every state would meet to choose the party's candidate for president. Everyone expected the choice to be

FRAN MEETS THE TERROR

FRAN O'BRIEN'S SUMMER IN VICKSBURG HAD
been quiet, compared with the mayhem that
scarred the other towns. One afternoon, two
white men had barged into her classroom.
Students froze. Fran hesitated. But the men just
stood, glared, then walked out. It had been Fran's
only brush with danger—but soon that would
change.

Each morning Fran waited inside her host
house until the SNCC car arrived to pick her
up. And each evening she and other volunteers
walked in a group down the long driveway of
the Freedom House to meet another SNCC car
that would take them home. Fran was following
SNCC's rules. But Mississippi held dangers she
did not foresee.

One evening, she and five others stood at the end of the driveway, waiting for the SNCC car. When it came, it had room for only five passengers. Fran let the others pile in. When she asked if she could squeeze in, the driver said that they could not risk overloading the car. It might draw attention and give a cop an excuse for an arrest. "Don't worry," Fran was told, "another car will be along in a minute."

Standing alone, Fran felt a shudder, but told herself not to be such a baby. Another car would be along soon. And there it was, headlights beaming down the road, slowing, slowing, stopping. Fran rushed toward it. Before she could pull back, she saw four men inside—in white robes and hoods. She was not imagining this. She was not dreaming. The quiet of her summer had ended.

Before Fran could turn and run, one hooded man jumped out, clapped a hand over her mouth, and dragged her into the car. It roared off, then stopped in a field or vacant lot. Darkness had fallen. The men dragged Fran out of the car. She tried to curl into a ball as she had been taught. They wouldn't let her. One of them said they were going to make her sorry she had ever come to Mississippi. Then they beat her, again and again, with a rubber hose, each time harder than before. They passed the hose around, taking turns.

Time slowed and seemed to stop. Fran's world dimmed. Even the agonizing pain faded.

When Fran came back to consciousness, she was lying in the driveway of the Freedom House, bruised but not bloody. She thought she must have been gone for hours—but when she ran

up the driveway, people were still on the porch, laughing and talking. They had no idea what had happened to her.

Fran let them know that she'd had a bad encounter, but she kept the details to herself. No one guessed what had just happened to the shy, dedicated teacher who loved children. Later Fran could not remember how she got home. She remembered little of her last few days in Mississippi, only that she counted the days until August 17, when she would leave for home. Fran made a rock-firm decision not to tell anyone. She refused to become a statistic or another newspaper story. So she kept her horrible secret inside. For years Fran kept quiet about her encounter with the Klan.

President Lyndon Johnson, successor to the slain John F. Kennedy. For some people, the real question of the convention was: What about the Freedom Democrats?

Despite certain nomination, President Johnson had not been sleeping well. For weeks, he had sat up at night, worrying about the Freedom Democrats. Some saw their challenge as hopeless. But Johnson saw them as a "ticking time bomb." He could imagine that if the Freedom Democrats came before the full convention, enough delegates might be moved by horror stories from Mississippi to give the Freedom Democrats seats on the convention floor. This would be a powerful snub to the white power elite, the governor and elected officials of Mississippi who were there to represent the state. They would almost certainly walk out. Other Southern states would follow. And come the November election, Johnson said, the Democrats "will lose fifteen states. . . ." In short, the Freedom Democrats' challenge could cost Johnson the presidency.

SNCC had its eyes firmly fixed on the convention, too. Members were writing papers on political issues and printing brochures.

They used Harry Belafonte's money to hire buses to carry Freedom Democrats to Atlantic City. Canvassers stepped up their last-ditch drive, piling up signatures. They had learned to link politics to people's lives. Are you tired of trudging dirt roads? Join the Freedom Democrats, and someday your streets will be paved.

Freedom Schools also did their part. Teachers canvassed on weekends. Some even sent their older students door-to-door. Back in class, the Freedom Schools continued to be more successful than anyone had expected. Two thousand students were enrolled. Most of the classrooms relied more on enthusiasm than on textbooks. Kids acted out scenes from African American history. They held formal debates on nonviolence. And almost every Freedom School published a newspaper, decorated with the students' drawings and typed by the teachers. These newspapers featured poetry, essays on civil rights, and news of the Freedom Democrat drive.

Yet even the most upbeat teachers could not hide the harsh truth that all students knew: when summer ended, the teachers would go home, but the children would still be in Mississippi. Volunteers encouraged the students to keep freedom's flame alive by questioning everything. Yet by the middle of August, students were already sad that the Freedom Schools were about to end.

A teacher in Canton noticed the change: "Some of them are beginning to realize, now that we're talking about the end of school and our departures, that we're not . . . staying forever and we're not leaving any miracles behind." But when children rushed to greet them in the mornings, or when an old man read his first words in the evening, most teachers knew their summer had been worth all the sweat, fear, and even chaos. "We're giving these kids a start," one said. "They'll never be the same again."

Learning Democracy by Trial and Error

The Democratic national convention had always been a big part of SNCC's plans for Freedom Summer. To create a path to the national convention, the Mississippi Freedom Democratic Party (MFDP) held its own local meetings, preparing for its own convention. At first, farmers and sharecroppers, maids and cooks were uncertain about the rules and regulations of politics. But with some guidance from SNCC, they learned democracy by trial and error. They elected chairmen, secretaries, and delegates. Then 2,500 of them went to a rousing MDFP state convention in Jackson.

There, when the Freedom Songs ended, a lawyer spoke. He told them that although the MDFP was not a legal political party, they still had a good chance in Atlantic City. A summer of lobbying in Washington, D.C. and elsewhere had won support for their case. Enough support, the lawyer thought, for them to bring their challenge to the convention, and enough votes to win the challenge and be accepted as delegates. Only President Johnson could stop them, and he wouldn't dare, not with the whole world watching.

The MFDP convention chose five party leaders, forty delegates, and twenty-two alternate delegates to go to Atlantic City. Unlike Mississippi's all-white delegation, MFDP delegates were not wealthy party bigwigs. They were barbers, teachers, farm laborers, and domestic workers. "This," one volunteer wrote home, "is the stuff democracy is made of."

They would leave for Atlantic City in thirteen days. During those days, new barriers were put in their way. Freedom Democrat meetings were firebombed in Hattiesburg. Delegates were arrested in Greenwood, and beaten by Klansmen near Vicksburg. Radio stations refused to run their ads. The state attorney general issued an order that denied they were a party and that forbade them to use the word "Democratic." The order also stated that they were prevented from leaving the state.

And yet, on August 19, three buses stood outside COFO headquarters in Jackson. The moment of truth for the Mississippi Freedom Democrats had arrived. Bob Moses had once hoped for 400,000 signatures, then 200,000, then 100,000. In the end, he had had to settle for 63,000. But the MDFP had followed Democratic Party rules with great care. They had filed all the necessary papers. As the delegates milled beside the buses, their hopes shone brightly.

One by one, they climbed aboard. Arms waved out windows. The buses pulled out at 10:00 p.m. A great cheer broke into song, and they rolled north toward the Tennessee line.

CHAPTER 10

"THE STUFF DEMOCRACY IS MADE OF"

IN LATE AUGUST 1964, THE FADED BEACH RESORT of Atlantic City welcomed 5,200 Democratic Party delegates from all over the county. They were in a mood to celebrate. President Lyndon Johnson would be their candidate in the presidential election, and he was likely to win. The delegates looked forward to a convention with more parties than politics. But for the sixty-seven Mississippians stepping off their buses, blinking in the morning sun, democracy was a matter of life and death.

The Freedom Democrats included two sons of slaves. Several had served in World War I or World War II. All of them were veterans of

Supporters of the Mississippi Freedom Democratic Party holding signs in front of the convention hall at the 1964 Democratic National Convention, Atlantic City, New Jersey.

life in Mississippi, which had peppered their front doors with bullet holes. One delegate wore the scars of bullet holes on his skin. Most had childhood memories of lynchings. Their adult lives had been full of insults and threats. Most were making their first trip out of Mississippi. They were all shades of brown, except for four delegates who were white—proof that the Freedom Democrats were a party for everyone.

In the eyes of the law, these delegates represented no one. Morally, they represented the very idea of democracy. Their presence in Atlantic City was a challenge to beliefs that Americans claimed to hold dear. Was the United States really a nation of "liberty and justice *for all*?" Was voting a right for everyone, or a privilege for some?

Work to Do

Now that the Freedom Democrats were in Atlantic City, they had no time to see the sights. They had work to do. The convention would begin on Monday. Over the weekend, in public and in private, the Freedom Democrats worked to build support for their claim to be part of the convention.

THE PRESIDENT'S NIGHTMARE

ON THE FREEDOM DEMOCRATS' FIRST MORNING
in Atlantic City, no one paid much attention
to them—except the president. Polls showed
that Lyndon Johnson had a good lead over the
Republican candidate, Barry Goldwater. Earlier
the press had said that the convention would
be his "coronation," not just as the Democratic
candidate but as the likely winner of the election.
But already, with the convention not yet under
way, the president's nightmare was unfolding.

The South was restless. Delegates from
Alabama were threatening to walk out of the
convention. The Civil Rights Act had infuriated
George Wallace, the governor of Alabama. He
was predicting an uprising against Johnson's

Delegates and
stage at the 1964
Democratic National
Convention, Atlantic
City, New Jersey.

Democratic party. Wallace said he might even run for president in November as the candidate of a third party. The governors of four southern states, including Alabama and Mississippi, had turned down the president's invitation to dinner at the White House.

Meanwhile, twenty-five Democratic congressmen—not from southern states—urged the president to give the Freedom Democrats seats at the convention. But the governor of Texas, John Connally, warned Johnson where that would lead. "If you seat those black buggers," the Texas governor warned the president, "the whole South will walk out!" Johnson sat in the White House, brooding over the spoiling of his "coronation."

Aaron "Doc" Henry, their chairman, spoke to the press. He said that although the official Mississippi delegates were Democrats, everyone knew they would support Goldwater in November, rather than the Democratic president who had signed the Civil Rights Act. This meant that the Freedom Democrats were Mississippi's only loyal Democrats. "If our case is fully heard we will be seated," Henry said. But if the Freedom Democrats were turned away, blacks across American might just "go fishing on election day."

While Henry talked to reporters, the Freedom Democrat delegates focused on the Credentials Committee, the group of delegates who would hear their challenge the next day. Freedom Democrats reviewed work sheets that listed each member of the committee and whether that member was a supporter or possible supporter. Then they set out to plead their case to delegations from Minnesota, Wisconsin, Oregon, and elsewhere. All that Friday afternoon, Mississippi's unofficial delegates invaded gatherings in the hotels where official delegates were staying.

Freedom Democrats handed out booklets that outlined the legal basis for their challenge. The booklets also told of crimes committed in Mississippi against African Americans who tried to register to vote. The booklets described the murders of Herbert Lee, James Chaney, Andrew Goodman, and Michael Schwerner. Members of the SNCC staff were also working the convention They had traded their overalls for three-piece suits to talk to politicians and bigwigs of the Democratic Party.

The Freedom Democrats had their sights set on two numbers: "eleven and eight." The Credentials Committee had 108 members. If 10 percent of them, eleven people, voted to support the challenge, it would move to the convention floor. There, if just eight states requested it, a roll call would unfold on national television—and most Freedom Democrats felt sure they would win the roll call.

The Challenge

Just after noon on Saturday, all sixty-seven Freedom Democrats set out from their hotel to walk to the convention. Strolling into the sea breeze, they reached Atlantic City's famous

Boardwalk and marched toward their meeting with democracy. Tourists turned to watch them. Crowds stopped to hear the stirring power of Freedom Songs. The group reached the convention hall early and stood outside to wait for the meeting of the Credentials Committee. Some of them admired the ocean. Others pointed to the street sign: N. Mississippi Avenue.

A tall, pale white man with glasses and a floppy bow-tie stood with them. He was Joseph Rauh, a Harvard-educated lawyer and longtime Washington insider. For decades Rauh had helped write laws, including the Civil Rights Act. By the summer of 1964, he was head lawyer for the Mississippi Freedom Democratic Party. He had promised them he would "move heaven and earth" to bring their challenge to the convention floor. But he would also have to move Lyndon Johnson. The president was controlling every detail of the convention, from the schedule of events to the contents of the souvenir book.

Party officials had moved the Credentials Committee meeting to a room that could hold only one network television camera. Rauh protested to a White House aide, and after half an hour of calls, the president agreed to let the

Freedom Democrats make their challenge in the much larger space of the convention hall.

In the hall, Rauh stood next to filing cabinets that held all 63,000 of the Mississippi Freedom Democrat Party registration cards that SNCC and the volunteers had gathered with so much effort. On one side of him sat Mississippi's all-white official delegates. On the other side sat the mostly-black group of Freedom Democrat delegates. Between them sat the Credentials Committee—men and women in dark suits, nodding off or scribbling notes.

Americans watching television that Saturday afternoon saw Rauh say that the Freedom Democrats had "only an hour to tell you a story of tragedy and terror in Mississippi." Aaron Henry then spoke of the state's "white power structure." It was responsible, he said, for the blood and the reign of terror. Next to speak was the Reverend Edwin King, who said, "I have been imprisoned. I have been beaten. I have been close to death. . . . All we ask is your help."

Neither Henry nor King was an especially moving speaker. Many viewers may have changed the channel. But when Rauh called his third witness, all the suffering, oppression, and hardship endured by generations of black people in Mississippi limped to the stage. Fannie Lou Hamer was ready to speak to the nation.

Among her many Freedom Songs, Hamer often sang "Go Tell it on the Mountain." Later she would tell friends that in speaking to the credentials committee and TV cameras, she felt she was on a mountaintop. But when she sat to speak, Hamer looked tired, even terrified, as the microphone was placed around her neck. She gave her name and address in her Deep Southern accent. Then she began: "It was the 31st of August in 1962 that eighteen of us traveled twenty-six miles to the county courthouse in Indianola to try to register to become first-class citizens. . . ."

Meanwhile, in Mississippi

As Fannie Lou Hamer spoke, TVs went on in black neighborhoods across the state. People gathered to watch the Freedom Democrats present their case. In Batesville, they hoped to catch a glimpse of Robert Miles, who was a delegate, or maybe of that nice white boy, Chris Williams. In Fannie Lou Hamer's hometown, her appearance on TV drew shouts.

"There's Fannie Lou!"

"Look at that!"

In Philadelphia, blacks and whites in the COFO office kept one eye on the television and the other on the street outside. It had been just ten days since COFO had opened its office in the town where Goodman, Schwerner, and Cheney had disappeared. Already the office, which was in a hotel, had been the target of white rage. The phone rang steadily with bomb threats. Sheriff Rainey and Deputy Price often burst in without warning. They stormed through, photographing people and papers. Price took delight in racing past the hotel with his siren blaring. One morning a man stood on the sidewalk across from the hotel, with a double-barreled shotgun aimed at the building. He aimed his shotgun for five full minutes before he drove away.

Each night, staffers stood guard on the hotel roof. One morning the group saw a package tossed to the steps from a passing car. Cautiously they tiptoed down. It turned out to be the newspaper. Volunteers could joke about the "comedy of terrors," but it wasn't funny to Philadelphia's black community. One woman told the volunteers, "If you people leave us,

SNCC office in Jackson, Mississippi, just before the MFDP delegation left for Atlantic City. Below, Fannie Lou Hamer on television.

they are going to kill us all. They gonna pile our bodies on top of one another." COFO put out a call for more volunteers, and several soon joined the night watch on the rooftop. They were among the eighty volunteers who had decided to stay on in Mississippi. One summer there, they concluded, was not enough to make a change.

All through August, many volunteers had wrestled with the idea of staying. First they convinced themselves, then they had to convince their parents. One woman decided to stay at the last minute, the night before she was supposed to leave and return to her studies. She wrote to her parents:

> I can simply no longer justify the pursuit
> of a Ph.D. When the folks in Flora
> have to struggle to comprehend the
> most elementary materials of history
> and society and man's larger life, I feel
> ashamed to be greedily going after
> "higher learning." . . . It would be living a
> kind of lie to leave here now.

A Dirty Trick

In the convention hall in Atlantic City, Fannie Lou Hamer's voice got stronger as she went on

speaking. She told the Credentials Committee—
and any Americans who were watching
television—what had happened after she tried to
register to vote.

Her boss ordered her to withdraw her
registration. But she told him, "I didn't try to
register for you. I tried to register for myself!"
Thrown off her plantation, she lost her job
and her place to live that same day. Committee
members leaned forward. Every eye was focused
on Hamer. Next, she spoke of the sixteen bullets
that had been fired into the home of friends who
took her in. Bullets that had been meant for her.
Then she began to talk about the time she and
nine others had gone to a registration workshop
and were coming back to Mississippi on a bus.

Suddenly the television networks cut into
Hamer's speech. The president had a statement
to make from the White House. Standing at
a podium, Johnson began: "On this day nine
months ago, at very nearly this same hour in the
afternoon, the duties of this office were thrust
upon me by a terrible moment in our nation's
history." Johnson reminded viewers that he was
president because President John F. Kennedy
had been assassinated. Then he kept talking.

THE MUD BETWEEN FRED'S TOES

Volunteer Fred Winn, who had started his time
in Mississippi by turning an old outhouse into
bookcases, came up with a joke to explain his
decision to remain after the end of Freedom
Summer. "I wasn't going to stay in Mississippi,"
he wrote to his father, "until I stepped outside
one day without my shoes on. . . . I got some mud
in between my toes. I haven't been able to get it
out since."

The truth was that after moving from town to
town, Fred felt at home in Indianola, working all
hours at the project office. He had gotten to know
people. There was "Smith," a seven-year-old boy
who came to the office, answered only to "Smith,"
and just stared at him. There was the middle-
aged woman who had been crippled by childhood

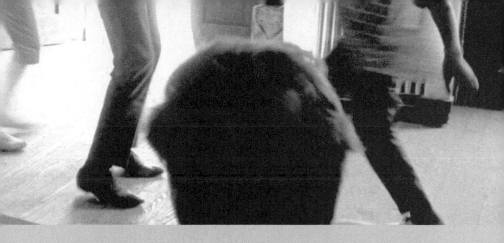

polio. Now she picked cotton on her knees. In just eight weeks, the slightly nerdy young carpenter had become a freedom fighter. He felt more at ease among both blacks and whites.

Fred had also learned to handle Mississippi cops. When an Indianola volunteer was arrested, Fred made three quick phone calls and had the man bailed out within an hour. Fred even played a little joke on the Indianola city council. The state had passed a ban on handing out leaflets without a permit. A COFO lawyer wanted to challenge that ban, but he needed evidence of a permit that had been unfairly refused. But the city council usually approved leaflets about mass meetings. What event was *certain* to be turned down?

The project office quickly printed up leaflets advertising the Freedom Hop, "Indianola's First

Integrated Dance." The leaflet said, "Let's see all you Southern Guys and Gals. . . ." Fred went before the city council with the leaflets in hand. He kept a straight face but chuckled silently at his little joke. An integrated dance in Mississippi? What could be more shocking? Reading the leaflet, a councilman barked, "What's this all about?"

Fred explained that an integrated dance, with black and white youngsters mingling on the dance floor, would be good for the community. The red-faced councilmen muttered among themselves. The permit was refused—just as COFO expected. Indianola never held its Freedom Hop, but the law against leafleting was challenged in court and eventually overturned.

And talking. The president knew he had to speak for at least ten minutes to keep Fannie Lou Hamer's speech off the airwaves. He filled the time with unimportant talk about how he would choose a vice president, but he *did* fill the time. When he was finished, so was Hamer.

Television coverage returned to the testimony in front of the Credentials Committee. Rita Schwerner, widow of the slain Michael Schwerner, told how the governor of Mississippi had slammed a door in her face. James Farmer and Roy Wilkins, important leaders of the civil rights movement, gave their support to the Freedom Democrats' challenge.

Finally, Martin Luther King, Jr. spoke to the committee. Any political party, he said, should be proud to give the Freedom Democrats a seat, because "it is in these saints of ordinary walks of life that the true spirit of democracy finds its most proud and abiding expression."

Then it was Mississippi's hour to speak. A state senator said that there had been no discrimination. The Freedom Democrats, he claimed, were "power-hungry soreheads." He accused their group of being full of Communists. He also said they were as secretive as the Ku Klux Klan.

Joseph Rauh was given the last word for the Freedom Democrats. He offered the Credentials Committee a choice. It could "vote for the power structure of Mississippi that is responsible for the deaths of those three boys, or . . . vote for the people for whom those three boys gave their lives." The committee members stood and applauded.

The meeting was over. Had it moved the Credentials Committee? The committee promised to deliver its decision by six o'clock Sunday evening. But Saturday still had a surprise in store.

Fannie Lou Hamer on the Mountaintop

President Johnson's dirty trick had taken Fannie Lou Hamer off the air during the afternoon. But not even the president could silence her. That evening all three television networks replayed her entire speech. It was seen by many more people than would have seen it in the afternoon. Americans saw and heard her, as her head shook and her voice rippled with emotion:

> . . . I was carried to the county jail and put in the booking room. They left some of the people in the booking room and

began to place us in cells. I was placed in
a cell with a young woman called Miss
Ivesta Simpson. After I was placed in
the cell I began to hear sounds of licks
and screams. I could hear the sounds of
horrible licks and screams.

Now the same booming voice that had filled
so many cramped churches in Mississippi filled
living rooms across America:

. . . And he said, "We're going to make
you wish you was dead." I was carried
out of that cell into another cell where
they had two Negro prisoners. The state
highway patrolmen ordered the first
Negro to take the blackjack. The first
Negro prisoner ordered me, by orders
from the state highway patrolman, for
me to lay down on a bunk bed on my
face. And I laid on my face, the first
Negro began to beat me.

Perhaps some shocked parents changed the
channels. The rest saw Hamer reach deep within
herself:

. . . After the first Negro had beat until
he was exhausted, the state highway
patrolman ordered the second Negro to

take the blackjack. The second Negro
began to beat. . . .

Tears welled up in Hamer's eyes, but they did
not soften her speech. She leveled her righteous
accusation at the whole nation:

All of this is on account of we want to
register, to become first-class citizens.
And if the Freedom Democratic Party is
not seated—NOW—*I question America.
Is this America?* The land of the free and
the home of the brave? Where we have to
sleep with our telephones off the hooks
because our lives be threatened daily.
Because we want to live as *decent* human
beings, in America?

Then Fannie Lou Hamer said a simple
"Thank you" and walked off the mountaintop.

Within minutes, telegrams flooded the White
House. Four hundred arrived that evening. Three
hundred and ninety-nine of them demanded
that the Freedom Democrats be given seats at
the convention. In Atlantic City, the Freedom
Democrats suddenly seemed to be everywhere.
Everyone was talking about their challenge.
Reporters interviewed sharecroppers and maids

who had come north to represent Mississippi.

By Sunday morning, support for the Freedom Democrats appeared to be well beyond the eleven committee members and eight states they needed on their side. Seventeen committee members backed their challenge. Ten state delegations were ready to call for a roll call vote.

Even Bob Moses, usually cautious, was optimistic. He told a crowd on the Boardwalk, "I don't think if this issue gets to the floor of this convention that they can possibly turn them down." Two thousand supporters gathered on the Boardwalk that afternoon. When Oregon congressman Wayne Morse told the crowd that every member of his delegation backed the challenge, cheers erupted. Over the cries of seagulls and the radios blaring Beatles hits, Fannie Lou Hamer belted out "This Little Light of Mine."

The Dark Side of Democracy

The Credentials Committee had three possible ways to handle the Freedom Democrats' challenge. One was to give all seats at the convention to the Freedom Democrats, instead of the white delegation. Another was to give no seats to the Freedom Democrats—they were not a legal party, after all.

The third possibility was to seat both delegations, if both of them signed loyalty oaths that they would support Johnson as their chosen candidate for president. In this case, each delegate would have half a vote. As the Freedom Democrats pointed out in their pamphlet, this solution had been used several times before. It had even helped Johnson in 1944, when he was a congressman who led a challenge against the delegation from his home state of Texas.

In 1964, though, Johnson would not accept the 50/50 "seat both delegations" solution. He had been warned that the entire South would walk out of the convention if he gave the Freedom Democrats even a partial vote. Instead, he wanted to seat them as "honored guests"—with no voting privileges. The Freedom Democrats were dead set against this "back of the bus" treatment. They had been treated as second-class citizens too often. In any case, the Credentials Committee voted down the 50/50 split.

Then an Oregon congressman suggested a fourth solution. Two Freedom Democrats could be seated "at large." This term is used for delegates who are chosen at the convention rather than by meetings in their home states. Joseph Rauh's heart sank at this suggestion. The committee, however, was not yet ready to vote.

Committee members discussed the challenge into the evening. At one point, a call to the White House told the president that the Freedom Democrats definitely had enough support to bring their challenge to the convention floor. And there, Johnson feared, it would be accepted. Terrified of a Southern walkout, Johnson sent a warning to Joseph Rauh. If he wanted any future cooperation or help from the Johnson administration, "he better not let that get out on the floor."

That weekend, FBI agents broke into an office just a block from the convention hall. The office was shared by SNCC and CORE (Congress of Racial Equality). The agents had just come from tapping Martin Luther King's hotel phone. It took them only minutes to wiretap the phones used by the Freedom Democrats. This illegal spying had been ordered by the president. J. Edgar Hoover hated King and was willing to spy on him, but even Hoover thought that the president wiretapping his own party's convention was "way out of line." Still, he had it done. And Johnson's second dirty trick paid off.

Information from the wiretaps was fed to the president's office each hour. By Sunday evening, he knew which delegates the Freedom Democrats were lobbying for their backing. He knew which governors Martin Luther King was pushing to support the Freedom Democrats on the convention floor. Perhaps most valuable of all, he had a list of the Credentials Committee members who backed the challenge.

Now the pressure tightened. Calls went out. Threats to end any political favors flowed from the White House. Appointments to judgeships and other positions, loans and promotions that were in the making—these would all vanish if credentials committee members did not turn their backs on the Freedom Democrats. Joseph Rauh kept counting, but now he found he had just eleven supporters. Then ten. Then eight.

The convention was set to begin Monday evening. That day, FBI agents went undercover as reporters for NBC. Black informers worked themselves into the SNCC/CORE office. Wiretaps bugged the hotel rooms of Freedom

Democrat delegates. SNCC knew nothing of this surveillance. Meanwhile, the Freedom Democrats and their supporters—150 people in all—sat on the Boardwalk outside the convention hall. Among them was Chris Williams. He was not a Freedom Democrat or a delegate, but he had come to Atlantic City to help in any way he could. He had driven Freedom Democrats around town and had sung in lively meetings. Now he was one of the protesters.

Most of them were silent. Many held signs:

SUPPORT THE FREEDOM DEMOCRATS
1964, NOT 1864

Three of the signs were drawings of James Chaney, Andrew Goodman, and Michael Schwerner. Chaney's picture was held by the murdered man's younger brother, Ben. Next to the group, as if in a museum, Mississippi-style democracy was on display. A burned and blackened car. Photographs of the miserable poverty of sharecroppers. The charred bell from the burned-out Mt. Zion Church.

The Boardwalk sit-in lasted all day. It grew to include hundreds of people. Tourists walked past and stared. A few stopped to talk. Some of them brought food for the protesters—hot dogs,

Martin Luther King addressing MFDP rally on Atlantic
City boardwalk in front of convention center, 1964. Pictures
behind him show slain civil rights workers Andrew Goodman,
James Chaney, and Mickey Schwerner.

apples, saltwater taffy. Meanwhile, President Johnson's fears were mounting. He told Hubert Humphrey to handle the Freedom Democrats.

Humphrey was a senator from Minnesota. He had a solid history of backing civil rights, but he also had ambition. Most people expected Johnson to pick Humphrey as his running mate, which would mean that Humphrey stood a good chance of becoming vice president. Johnson dangled that prize in front of Humphrey when he gave him the task of bringing the Freedom Democrats under control. The president told a friend that Humphrey had "no future in this party at all if this big war comes off and the South walks out and we all get in a helluva mess."

On Monday afternoon, Humphrey held a meeting in his hotel suite. His goal was to talk the Freedom Democrats into accepting the two-seat suggestion that had upset Joseph Rauh but had not yet been approved by the Credentials Committee. Aaron Henry, chairman of the Freedom Democrats, was invited to represent the group. Humphrey also invited several members of the committee, as well as Martin

Luther King, King's assistant, and James Farmer of CORE. These black leaders were moderate, not extreme, in their views and positions. They might be convinced to compromise on two seats. But Henry brought two guests of his own: Bob Moses and Fannie Lou Hamer.

The conversation went on for three hours. When the two-seat compromise came up, Bob Moses quietly stated that the Freedom Democrats could "accept no less than equal votes at the convention." Humphrey fought back. He reminded everyone of his record on civil rights. Among other things, he had single-handedly integrated the dining room of the U.S. Senate when he invited a black assistant to lunch and refused to leave. Humphrey ended by saying that his nomination for vice president depended on getting the Freedom Democrats to accept the two-seat compromise.

Fannie Lou Hamer had listened in silence, sitting in a corner. She had heard about Humphrey's civil rights record before coming to Atlantic City, and she had looked forward to meeting him. Now she struggled to see the good heart behind the smile of a politician. Finally, she spoke out: "Senator Humphrey, I've been praying about you and you're a good man, and you know what's right. The trouble is you're afraid to do what's right." When she finished, Hamer had tears in her eyes. Some said that Humphrey also cried. An hour later the meeting broke up. No deal had been made.

The Credentials Committee told reporters that its decision about the Mississippi delegations was postponed until the next day. Joseph Rauh talked to reporters, too. He tried to hide his sinking sense of betrayal. "We can win on the floor and we'll take it all the way," he vowed.

That night the convention began. Where Mississippi's delegation should have been sitting there were rows of empty seats. Members of the Credentials Committee argued over the Mississippi problem until dawn.

A Door Slams

All Tuesday, while the president wrestled with himself over the convention crisis, the Freedom Democrats kept up their protest on the Boardwalk. Hundreds sat in silence outside the convention hall, under a forest of picket signs. Rumors passed in whispers: about the two-seat compromise, about the Credentials Committee.

BETWEEN HIS CONSCIENCE AND HIS FEARS

BY TUESDAY MORNING, PRESIDENT JOHNSON
was in despair. Humphrey had reported back
to the president about his private meeting.
Humphrey said that he had listened patiently,
argued passionately, and "made no headway"
toward a compromise with the Freedom
Democrats. The night before, a news broadcast
of the convention had predicted a "floor fight" or
even a full Southern walkout. The White House
was now receiving telegrams complaining that
"the Negroes have taken over the country."

Johnson felt caught in a racial crossfire. He had
steamrolled the Civil Rights Act into law, only to
see African American ghettos erupt in riots. He
had defied southern segregationists, only to have
a ragtag band from Mississippi threaten to tear

the Democratic Party apart. Now he was losing control of *his* convention. He told a friend, "The Freedom Party has control of the convention." He also suspected that the whole thing was a "trap" by Attorney General Robert Kennedy to embarrass him, because the two men had been at odds for a long time.

As Johnson's mood darkened, he saw only one choice: quitting. He would finish his term and go home to Texas. Around noon he told his press secretary to order a helicopter. He would fly to Atlantic City and read the speech he had just written: "The times require leadership about which there is no doubt and a voice that men of all parties, sections, and color can follow. I have learned after trying very hard that I am not that voice or that leader."

The press secretary tried to remain calm. He pointed out that stepping down from the nomination "would throw the nation in quite an uproar." All afternoon, Johnson wavered between his conscience and his fears. He admitted that the Freedom Democrats were morally right. It was wrong to "salute" the "lily-white babies" of the official delegation from a state that had repeatedly broken the law by refusing to let its black citizens vote. But southern politicians were calling with complaints and warnings. Johnson kept insisting he would quit. He may have meant it as a bluff, not a serious threat, but in the end his wife talked him out of it. She wrote him a note: "To step out now would be wrong for your country, and I see nothing but a lonely wasteland for your future. . . ."

That afternoon Joseph Rauh talked by phone with Walter Reuther, president of the United Auto Workers union. Reuther was convinced that the two-seat compromise was the only possible solution to the crisis—and the UAW employed Rauh as a lawyer. Reuther told Rauh to march straight to the Credentials Committee and accept the two seats, or he would no longer work for the UAW.

The challenge was unraveling. Rauh went before the Credentials Committee. Struggling to be heard over cries of "Vote! Vote!" he argued desperately for a recess, or break. Across the street, in Humphrey's hotel suite, another meeting was taking place. This time there would be no tears and no appeal to softer feeling. Tempers would flare. Political pressure and trickery were the order of the day.

When Martin Luther King backed away from the two-seat compromise, Walter Reuther reminded him that the UAW had bankrolled King in Atlanta. "Your funding is on the line," Reuther said. King quickly agreed to the compromise.

Which two delegates at large would represent the entire Freedom Democrat delegation under this arrangement? Aaron Henry and Edwin King were recommended. King said that he would give his seat to Fannie Lou Hamer. Humphrey refused: "The President has said he will not allow that illiterate woman to speak on the floor of the Democratic convention." Then a television was wheeled into Humphrey's room. While the entire group watched, newsmen announced that the Credentials Committee had just approved the two-seat compromise. The startling news caused Bob Moses to lose his legendary cool.

In spite of beatings, burnings, and killings, the brutality of Mississippi had not destroyed Moses' faith that American democracy could work. SNCC and Moses and the summer volunteers had visited thousands of shacks to preach democracy. Blood had been shed all summer in the name of democracy. Now America had slapped Bob Moses in the face. Now he saw what he may have suspected all along. Threats, pressure, and sneaky backroom deals were also "the stuff democracy is made of."

Moses was now sure that Humphrey had summoned the Freedom Democrats to his hotel to keep them from arguing their case where it mattered—before the credentials committee. "You cheated!" Moses shouted. He strode out of the crowded suite and slammed the door.

The echo of that slam was the sound of SNCC giving up on the American political process. Moses soon declared that he would never again trust a politician. Other SNCCs agreed. James Forman said, "Atlantic City was a powerful lesson. . . . No longer was there any hope, among those who still had it, that the federal government would change the situation in the Deep South." Ella Baker, founder of SNCC, said, "The kids tried the established methods, and they tried at the expense of their lives. . . . But they were not willing to wait and they had paid a high price. So they began to look for other answers."

Empty Chairs
When the demonstrators sitting on the Boardwalk heard that the two-seat compromise had been accepted, they stood in silence. SNCCs and volunteers felt the same gut-wrenching fury they had known each day in Mississippi. Tourists passed them. Waves crashed on the beach. Seagulls circled overhead. The summer

that had begun innocently on an Ohio college campus, the summer that had grabbed headlines and trudged on through fear to bring its hopes before a national audience, was over.

That evening on the convention floor, the two-seat compromise was explained and adopted in less than a minute. Joseph Rauh arrived on the floor with tears in his eyes. He had just come from a meeting where the Freedom Democrats formally voted down the compromise. Rauh marched up to the podium to turn in the badges labeled "At Large."

The compromise had included more than the two seats. It also included a promise that future conventions would never again seat an all-white delegation. (They never did.) It required Mississippi's all-white official delegation to swear loyalty to the Democratic candidates that would be chosen at the convention. This outraged the Mississippi delegates. They felt their state had been "horse-whipped" and subjected to "cheap, degrading insults." How dare they be required to prove themselves loyal Democrats! Governor Johnson phoned from Mississippi, and the delegates began packing. They were walking out. The convention continued with just four loyal Mississippi delegates seated among rows of empty chairs.

The chairs didn't stay empty for long. The usual convention speeches were interrupted when news reporters noticed a commotion. John Chancellor of NBC shouted that the Freedom Democrats were marching into the convention hall! He followed them past New Jersey state troopers and onto the floor. First ten, then twenty or more Freedom Democrats took the seats that had been denied them.

From the White House, Johnson ordered the Freedom Democrats removed. One of his aides, however, realized how bad it would look if cops were seen struggling with African Americans on the convention floor. One Freedom Democrat was taken out, but the rest remained. Fannie Lou Hamer said, "All we want is a chance to be a part of America."

Atlantic City's Union Temple Baptist Church had been the gathering place of Freedom Democrats and their supporters. That night it overflowed with bitterness. Moderate black leaders told the delegates that two seats amounted to victory. More progress would come. SNCC leaders strongly disagreed. "We've shed

too much blood," John Lewis said. "We've come too far to back down now." Fannie Lou Hamer said, "We didn't come all this way for no two seats. All of us is tired."

On Wednesday morning, the moderates made a final plea for unity. The two-seat compromise had been formally accepted by the convention—couldn't the Freedom Democrats accept it, too? Johnson needed their full support. If he lost the election in November, it would be a disaster for civil rights. Talk became argument. People who had been on the same side just days earlier were turning against each other. Roy Wilkins of the National Association for the Advancement of Colored People (NAACP) told Fannie Lou Hamer, "You have made your point, but you don't know anything and you should go home to Mississippi."

Freedom Democrats found themselves split by class. Aaron Henry and the few other well-educated, white-collar delegates supported the two-seat compromise. Fannie Lou Hamer and the rest of the sharecroppers and blue-collar workers stood firm against it. Martin Luther King was torn between politics and principle. He said, "Being a Negro leader, I want you to take

MFDP delegates occupy seats of regular Mississippi Democratic delegates. Lulabelle Johnson, seated, bottom. Jimmy Travis, seated, third from bottom.

this, but if I were a Mississippi Negro, I would vote against it."

For most of the meeting, Bob Moses had stared at the floor. He seemed to be somewhere else. Now he rose and summed up the exhausting week in one sentence: "We're not here to bring politics into our morality but to bring morality into our politics."

Moses did not speak for or against the two-seat compromise. That was for the delegates of the Mississippi Freedom Democratic Party to decide. Around noon they were left alone to vote on it. Everything Freedom Summer had stood for was at stake. As Democrats, they should back their party. But as *Freedom* Democrats, they had a principle to live up to. Finally the vote was taken. The Freedom Democrats turned down the compromise.

On Thursday night, a happy Lyndon Johnson came to Atlantic City to accept his party's nomination. He and Hubert Humphrey, his running mate, linked hands in triumph. The following morning, sixty-seven Freedom Democrats filed onto buses.

Across America, the two-seat compromise was being hailed in the newspapers as a "moral and political victory" and "nothing short of heroic." But the Freedom Democrats did not feel victorious. Soon the volunteers of Freedom Summer would be gone, taking the national spotlight away with them. Sharecroppers and maids and cooks would be back at work. They dreaded the treatment they could receive. The long, sad bus ride continued: west across Pennsylvania and Ohio, then south through Kentucky and Tennessee, and back to Mississippi.

CHAPTER 11

"BEAUTY FOR ASHES"

SOMETIME DURING THE LAST WEEK OF FREEDOM
Summer, an investigator from Mississippi's State
Sovereignty Commission went to Batesville.
He had come to check up on voter registration
in Panola County. When he parked behind the
courthouse, he spotted several black women
standing with a young white man. They were
talking about voter registration.

The investigator stepped inside the
courthouse. He asked the registrar how voting
registration was going.

"Fine," the registrar answered.

And how many Negroes had registered that
summer?

"Something over seven hundred."

Bob Moses, 1963.

The investigator was shocked. The registrar reminded him that Panola County was under an order from a federal court. For one year, registrars could not make people "interpret" the state constitution or pay a poll tax.

"Yes, I'm aware of that but I still can't see how that many could qualify in so short a period of time."

The registrar wearily explained. Some clerks had taken the court order very seriously. They were actually *helping* Negroes fill out forms. They were pointing out mistakes and letting the Negroes correct them.

The investigator tried to control his anger. This was not what the court order meant. But the registrar insisted that he wouldn't interfere. He wouldn't risk another trip to federal court.

Down the hall, in the district attorney's office, the investigator heard even worse news. The COFO drive to register voters had "snowballed," the district attorney said. It had gotten "completely out of control." Negroes were coming in from all over the county. Nothing seemed to stop them. They just kept filling out forms and getting approved as voters. It was bound to spread. Another county was also under an order from federal court. More would surely come.

The investigator said he would take up the matter with the state attorney general. Something had to be done. On his way out, he saw more blacks coming up the steps, out of the heat, into the coolness of the courthouse.

The Ashes and the Beauty

By mid-September, the summer of 1964 was over. The muggy haze of August had lifted, leaving a pale beauty on the land. Crisp air smelled of smoldering leaves. Even the swamps seemed magical, tinged with gold and green. The black schools in the Mississippi Delta closed, so that children could work alongside their parents in the cotton fields. It had been that way for a century, but that would change before long.

SNCCs felt bitter over the death of their hopes in Atlantic City. Yet bitterness was mingled with relief that Freedom Summer was over. Some eighty volunteers were staying on in Mississippi, but for the most part, SNCCs could go back to helping the local people shine their own lights. Or could they? Hollis Watkins of SNCC had been against the summer project. "I knew I had been right in opposing the project," he remembered later. "Trying to reactivate and get people motivated was much, much harder." Freedom Summer had left the SNCC staff drained of energy.

Freedom Summer had also left white Mississippi filled with shock, shame, and outrage. The anger did not take long to come to the surface, especially in McComb.

Throughout the fall, McComb became a battleground. Jesse Harris, COFO's project director for McComb, wrote to the Justice Department. He warned that the increasing violence was "almost certain" to lead to the murder of another civil rights worker. The Justice Department offered no protection. When COFO called the FBI to complain about police harassment, they were told that McComb cops were "very fine people and you shouldn't criticize them."

The Klan was free to strike at will in McComb. Bombs hit another church and a preacher's house. Thugs beat volunteers in broad daylight. Pickups circled the Freedom House every night. Meanwhile, the police set up roadblocks and arrested dozens of blacks on trumped-up charges. There were more bombs, midnight explosions that splintered homes and spread terror.

While McComb came close to a state of siege, people from across the country showed how Freedom Summer had inspired them. Volunteers' parents continued to meet, raise funds, and send money south. Pharmaceutical companies sent vitamins and first aid kits. Public schools adopted Freedom Schools, sending them books and supplies.

Nearly three dozen black churches had been destroyed. Now Mississippi clergy, black and white, formed a committee to raise money to build new ones. The committee collected $10,000 in its first week—enough to begin building. The committee's campaign was called Beauty for Ashes. The name came from a line in the book of Isaiah in the Bible: "The Lord hath anointed me to preach good tidings unto the meek . . . to give unto them beauty for ashes. . . ." By Christmas, college students were giving up their vacations to build churches in Mississippi.

Changed by Mississippi

Ten weeks of Freedom Summer had frayed the nerves of the project volunteers. Many of them had thought they'd gotten used to the stress of life in Mississippi, but when they got home, they discovered that they would never feel the same.

Psychiatrist Robert Coles studied some of the returned volunteers. He saw signs of "battle fatigue . . . exhaustion, weariness, despair, frustration and rage." Many of them wanted to talk about Mississippi, but how could they describe a sharecropper's shack or a Mississippi jail to people who had never imagined such things?

Some of the returned volunteers did give talks about their experiences. Many more refused to talk to anyone. At home or back on a college campus, their white world seemed isolated and pointless. Summer had thrown them into a movement and a struggle for others. Now they were expected to return to the world of classes, parties, and career plans. They could not explain how this made them feel. One mother said sadly, "Our very normal, bright young child has changed."

Some of the returned volunteers spent long hours in their rooms. Many were overwhelmed with guilt at leaving the black people of Mississippi—"the best people I ever met," as one volunteer said. When they went out, they found themselves dodging white people and drawn to any passing black face. Politics was a distant background noise. America's talk of equality seemed laughable. Decades later, a survey of about 250 of the Freedom Summer volunteers showed that their experience had made two-thirds of them more politically liberal. Large percentages of them had lost respect for the president, Congress, the Justice Department, and the FBI.

Before Mario Savio went to Mississippi, a SNCC interviewer described him as "not a very creative guy . . . [who] did not play much of a leadership role." A summer in McComb changed that. When a protest broke out at the University of California in Berkeley in October 1964 over the arrest of a student for handing out CORE leaflets, students spoke out about free speech. Savio was one of the most effective speakers. In the months that followed, he led protests for what became known as Berkeley's Free Speech Movement.

Inspired by Berkeley, student protests broke out across America—against the Vietnam War, against the military draft, against the fact that women's rights were unequal to men's. In the forefront of all these movements were veterans of Freedom Summer. Again and again, leaders of the protest movements of the 1960s—not just Mario Savio but Tom Hayden, Abbie Hoffman, and others who supported the Summer Project even though they were not part of it—would say that Mississippi had taught them to question America.

SNCC Unravels

The returned volunteers struggled to cope with an America they suddenly found unbearably white. Meanwhile, tensions were rising among the SNCCs in Mississippi. Staff members were working without pay. Their cars, after a summer of racing around the state, were lost, wrecked, or scattered. A year earlier, SNCCs would have faced down these problems, but Freedom Summer had left them even more exhausted than the volunteers.

SNCC was coming apart. Once the group had been just a handful of the bravest and boldest

FRAN: UNHEALED WOUNDS

BACK AT HER OREGON COLLEGE, FRAN O'BRIEN was restless and angry. Once she had been quiet and shy. But after her summer teaching in Vicksburg's Freedom House, she argued with old friends who seemed to have become bigots. No one understood what Fran had been through in Mississippi, but everyone noticed her new, prickly attitude. "I didn't realize yet that it was because I was a different person, so my whole senior year was confusing," she later said.

Fran talked about the children of Vicksburg, but she told no one about her beating by the Klansmen. She kept the horror to herself, and it left her feeling alone and apart. Strangest of all, she dreamed of returning to Mississippi the following summer. Other young people in other colleges around the country were feeling the same sense of separation from their former lives.

After one week of intensive training, volunteers bid tearful goodbyes and headed south.

In Chicago, former volunteer Len Edwards was back in law school. He was out with friends one evening, talking about baseball, girls, politics. Someone asked, "Well, what was happening down there in Mississippi?" Edwards managed to get out two sentences. Then, he said, "I started crying, I just burst out crying."

In Massachusetts, Linda Wetmore found that "everything was awful." Wetmore had been arrested on Freedom Day in Greenwood. That news had been on the front page of the *Boston Globe*. It made her notorious in her home town. At church someone asked her, "You're telling me you'd want to live next door to a [racial slur]?"

Wetmore's boyfriend came over to say, "I could never kiss anybody who'd kissed a black man." Wetmore had not kissed a black man—but she answered, "Then I guess we can't go out anymore."

fighters for civil rights. Now the organization had 400 staff members. A fifth of them were white. Bob Moses saw racial resentment "welling out like poison." Too many blacks called whites smug and superior. Too many whites saw blacks as slow or lazy. SNCC was also nagged by questions about the future. Should it become a structured organization, like CORE? Or should it remain a free-wheeling movement whose members did what they felt inspired to do?

In November, 160 SNCC staffers gathered in Waveland, Mississippi. James Forman opened the meeting by calling SNCC "a band of brothers." He said, "We must decide if the circle will be unbroken. If we remain a band of brothers, a circle of trust, we shall overcome!"

But few Freedom Songs followed these stirring words. Slumped in their chairs, blacks and whites seemed more at odds than ever. Disputes broke out over the smallest details. Forman thought that SNCC was suffering from "too many people high on freedom, just going off and doing what they want." The road ahead looked rocky. Race and class were dividing people. And there was a new obstacle—gender.

One of the papers presented at the gathering was "Women in the Movement," by Casey Hayden and Mary King, two SNCC veterans. It outlined how men in the movement kept women out of top decision-making positions and treated female staffers as mere "girls." The paper "hardly made a ripple" at the SNCC gathering, as the authors had predicted. But it would ripple far beyond that Mississippi beach town. The SNCC paper became a foundation of the fast-growing women's liberation movement.

Meanwhile, the Waveland conference continued. Several SNCC members walked out, disgusted by the air of hostility. Others kept bickering. When they returned to their projects, the conflict continued. Volunteers sat at typewriters banging out long lists of complaints. Project directors saw workers wandering in and out. Muriel Tillinghast had moved to Jackson to run the COFO office. She saw that SNCC was becoming "a different kind of organization, but we don't know where we're going."

Within a year, Bob Moses would resign from SNCC and leave Mississippi. Many SNCCs would no longer be on speaking terms with one another. Within two years, SNCC's new

SNCC conference
in Waveland,
Mississippi,
November 1964.

chairman, Stokely Carmichael, would be arrested in Greenwood and would lead the crowd in chanting, "Black Power!" Many SNCCs were now carrying guns, even to meetings. Soon a SNCC meeting in New York State would vote, against the wishes of Carmichael and others, to kick all whites out of the organization.

SNCC surrendered to rage and resentment. This new, angrier SNCC shifted its focus to urban ghettos, where the enemy was not the local sheriff but police raids and FBI spying. When SNCC voiced support for freedom movements around the world, some violent, it lost much of the funding that came from white liberals. The only thing everyone could agree on was that even though Freedom Summer had cracked Mississippi's closed society, it had also shattered SNCC's circle of trust.

The Inside Story of the Killings

While SNCC unraveled, the FBI finally cracked the Klan in Mississippi. Two weeks after Freedom Summer, a Klansman broke his vow of silence.

He was a police officer named Wallace Miller. He had joined the Klan more to fit in than to fight integration. "I got the feeling that anyone who wasn't a Klansman wasn't anything," he said. But Miller hadn't counted on covering up murder. In mid-September, he met FBI agents in a restaurant and told how the Klan had planned to get rid of Michael Schwerner. The Grand Wizard had issued the extermination order. The Mt. Zion Church had been burned to lure Schwerner and Goodman into Neshoba County. Miller outlined what happened when they came.

Just as Deputy Cecil Price had said, Schwerner, Goodman, and James Chaney had been released from the county jail at 10:30 p.m. But Price had not watched their taillights disappear, as he claimed. The three men had been chased, cornered, and trapped. Taken up a dirt road, they were murdered in cold blood, and buried beneath the dam. Miller gave the FBI the name of the man he said had killed Schwerner and Goodman, but he would provide no more details.

To make a case that would stick, the FBI needed more evidence. Agents went looking for more informants. They knew that Klansman James Jordan had had a role in the killings. They interrogated him repeatedly. Finally, for $3,500 and a promise of federal protection, Jordan talked. A Klansmen named Edgar Ray Killen had heard that Schwerner and others were in the Philadelphia jail. Killen rushed to gather a lynch mob. It was not every day that the Klan carried out an extermination order. As the summer project volunteers settled in for their first night in Mississippi, more than a dozen Klansmen in three cars and a pickup converged on the jail. They were a mixed group: a preacher, a former sheriff, truck drivers, contractors, and cops young and old.

Now the killings were detailed in full. When the three civil rights workers left the jail, three cars set out after them. Deputy Price joined them in his patrol car. They chased the station wagon over roller-coaster hills, faster and faster. They were going a hundred miles an hour when Chaney decided to pull over. No one ever found out why. Price ordered the three men into his patrol car. He turned up a narrow gravel road that led to the murder site. Cars stopped, doors slammed, then came shots. Someone called a bulldozer operator to bury the bodies. The owner of the landfill filled a jar with gasoline to burn the car. Back in Philadelphia, the killers met with Sheriff Rainey. "I'll kill anyone who talks," Rainey told them, "even if it's my own brother." The men swore each other to silence and went home. Mississippi had been "redeemed" again.

A few weeks later, another informant filled in the final details. James Jordan, it turned out, had ridden with Price. A man named Wayne Roberts had fired the shots that killed Schwerner and Goodman. Jordan then got out of Price's patrol car, crying, "Save one for me!" He gunned down Chaney as he scrambled to get away.

On December 4, sixty FBI agents fanned out across Mississippi with arrest warrants. By that afternoon, nineteen men sat in the courthouse under arrest. Two of them were Sheriff Rainey and Deputy Price. A photographer from *Life* magazine photographed the sheriff chewing tobacco and laughing at a joke. He did not look worried.

Six days later, the federal commissioner in Meridian ruled that the latest Klan confession was "hearsay" evidence. She dismissed all charges. Shaking hands, slapping each other on the back, the nineteen men went free. Outside the courthouse someone said, "Ol' Rainey could be elected governor now."

The Justice Department filed new charges against the men on New Year's Day. It would be almost three years before they would go to trial. Meanwhile, Rainey and Price were more popular than ever in Neshoba County. Locals doubted that they or anyone would ever be convicted of the murders. Elsewhere in the state, Klansmen met in open rallies that drew hundreds of people. Crosses blazed at night, and so did a COFO office. But something was changing. Shame was bringing moderate Mississippians out of hiding.

The Tide Begins to Turn

Throughout 1965, Mississippi was torn between the present and the past, between the law and the way things had always been. Years later, writer Willie Morris remembered "a feeling that we hit the bottom of the barrel with these three murders in 1964." Mississippi's reputation was in tatters. Investment in the state dropped. Tourism on the Gulf Coast was cut in half.

Faced with economic damage and the scorn and disgust of much of the nation, Mississippi realized it had to change.

After more than a dozen bombings, McComb had fought back against the Klan. Citizens who saw that the life of their community was at stake offered rewards for information about the bombings. Business and community leaders formed Citizens for Progress. They called for "equal treatment under the law for all citizens regardless of race, creed, position, or wealth." Local businesses started to desegregate at last, accepting black customers.

Similar things were happening across the state. Public schools in several counties desegregated first-grade classes. (New all-white private schools sprang up wherever integration seemed near.) Two African Americans enrolled at Ole Miss, and no one rioted. The Mississippi Economic Council said that the state should follow the Civil Rights Act to the fullest, and the governor approved. But those good intentions didn't mean much in the backwoods or the Delta.

Full democracy would come to Mississippi only by federal law. In August 1965, the U.S.

Congress passed the Voting Rights Act. President Lyndon Johnson, responding to the violence of Freedom Summer, had ordered his attorney general to write the legislation. The Voting Rights Act made the federal government a watchdog to protect black voting across the South. Before Freedom Summer, just 7 percent of blacks in Mississippi could vote. Within six months after the Voting Rights Act, that number had risen to 60 percent. Things were "sure enough" changing.

The Wheels of Justice
It was not until 1967 that the trial took place. Sheriff Lawrence Rainey, Deputy Cecil Price, Imperial Klan Wizard Sam Bowers, and fifteen other men faced charges relating to the murders of the three slain civil rights workers during Freedom Summer. As the trial began, all of them seemed to be in high spirits. They were confident no jury would convict them. Rainey and Price had been touring the South to cheering crowds of Klansmen. Now a Confederate flag was hoisted as they reached the courthouse door in Meridian.

By this time, Mississippi was deeply divided on the case that had brought national shame. The state still refused to bring murder charges against the accused men, so they were being tried in federal court on charges of violating the murdered men's civil rights. Some Mississippians hoped that justice would be served to them. Others still saw them as heroes who had stood up for their state.

The trial was remarkably short. It took place before a judge who was a known racist. The verdict was mixed. Seven men, including Bowers, Price, and the shooter Wayne Roberts, were found guilty. Seven others, including Rainey, were found not guilty. The jury could not reach a decision on the remaining four, including Edgar Ray Killen, who had organized the lynch mob. Michael Schwerner's father hoped that the state would bring murder charges. James Chaney's mother said, perhaps more realistically, "They did better than I thought they would."

A few months later, the judge handed down sentences. Roberts and Bowers got ten years in prison. The others who had been found guilty got three to six years. After two years of appeals, the convicted men went to federal prison in 1970. The case was the first time since Reconstruction that any white person had been convicted of civil rights violations in Mississippi.

Another chapter in the case opened in 1998. Imperial Wizard Sam Bowers had finally been convicted of a 1966 murder. That victim was Vernon Dahmer, the farmer who had hosted a picnic for volunteers during Freedom Summer. Now Bowers was boasting about what he considered his most famous "elimination": the murders of Schwerner, Goodman, and Chaney. Those deaths had sent Bowers to prison for civil rights violations, but he said, "I was quite delighted to be convicted and have the main instigator of the entire affair walk out of prison a free man."

That instigator, the man whom Bowers said was responsible for the crimes, was Edgar Ray Killen. When the families of Schwerner, Goodman, and Chaney heard of Bowers's boast, they called for the case to be reopened. Mississippi's attorney general started investigating in 1999. The investigation dragged on for years. Finally, in 2005, police arrested Killen. He went to trial forty-one years after the three murders, with family members of the three men in the courtroom.

Killen was found guilty on three counts of manslaughter and sentenced to sixty years in prison. He died there in 2018.

Long before the wheels of justice turned, the site of the murders had become a place of memorial. And Route 19, the road where the three men had been seized by their killers, had been renamed the Chaney, Goodman, and Schwerner Memorial Highway.

WE ARE
TIRED
OF BEING
RULED BY
RACISTS

AFTER

ORDINARY PEOPLE
MADE A DIFFERENCE

THROUGHOUT THE 1970S, WHITE AND BLACK
slowly came together in Mississippi. John
Howell, who became a publisher in Batesville,
had been a teenager in 1964. "After Freedom
Summer," he said, "we met black people who,
when we got over our grudge at them for having
the audacity to want to do things like vote and
go to decent schools, were . . . such sweet and
forgiving people."

Bigotry and racial prejudice did not disappear,
but things were changing. Robert Miles, who
had risked his life to host Freedom Summer
volunteers, ran for supervisor of Panola County.
He didn't win, but he was stunned when a white
man handed him fifty dollars to help take black

This photo of an
earlier civil rights
protest was used
in an educational
filmstrip prepared
by the Mississippi
Freedom Democratic
Party used in Free-
dom Schools during
Freedom Summer.

voters to the polls. Miles said, "I never dreamed I'd live to see such a day."

Charles Evers, brother of murdered activist Medgar Evers, was elected mayor of Fayetteville, Mississippi. He was the first black mayor elected in the state since Reconstruction. In 1986, Mike Espy became the first African American elected to the U.S. Congress from Mississippi since Reconstruction. The following year, a black woman was crowned Miss Mississippi. Throughout the state, African Americans became cops, sheriffs, and elected politicians. In 2009, even Philadelphia, the town that had seen so much anger and agony during Freedom Summer, elected a black mayor.

But had Mississippi really changed? Hodding Carter, Jr., who was at one time the editor of the *Delta Democrat Times* in Greenville, thinks it has. "What is in the hearts of individuals is one thing," Carter said. "How they now find they must operate in public is another. We are talking about fundamental change, which has left the state still far from the mountaintop, but it has been climbing for some time. It may go sideways from time to time, but it isn't going back."

In just a generation, Mississippi progressed so far that its children were shocked by stories from the recent past. In 1984, when a former activist told kids about having to duck down so he wouldn't be seen in an integrated car, the kids gasped. "Not in Mississippi!" some said.

Mississippi still holds deep pockets of poverty. The state faces the same racial tensions and challenges as the rest of the country, along with echoes of its own racial history. But no one would deny that ordinary people had made a difference.

Later Lives
After the savage summer of 1964, the volunteers had gone their separate ways. The tenth anniversary of Freedom Summer passed, then the twentieth. But in 1989, the twenty-fifth anniversary, people reached out to each other. Dozens of former volunteers came to the first full reunion. After meeting in Jackson, they toured the state. Outside Philadelphia, they toured the rebuilt Mt. Zion Church. They heard Mississippi's attorney general formally apologize to the families of Michael Schwerner, Andrew

Goodman, and James Chaney. It was a short reunion, but it had started something.

Five years later, on the thirtieth anniversary, nearly four hundred of the volunteers came to Mississippi. This time, no one called it an invasion. A banner at the Jackson airport welcomed them. Most of the volunteers were returning to Mississippi for the first time since Freedom Summer. After crossing hands to sing tearful Freedom Songs, they took buses to the places they had worked. They could hardly believe they were in Mississippi. The sight of black cops startled them. Freedom School teachers met with their former students who had gone on to earn college degrees and run for political office.

Bigotry still seethed beneath the surface, however. Volunteers who visited James Chaney's grave found it had been vandalized. Chaney's brother Ben, a civil rights activist, told them, "There has not been meaningful change in Mississippi." Many agreed. They felt that even though the state had recently convicted the killer of Medgar Evers, "ghosts of Mississippi" remained.

It took Fran O'Brien twenty-five years to be free of the demons of a single summer night in Mississippi. She had buried that memory. She had even gone back to Mississippi in 1965, but the volunteer situation was so chaotic that she returned to California and became a teacher. During her first spring in the classroom, Martin Luther King, Jr. was assassinated. Fran overheard kids say, "It's a good thing they got that Communist." She later recalled, "I told them that Martin Luther King was not a Communist and I knew because I had met him."

Fran spoke as a veteran of the civil rights movement. But not until she went to the first Freedom Summer reunion in 1989 did she finally confront the ghost in her own past—the memory of the beating. Writing about it helped her overcome her fear and humiliation. Fran taught for thirty-four years before retiring. Most of her classrooms were for physically or mentally handicapped children. Fran saw parallels to the civil rights movement in her students' struggle for independence.

Fred Winn stayed on in Mississippi for nine months after Freedom Summer. It was a hard time. He was arrested five times, targeted by whites, and hounded by the draft board. A hasty wedding to a female coworker and his arrest record kept him from being drafted. The marriage ended later that year. In the spring of 1965, Indianola's Freedom School was firebombed. Not long afterward, the house where Fred and other volunteers were staying was also set ablaze, along with other buildings in the black neighborhood. All Fred could save before fighting the fires was the project's account books and his father's Bible.

A few days later, Fred and his new girlfriend, a young African American woman, left for San Francisco, Fred's home town. To his dismay, he found that black-run civil rights groups were not interested in him. Black separatism—the feeling that African Americans had to fight their own battles and not get involved with whites—was on the rise. Soon black people on Fred's street would talk to his girlfriend but not him. She continued to work in civil rights, but the two drifted apart. Fred felt crushed, rejected not just by a woman but by the race he had befriended. He looked for teaching jobs, but they were scarce, so he took off on a series of rambling trips through Europe, North Africa, and South America.

Back in San Francisco, Fred took up the plumbing trade. He dropped "Fred" and began going by his middle name, "Bright." He remained in touch with the half-sister whose birth split his family and sent him to Mississippi. Decades after signing his letters with "We Shall Overcome," Bright Winn remained devoted to civil rights.

Muriel Tillinghast left Mississippi in 1965, moving to Atlanta to work with SNCC. Later she worked for SNCC and various social programs in New York and elsewhere. She applied the lessons of Mississippi throughout her life. "I've worked in prisons, Head Start, for immigrants, health rights—pretty much everything," she said.

Whenever possible, Muriel has spoken of Mississippi. "It was like going to war," she remembered. "A lot of veterans will tell you they don't discuss war stories. But sometimes you have to—to let your children know. 'That's why we don't do this in this family.' Because of the way things were in Mississippi."

During Chris Williams's final months in Mississippi, his luck ran out. In November, while

canvassing on a plantation in Panola County, he was surrounded by raging whites who threatened to throw him into the Tallahatchie River. They settled for having him arrested. After two days in jail, he went back to work, driving the muddy back roads of winter to hold registration meetings and speak in churches. He also fell in love with Penny Patch, who had become the first white female SNCC in the Deep South even before Freedom Summer. Soon they were a couple, but violence was changing Chris's life in Mississippi. He and Penny barely escaped being attacked by a white mob. Chris and Robert Miles were attacked in downtown Batesville. Shots were fired into the Miles home.

Chris and Penny left Mississippi for California. Soon they moved to Vermont, where, with other civil rights veterans, they farmed and tried to live off the land. The couple had married, but the marriage ended in 1970. Eventually Chris returned to school to study architecture. He married again, raised a family, and in 1989 he became director of architectural services at a college in his home state of Massachusetts— twenty-five years after hitchhiking out of it.

Muriel Tillinghast, 2009, above; and Chris Williams, 2014.

"Other people went to Vietnam and that impacted their lives," Chris said, "but Mississippi was the thing in my life that has resonated down through the years. I'm very clear that the person who got the most out of it was me. I feel grateful every day to have been part of it."

A majority of the Freedom Summer volunteers remained involved in social causes. Dozens became lawyers who fought for the poor. Others became full-time activists and ran nonprofit organizations. Many Freedom Summer teachers continued to teach, sometimes in college. Several became writers. Just a handful of them, having seen first-hand "the stuff democracy is made of," went into politics. One of those, Barney Frank, became a Massachusetts congressman in 1980. He spoke for many volunteers when he said about Freedom Summer, "I am prouder of being there than of anything else in my life."

Bob Moses followed a winding path after Freedom Summer. Among other things, he taught in a rural school in the African nation of Tanzania for eight years with his second wife, a former SNCC field secretary. One day after coming back to the United States, he visited his daughter's algebra class. Moses saw that inner-city students were falling behind in math, so he created ways to get them involved in his favorite subject. He received a MacArthur genius grant—a gift of money from a private foundation—that helped turn his lessons into the Algebra Project. By 1990, Moses was traveling all over the United States, even Mississippi, to work with teachers and parents who often did not regard math as important. He said, "Like working with sharecroppers demanding the right to vote, we're trying to get students demanding quality public education in algebra."

Moses continued to speak not just at math conferences but at civil rights conferences around the country. Although he is less well-known than many who have worked for civil rights, no one did more to make America a full democracy.

Moses always spoke of Fannie Lou Hamer as a symbol of empowerment. Sadly, Hamer did not share in the gains she helped the black people of Mississippi achieve. She was soon pushed to the fringes of the movement by younger activists. She suffered a tragic loss in 1967, when her daughter was injured in a car accident. No medical facility in the Mississippi Delta would treat her, and the young woman died on the way to a Tennessee hospital.

Hamer's own health failed after a life of poor nutrition, stress, and the brutal beating in jail. She died penniless in 1977. A thousand people came to her funeral and sang her favorite song, "This Little Light of Mine." The town of Ruleville put up a sign reading "Home of Fannie Lou Hamer." Her gravestone, though, best sums up her strength. It displays her motto: "I'm sick and tired of being sick and tired."

The Legacy of Freedom Summer
The legacy of Freedom Summer is a question that has never been settled. Was the summer project a spark for change? Or was it an unnecessary interference in Mississippi's affairs that actually gave poisonous new life to a dying culture of racism and violence?

Charlie Cobb of SNCC felt it was both. The summer "changed Mississippi forever," he said, but he believed the changes were going to happen anyway: "You were going to get these federal laws—the Civil Rights Bill in '64 and the Voting Rights Act in '65. And eventually you

were going to get some slowing of the violence."
Cobb felt that Freedom Summer had slowed the
drive of activism among local people. "It would
have been better," he said, "to go the other way."

But many others have high praise for Freedom
Summer. Aaron Henry, who served as chairman
of the Freedom Democrat delegation, called it
"the greatest sociological experiment the nation
has ever pulled off." It changed the minds of
black Mississippians, who "began to look upon
themselves as somebody." Fannie Lou Hamer
said about the volunteers, "Nobody never come
out into the country and talked to real farmers
and things. . . . And it was these kids what broke
a lot of this down. They treated us like we were
special and we loved 'em."

John Lewis, the SNCC chairman who became
a U.S. congressman from Georgia, sees a longer
legacy for Freedom Summer. Speaking in
2008, when Barack Obama was campaigning
to become the nation's first black president,
Lewis said, "Freedom Summer injected a new
spirit into the very vein of life in Mississippi
and the country. It literally brought the country
to Mississippi. People were able to see the
horror and evil of blatant racial discrimination.

If it hadn't been for the veterans of Freedom Summer, there would be no Barack Obama."

When Obama was elected, some in Mississippi (and elsewhere) had a hard time getting used to the idea of a black family in the White House. By the time Obama took office in January 2009, though, Mississippi seemed more amazed than upset. Blacks and whites watched his inauguration in classrooms, cafes, and courthouses. A lot of people in those crowds cheered.

On Obama's Inauguration Day, Chris Williams told his colleagues at Williams College that he had once been a civil rights worker, that he had been part of Freedom Summer, that three men had been murdered on his first day. America had changed since then, he said. Fran O'Brien thought that Obama's Inauguration Day was "the closest thing to a perfect day one can experience in this world." She didn't have a television, so she listened on the radio. Afterward she went to a diner to eat and watch news clips of the inauguration. An African American waitress noticed the white-haired white woman crying. So Fran told Ebony about her summer of teaching in Vicksburg. She spoke of fear and hope, but not of horror. Bright Winn watched the inauguration on TV. His son was there, in Washington, and during a phone call, Bright heard the cheering in the background.

That day, many of the former volunteers thought about those who had died in Mississippi in the name of civil rights. Not just Schwerner, Goodman, and Chaney, but Herbert Lee and Medgar Evers and Emmett Till, and more than a dozen others. Some Freedom Summer veterans called each other after more than a decade. One of them said, "It took forty-five years, but we helped make this day."

The volunteers knew that they had not been heroes like the local people, nor pioneers like the first civil rights workers. They had merely gone to a place where many outsiders feared to go. They had been witnesses and spotlights. They had risen above hatred and spread hope. "At the end of it all," said Chris Williams, "I guess what really caught me by surprise is that my fellow citizens voted for Obama in such large numbers, giving him a resounding victory. I didn't think we had reached that place yet. How can we not be optimistic?"

Mississippi Freedom Democratic Party volunteer registering voters in front of Mt. Zion Baptist Church in Hattiesburg, Mississippi, 1964.

Notes

BEFORE   **MISSISSIPPI AT A CROSSROADS**

"There is no state with a record": Henry Hampton, dir., "Mississippi—Is This America?" episode 5 of *Eyes on the Prize: America's Civil Rights Movement* (Boston: Blackside, 1987).

"as common as a snake": Roy Torkington Papers, Civil Rights Collection, McCain Library and Archives, University of Southern Mississippi.

"the Negroes of Mississippi": John Dittmer, *Local People: The Struggle for Civil Rights in Mississippi* (Urbana: University of Illinois Press, 1994), p. 206.

"We are going to see that law and order is maintained": Marilyn Mulford and Connie Field, dirs., *Freedom on My Mind* (Berkeley, Calif.: Clarity Film Productions, 1994).

"We're going to be ready for them": "Mississippi: Allen's Army," *Newsweek*, February 24, 1964, p. 30.

"Mississippi changed everything": Gloria Clark, personal interview, October 3, 2007.

CHAPTER 1   **A RISKY BUS RIDE**

"At Oxford, my mental picture of Mississippi": Elizabeth Martinez, ed., *Letters from Mississippi* (Brookline, MA.: Zephyr Press, 2006), p. 186.

"I may be killed and you may be killed": *New York Times*, June 17, 1964.

"They—the white folk": John Lewis, *Walking with the Wind: A Memoir of the Movement* (New York: Simon & Schuster, 1998), p. 249.

"They take you to jail": *New York Times*, June 21, 1964.

"A great change is at hand": John F. Kennedy, "Radio and Television Report to the American People on Civil Rights," June 11, 1963, http://www.jfklibrary.org/Historical+Resources/Archives/Reference+Desk/Speeches/JFK/003POF03CivilRights06111963.htm.

"honor the memory" and "carry out the legacy": Doug McAdam, *Freedom Summer* (New York: Oxford University Press, 1988), p. 48.

"a learning attitude": Student Non-Violent Coordinating Committee Papers, Harvard University, reel 39.

"A student who seems determined": SNCC Papers, reel 39.

"I don't see how I have any right": *New York Times*, July 11, 1964, p. 22.

"I want to do my part": *McAdam*, p.46.

"to actually do something worthwhile": Chris Williams, personal interview, October 9, 2007.

"just scared the crap out of us": Williams, journal, Summer 1964, pp. 8–9.

"We don't know what it is to be a Negro": Martinez, *Letters from Mississippi*, p. 5.

"You killed my husband!": Taylor Branch, *Parting the Waters: America in the King Years*, 1954–1963 (New York: Simon and Schuster, 1988), p. 510.

"For me, it was as if everything": Robert P. Moses and Charles E. Cobb Jr., *Radical Equations: Math Literacy and Civil Rights* (Boston: Beacon Press, 2001), p. 76.

"dedicate our lives": Bob Moses, personal interview, December 10, 2008.

"either an act of madness": Stokely Carmichael, *Ready for Revolution: The Life and Struggles of Stokely Carmichael* (Kwame Ture), with Ekwueme Michael Thelwell (New York: Scribner, 2003), p. 350.

"bringing a large number": Hollis Watkins, personal interview, June 16, 2008.

"If we're trying to break down": Howard Zinn, *SNCC: The New Abolitionists* (Boston: Beacon Press, 1964), p. 188.

"I'm sorry it isn't more": SNCC Papers, reel 64.

"When the kids in Birmingham were killed": SNCC Papers, reel 38.

"Don't come to Mississippi": *New York Times*, June 21, 1964; Seth Cagin and Philip Dray, *We Are Not Afraid: The Story of Goodman, Schwerner, and Chaney, and the Civil Rights Campaign for Mississippi* (New York: Nation Books, 2006), p. 30.

"You should be ashamed!": Dittmer, *Local People*, p. 243.

"The flash point": Mulford and Field, *Freedom on My Mind*.

"If you don't get scared": "Mississippi—Summer of 1964: Troubled State, Troubled Time," *Newsweek*, July 13, 1964, p. 20.

"The crisis is past, I think": William Hodes Papers, State Historical Society of Wisconsin (SHSW).

"When you turn the other cheek": Nicholas Von Hoffman, *Mississippi Notebook* (New York: David White, 1964), p. 31.

"You must understand that nonviolence": Tracy Sugarman, *Stranger at the Gates: A Summer in Mississippi* (New York: Hill and Wang, 1966), p. 28.

"morally rotten outcasts of the White race": SNCC Papers, reel 38.

"The responsibility for protection": Len Holt, *The Summer That Didn't End* (New York: William Morrow, 1965), p. 50.

"These were my friends": Muriel Tillinghast, interview, October 31, 2007.

"Part of it is the American dream": James Atwater, "If We Can Crack Mississippi . . . ," *Saturday Evening Post*, July 25, 1964, p. 18.

"The injustices to the Negro in Mississippi": *Los Angeles Times*, June 20, 1964.

"a long, hot summer" and "racial explosion": "Mississippi Girds for its Summer of Discontent," *U.S. News & World Report*, June 15, 1964, p. 46.

Dear People at home: Martinez, *Letters from Mississippi*, p. 10.

"We hit the Mississippi state line": Tillinghast, interview, November 28, 2007.

CHAPTER 2   THE PAST IS "NOT EVEN PAST"

"The past is never dead": William Faulkner, *Requiem for a Nun* (New York: Penguin Books, 1953), p. 81.

"The whole public are tired out": William C. Harris, *The Day of the Carpetbagger: Republican Reconstruction in Mississippi* (Baton Rouge: Louisiana State University Press, 1979), p. 668.

"an era of second slavery": Eric Foner, *A Short History of Reconstruction, 1863–1877* (New York: Harper & Row, 1990), p. 236.

"so dangerous": W. J. Cash, *The Mind of the South* Random House, New York, NY, 1941, p. 93.

"the supreme law of self-preservation": C. Vann Woodward, **The Strange Career of Jim Crow**, 3d ed. (New York: Oxford University Press, 1974), p. 73.

"When civil rights came along": Jason Sokol, *There Goes My Everything: White Southerners in the Age of Civil Rights, 1945–1975* (New York: Alfred A. Knopf, 2006), p. 63.

"The Negro is a lazy": Curtis Wilkie, *Dixie: A Personal Odyssey through Events That Shaped the Modern South* (New York: Simon & Schuster, 2003), p. 57.

"every red-blooded American": John Ray Skates, *Mississippi: A Bicentennial History* (New York: W. W. Norton, 1979), p. 155.

"Segregation will never end in my lifetime": Hodding Carter III, *The South Strikes Back* (Garden City, N.Y.: Doubleday, 1959), p. 13.

"shocked and stunned": Neil R. McMillen, *The Citizens' Council: Organized Resistance to the Second Reconstruction, 1954–1964* (Urbana: University of Illinois Press, 1971), p. 15.

"We will not be integrated!": Carter, *South Strikes Back*, p. 43.

"the uptown Klan": Hodding Carter quoted in James W. Silver, *Mississippi: The Closed Society*, rev. ed. (New York: Harcourt, Brace & World, 1966), p. 36.

"If we in America": John Dittmer, *Local People: The Struggle for Civil Rights in Mississippi* (Urbana: University of Illinois Press, 1994), p. 57.

"There's open season on Negroes now": Dittmer, *Local People*, p. 58.

"From that point on": Howell Raines, *My Soul Is Rested: Movement Days in the Deep South Remembered* (New York: Penguin, 1977), p. 235.

"It was the so-called dumb people": Youth of the Rural Organizing and Cultural Center, *Minds Stayed on Freedom: The Civil Rights Struggle in the Rural South, an Oral History* (Boulder, Colo.: Westview Press, 1991), p. 59.

"Sorry, Cable Trouble": Dittmer, *Local People*, pp. 65–66.

"The following program": Sally Belfrage, *Freedom Summer* (New York: Viking, 1965), p. 109.

"Negro cow-girl": Dan Classen, *Watching Jim Crow: The Struggles over Mississippi TV, 1955–1969* (Durham, N.C.: Duke University Press, 2004), pp. 101–3.

"a veiled argument for racial intermarriage:" Harris, Mark, *Pictures at a Revolution: Five Movies and the Birth of the New Hollywood*, (New York: Penguin Press), p. 57.

"Today we live in fear": Silver, Mississippi, p. 39.

"We hate violence": Silver, Mississippi, p. 46.

"The project is concerned with construction": COFO letter to Mississippi sheriffs, May 21, 1964, Hillegas Collection.

"communists, sex perverts": Yasuhiro Katagiri, *The Mississippi State Sovereignty Commission: Civil Rights and States' Rights* (Jackson: University Press of Mississippi, 2001), p. 159.

"This is just a taste": *Chicago Tribune*, June 9, 1964.

CHAPTER 3   **FREEDOM STREET**

"unpleasant, to say the least": Chris Williams, correspondence, June 21, 1964.

"Y'all gonna hear": Chris Williams, personal interview, February 1, 2008.

"I've waited eighty years": Martinez, *Letters from Mississippi*, p. 51.

"There are people here": Martinez, *Letters from Mississippi*, p. 61.

"a fiery and fast moving old woman": Martinez, *Letters from Mississippi*, pp. 47–48.

Dear People: Greetings from Batesville, Miss: Williams, correspondence, June 21, 1964.

"I was petrified": Muriel Tillinghast interview, November 28, 2007.

"rather get arrested in Greenville": Tracy Sugarman, *Stranger at the Gates: A Summer in Mississippi* (New York: Hill and Wang, 1966), p. 167.

"We don't bother no white folks": William Bradford Huie, *Three Lives for Mississippi* (New York: WCC Books, 1964, 1965), p. 140.

"Yesterday morning, three of our people": Sally Belfrage, *Freedom Summer* (New York: Viking, 1965), p. 11.

"You are not responsible": Taylor Branch, *Pillar of Fire: America in the King Years, 1963–65* (New York: Simon & Schuster, 1998), p. 363.

"More than any white person": William Bradford Huie, *Three Lives for Mississippi* (New York: WCC Books, 1964, 1965), p. 114.

"I am now so thoroughly identified": Seth Cagin and Philip Dray, *We Are Not Afraid: The Story of Goodman, Schwerner, and Chaney, and the Civil Rights Campaign for Mississippi* (New York: Nation Books, 2006), p. 259.

"We're actually pretty lucky here": Richard Woodley, "A Recollection of Michael Schwerner," *Reporter*, July 16, 1964, p. 23.

"a marked man": Huie, *Three Lives*, p. 81.

"I belong right here in Mississippi": Huie, *Three Lives*, p. 117.

"Mickey could count on Jim": Huie, *Three Lives*, p. 95.

"a born activist": Carolyn Goodman, "Andrew Goodman—1943–1964," in Erenrich, *Freedom Is a Constant Struggle*, p. 321.

"Because this is the most important thing": *New York Times*, June 25, 1964.

"We couldn't turn our backs": *New York Times*, June 25, 1964.

"I'm scared": Carolyn Goodman Papers, State Historical Society of Wisconsin.

"The people in this city": Federal Bureau of Investigation, Mississippi Burning Case, File 44-25706, (hereafter MIBURN), part 3, p. 53.

"Don't you know": COFO, Mississippi Black Paper, pp. 67–68.

"Which side is the federal government on?": Howard Zinn, *SNCC: The New Abolitionists* (Boston: Beacon Press, 1964), p. 215.

"There is a street in Itta Bena": Martinez, *Letters from Mississippi*, p. 192.

"Good evening. Three young civil rights workers": Walter Cronkite, "History Lessons: Mississippi 1964—Civil Rights and Unrest," June 16, 2005, http://www.npr.org/templates/player/mediaPlayer. html?action=1&t=1&islist=false&id=4706688&m=4706689."

"a bunch of killings": Michael R. Beschloss, ed., *Taking Charge: The Johnson White House Tapes, 1963–1964* (New York: Simon & Schuster, 1997), p. 313.

"I'm afraid that if I start": Beschloss, *Taking Charge*, p. 431.

"I would not be surprised": Beschloss, *Taking Charge*, pp. 431–32.

"no white organizations": Beschloss, *Taking Charge*, p. 434.

"Wreckage Raises New Fears": New York Times, June 24, 1964.

"They had no business down here": Florence Mars, *Witness in Philadelphia* (Baton Rouge: Louisiana State University Press, 1977), pp. 87–88.

"Where do you think you're goin'?": Cagin and Dray, We Are Not Afraid, p. 343.

"destroy evidence": John Lewis, *Walking with the Wind: A Memoir of the Movement* (New York: Simon & Schuster, 1998), p. 257.

"If there has been a crime": Lewis, *Walking with the Wind*, p. 257.

"We don't want anything to happen": James Farmer, *Lay Bare the Heart: An Autobiography of the Civil Rights Movement* (New York: New American Library, 1985), p. 276.

"a thousand of these youngsters": Nick Kotz, *Judgment Days: Lyndon Baines Johnson, Martin Luther King Jr., and the Laws that Changed America* (Boston: Houghton Mifflin, 2005) , p. 171.

"I'm not going to send troops": Randall B. Woods, *LBJ: Architect of American Ambition* (New York: Free Press, 2006), p. 479.

"to all parents everywhere": *New York Times*, June 26, 1964.

"Don't you know we'll never": Cagin and Dray, *We Are Not Afraid*, p. 366.

"I'm just hoping": *New York Times*, June 25, 1964.

"I am going to find my husband": Marco Williams, dir., *Ten Days that Unexpectedly Changed America—Freedom Summer* (New York: History Channel, 2006).

"Is it true that you and Governor Wallace here": Robert Zellner, *The Wrong Side of Murder Creek: A White Southerner in the Freedom Movement, with Constance Curry* (Montgomery, Ala.: NewSouth Books, 2008), p. 250.

"I don't want your sympathy!": *Los Angeles Times*, June 26, 1964.

"Sheriff Rainey, I feel": Cagin and Dray, *We Are Not Afraid*, p. 360.

"Bloody Neshoba": Howard Ball, *Murder in Mississippi: United States v. Price and the Struggle for Civil Rights* (Lawrence: University of Kansas Press, 2004), p. 64.

"I believe them jokers": Marilyn Mulford and Connie Field, dirs., *Freedom on My Mind* (Berkeley, Calif.: Clarity Film Productions, 1994).

"like termites on old lumber": *Jackson Clarion Ledger*, July 7, 1964.

"Beware, good Negro citizens": Mississippi Summer Project, running summary of incidents, transcript, USM (COFO incidents).

"Want us to do to you": *New York Times*, June 27, 1964.

"You dig it?": Hodes Papers, State Historical Society of Wisconsin.

"like a funeral parlor": Martinez, *Letters from Mississippi*, p. 33.

"Suddenly hundreds of young Americans": Robert Coles, *Farewell to the South* (Boston: Little, Brown, 1972), pp. 269.

"You know what we're all doing": Doug McAdam, *Freedom Summer* (New York: Oxford University Press, 1988), p. 71.

Dear Mom and Dad: Martinez, *Letters from Mississippi*, p. 26.

"The kids are dead": Belfrage, *Freedom Summer*, pp. 25–27.

"I don't know what all the fuss is about": Belfrage, *Freedom Summer*, p. 29.

CHAPTER 5   "IT IS SURE ENOUGH CHANGING"

"I'm sorry, Mr. President": Cheryl Lynn Greenburg, ed., *Circle of Trust: Remembering SNCC* (New Brunswick, NJ: Rutgers University Press, 1998), p. 191.

"Now it wasn't just these 'Negroes'": Fred Bright Winn, personal interview, November 13, 2007.

"Wherever there is a fight of equality": Fred Bright Winn, correspondence, June 15, 1964.

Holly Springs": WATS Line, June 30, 1964.

"Violence hangs overhead like dead air": Martinez, *Letters from Mississippi*, p. 168.

"reckless walking": Martinez, *Letters from Mississippi*, p. 147.

"Know all roads": SNCC Papers, reel 40.

"surviving and just walking around": Howell Raines, *My Soul Is Rested: Movement Days in the Deep South Remembered* (New York: Penguin, 1977), pp. 239–40.

"The whole scene": Martinez, *Letters from Mississippi*, p. 55.

"It's the best thing that's happened": John Hersey, "A Life for a Vote," Saturday Evening Post, September 26, 1964; reprinted in Library of America, Reporting Civil Rights, p. 223.

"agitators. . . come to Mississippi": Chris Williams, journal.

"He said they ought to send me home": Chris Williams, correspondence.

"I have developed a real taste": Chris Williams, correspondence.

"hard on the Negroes": Florence Mars, *Witness in Philadelphia* (Baton Rouge: Louisiana State University Press, 1977), p. 76.

"I bet you every one": Seth Cagin and Philip Dray, *We Are Not Afraid: The Story of Goodman, Schwerner, and Chaney, and the Civil Rights Campaign for Mississippi* (New York: Nation Books, 2006), p. 340.

"Now come on sheriff": Mississippi State Sovereignty Commission Files, Mississippi Department of Archives and History, Jackson, MS, (MDAH) SCR ID # 1-8-0-18-2-1-1.

"close the springs of racial poison": *Los Angeles Times,* July 5, 1964.

"time of testing": Beschloss, *Taking Charge,* p. 450.

"Had it up as high": Fannie Lou Hamer, "To Praise Our Bridges," in Abbott, Mississippi Writers, p. 324.

"I knowed as much about a facto law": Kay Mills, *This Little Light of Mine: The Life of Fannie Lou Hamer* (New York: Penguin Books, 1993), p. 37.

"The only thing they could do": Hamer, "To Praise Our Bridges," p. 324.

"I feel like a man": Tracy Sugarman, *Stranger at the Gates: A Summer in Mississippi* (New York: Hill and Wang, 1966), p. 116.

"These young white folks": Martinez, *Letters from Mississippi*, p. 72.

"I couldn't register people": Muriel Tillinghast, interview, November 28, 2007.

"The food was good": *New York Times*, July 6, 1964.

"We are just going to abide": *New York Times*, July 6, 1964.

CHAPTER 6   THE SICKNESS AND THE SCARS

"What will it take": Martinez, *Letters from Mississippi*, p. 138.

"lying on the ground": Martinez, *Letters from Mississippi*, p. 137.

"Tonight the sickness struck": Martinez, *Letters from Mississippi*, p. 137.

"Closed in Despair": "Civil Rights: And the Walls Came Tumbling Down," *Time*, July 17, 1974, p. 25.

"I'm free!": *Los Angeles Times*, July 16, 1964.

"unless these people get out": *New York Times*, July 5, 1964.

"Who are these fiends": Carolyn Goodman, "My Son Didn't Die in Vain!" with Bernard Asbell, *Good Housekeeping*, May 1965, p. 158.

"share the terror": *New York Times*, July 6, 1964.

"Morale is building": WATS Line, July 7, 1964.

"We are going ahead": WATS Line, July 8, 1964.

"Please try not to worry": Fran O'Brien, correspondence, July 6, 1964.

"You will be teaching": Charlie Cobb, "Organizing Freedom Schools," in Erenrich, *Freedom Is a Constant Struggle*, p. 136.

"be creative": "A Note to the Teacher, undated," Michael J. Miller Civil Rights Collection, Historical Manuscripts and Photographs, University of Southern Mississippi.

"The atmosphere in class": Martinez, *Letters from Mississippi*, p. 108.

"I kept thinking": Marilyn Mulford and Connie Field, dirs., *Freedom on My Mind* (Berkeley, Calif.: Clarity Film Productions, 1994).

"savage blacks and their communist masters": Sally Belfrage, *Freedom Summer* (New York: Viking, 1965), pp. 104–5.

"the goon squad": Florence Mars, *Witness in Philadelphia* (Baton Rouge: Louisiana State University Press, 1977), p. 101.

"extermination": John Dittmer, *Local People: The Struggle for Civil Rights in Mississippi* (Urbana: University of Illinois Press, 1994), p. 217.

"I have little doubt": Dittmer, *Local People*, p. 238.

"I don't want the Klansmen": Michael R. Beschloss, ed., *Taking Charge: The Johnson White House Tapes, 1963–1964* (New York: Simon & Schuster, 1997), p. 450.

"We haven't even started leaning": "Mississippi—Summer of 1964: Troubled State, Troubled Time," *Newsweek*, July 13, 1964, p. 20.

"I don't close it": Don Whitehead, *Attack on Terror: The FBI Against the Ku Klux Klan in Mississippi* (New York: Funk & Wagnalls, 1970), p. 96.

"We most certainly do not": *New York Times*, July 11, 1964.

"deep sorrow for Mississippi": *Los Angeles Times*, July 12, 1964.

"Mississippi is the only state": Doug McAdam, *Freedom Summer* (New York: Oxford University Press, 1988), p. 97.

"running my rear end off": Fred Bright Winn, correspondence, mid-July 1964.

"dirty" and "unclean": *New York Times*, July 17, 1964.

"to keep a lid on things": Fred Bright Winn, email, May 26, 2008.

"I was and am furious": Fred Bright Winn, correspondence, July 14, 1964.

"before a tragic incident": Hodes Papers, State Historical Society of Wisconsin.

"Sometimes when I lie awake": *Boston Globe*, July 4, 1964.

"I'm hot, I'm miserable": *Los Angeles Times*, July 19, 1964.

JULY 16   ANOTHER SO-CALLED "FREEDOM DAY"

"another so-called 'Freedom Day'": *Greenwood Commonwealth*, July 15, 1964.

"Jim Crow . . . Must go!": Tracy Sugarman, *Stranger at the Gates: A Summer in Mississippi* (New York: Hill and Wang, 1966), p. 160.

"I want to go to jail": Sally Belfrage, *Freedom Summer* (New York: Viking, 1965), p. 136.

"No one will interfere": *Greenwood Commonwealth*, July 17, 1964.

"When are they going to do something": *New York Times*, August 3, 1964.

"It's too much like": Louis Harris, "The Backlash Issue," *Newsweek*, July 13, 1964, p. 24.

"Without condoning racist attitudes": *Wall Street Journal*, June 30, 1964.

"no-good rabblerousers": Letters, *Newsweek*, July 17, 1964.

"By what stretch of the imagination": New York Times, July 10, 1964.

"Isn't there a way": Letters, *Life*, July 24, 1964.

"the whole scheme": *Greenwood Commonwealth*, July 17, 1964.

"the biggest faker": *New York Times*, July 16, 1964.

"We will sing loud": Sally Belfrage, *Freedom Summer* (New York: Viking, 1965), p. 145.

CHAPTER 7 "WALK TOGETHER, CHILDREN"

"Hello, Freedom!": Ira Landess, personal interview, November 28, 2007.

"When you're not in Mississippi": Martinez, Letters from Mississippi, p. 18.

"engaged in widespread terroristic acts": COFO v. Rainey, et al., Meikeljohn Civil Liberties Institute Archives, Bancroft Library, University of California, Berkeley, http://sunsite.berkeley.edu/meiklejohn/meik-10_1/ meik-10_1-6.html#580.7

"everyone who is not working": SNCC Papers, reel 40.

"Not me": Sally Belfrage, *Freedom Summer* (New York: Viking, 1965), p. 187.

"battle royal": *Washington Post*, July 23, 1964.

"potentially explosive": *Los Angeles Times*, July 26, 1964.

"a good bet": Charlie Cobb, personal interview, July 16, 2008.

"For someone so young": Unita Blackwell, *Barefootin': Life Lessons from the Road to Freedom*, with JoAnne Prichard Moore (New York: Crown, 2006), p. 79.

"We couldn't have lasted": Muriel Tillinghast, interview, December 16, 2008.

"If he gets killed": Michael R. Beschloss, ed., *Taking Charge: The Johnson White House Tapes, 1963–1964* (New York: Simon & Schuster, 1997), p. 460.

"There are threats" and "So that we don't have": Beschloss, *Taking Charge*, p. 461.

"We knew better": Charles Payne, *I've Got the Light of Freedom: The Organizing Tradition and the Mississippi Freedom Struggle* (Berkeley and Los Angeles: University of California Press, 1995), p. 103.

"the most creative thing": Mary King, *Freedom Song: A Personal Story of the 1960s Civil Rights Movement* (New York: Quill/William Morrow, 1987), p. 307–308.

"the unspeakable Martin Luther King": David R. Davies, ed., *The Press and Race: Mississippi Journalists Confront the Movement* (Jackson: University of Mississippi Press, 2001), p. 41.

"to demonstrate the absolute support": Taylor Branch, *Pillar of Fire: America in the King Years, 1963–65* (New York: Simon & Schuster, 1988), p. 410.

"You must not allow anybody": *New York Times*, July 22, 1964.

"turn this nation": *Washington Post*, July 23, 1964.

"Seat the Freedom Democratic Party!": James Forman, *The Making of Black Revolutionaries* (Washington, DC: Open Hand, 1985), p. 384.

"Small Crowd Greets King": *Jackson Clarion Ledger*, July 22, 1964.

"civil rights workers and troublemakers": Shirley Tucker, *Mississippi from Within* (New York: Arco, 1965), p. 130.

"Latest Wave of Invaders": *Jackson Clarion-Ledger*, July 22, 1964.

"We do know that Communist influence": *New York Times*, April 22, 1964.

"all communists speak Russian": *Panolian*, July 4, 1984.

"If they ain't calling you a Communist": Blackwell, *Barefootin'*, p. 118.

"The history of America": Fran O'Brien, interview, November 12, 2007.

"Well, you just read the book": O'Brien interview.

"Sometimes I feel I'm not doing much": Fran O'Brien, correspondence, July 18, 1964.

"the worst state in the Union": *Los Angeles Times*, July 24, 1964, p. 21.

"And what about you, young lady?": Fran O'Brien, interview, November 12, 2007.

"Three young men came here": *New York Times*, July 25, 1964.

"people of ill will": *New York Times*, July 25, 1964.

"I know what fear is": Belfrage, *Freedom Summer*, p. 169.

"Listen," the man said: Fran O'Brien, correspondence, July 28, 1964.

CHAPTER 8   **"A BLOT ON THE COUNTRY"**

"I believe with all my heart" and "I just hope": Florence Mars, *Witness in Philadelphia* (Baton Rouge: Lousiana State University Press, 1977, p. 105.

"There is no reason": *Jackson Clarion-Ledger*, August 4, 1964.

"95 percent of our blacks": *New York Times*, August 9, 1964.

"Only a fool" and "If Capps thinks": *New York Times*, August 9, 1964.

"Where have you people been?": Tracy Sugarman, *Stranger at the Gates: A Summer in Mississippi* (New York: Hill and Wang, 1966), p. 173.

"To be quite frank with you": Fred Bright Winn, correspondence, no date.

"counting them like a jail sentence": Winn, correspondence, August 13, 1964.

"wasn't going to turn the government over": Chris Williams, correspondence, July 13, 1964.

"very violent town": Chris Williams, correspondence, July 13, 1964.

"The whole state is beginning to tighten up": Chris Williams, correspondence, July 28, 1964.

"pay a million more": MDAH SCR ID # 2-112-1-49-1-1-1.

"We've spotted the dam": Don Whitehead, *Attack on Terror: The FBI Against the Ku Klux Klan in Mississippi* (New York: Funk & Wagnalls, 1970), p. 128.

"their enemy was not": COFO brochure, White Folks Project Collection, Univerisity of Southern Mississippi.

"Why Mississippi?": Ed Hamlett Papers, White Folks Project Collection, USM.

"get the feel": William and Kathleen Henderson Papers, State Historical Society of Wisconsin.

"It looks like the pilot phase": Elizabeth Martinez, ed. *Letters from Mississippi* (Brookline, MA: Zephyr Press, 2007), p. 181.

"Would you marry a Negro?": Martinez, *Letters from Mississippi*, p. 179.

"If you print my name": *Washington Post*, August 16, 1964.

"responsible citizens" and "I am an insurance man": MDAH SCR ID # 99-38-0-493-2-1-1.

"to let the Civil Rights workers": Hodding Carter III, *So the Heffners Left McComb* (Garden City, NY: Doubleday, 1965), p. 80.

"You're gonna get": Carter, *So the Heffners Left McComb*, p. 79.

"Mickey could count on Jim": William Bradford Huie, *Three Lives for Mississippi* (New York: WCC Books, 1964, 1965), p. 95.

"is not private": *New York Times*, August 6, 1964.

"My boy died a martyr": *McComb Enterprise-Journal*, August 6, 1964.

"The closed society that is Mississippi": *Hartford Courant*, August 6, 1964.

"a horrendous example": *New York Times*, August 6, 1964.

"witnesses to a way of life": *Washington Post*, August 6, 1964.

"We must track down the murderers": *Vicksburg Post*, August 6, 1964.

"Many of us in Mississippi": *Delta Democrat-Times*, August 9, 1964.

"a new hate campaign": *Meridian Star*, August 6, 1964.

"It was those integration groups": *Delta Democrat-Times*, August 6, 1964.

"If they had stayed home": *Hattiesburg American*, August 5, 1964, cited in Tucker, *Mississippi from Within*, p. 136.

"hate to be in his shoes": MDAH SCR ID # 2-112-1-49-1-1-1.

"I want people to know": *New York Times*, August 6, 1964.

"have some race pride": Belfrage, *Freedom Summer*, p. 182.

"What I think we ought to do": Belfrage, *Freedom Summer*, p. 183.

"Sorry, but I'm not here to do": Bradley G. Bond, *Mississippi: A Documentary History* (Jackson: University of Mississippi Press, 2003), pp. 254–59.

"The tragedy of Andy Goodman": *New York Times*, August 10, 1964.

"Success?": Moses told the press: *Newsweek*, August 24, 1964, p. 30.

"the unjust laws of Mississippi": SNCC Papers, reel 39.

"It was the single time in my life": John Dittmer, *Local People: The Struggle for Civil Rights in Mississippi* (Urbana: University of Illinois Press, 1994), p. 260.

"I am tired": Elizabeth Martinez, ed., *Letters from Mississippi* (Brookline, MA: Zephyr Press, 2007), p. 225.

"depression session": Curtis Wilkie, *Dixie: A Personal Odyssey through Events That Shaped the Modern South* (New York: Simon & Schuster, 2003), p. 144.

"If I stay here much longer": Robert Coles, *Farewell to the South* (Boston: Little, Brown, 1972), pp. 252–53.

"a ballet": Sidney Poitier, *Life beyond Measure: Letters to My Great-Granddaughter* (New York: HarperCollins, 2008), p. 174.

"I have been a lonely man": Adam Goudsouzian, *Sidney Poitier: Man, Actor, Icon* (Chapel Hill: University of North Carolina Press, 2004), p. 224.

"Each morning I wake": Julius Lester, *All is Well* (New York: William Morrow, 1976), p. 112.

"courage overcame fear": Muriel Tillinghast, interview, November 28, 2007.

"They've shot Silas!": Sally Belfrage, *Freedom Summer* (New York: Viking, 1965), p. 222.

"colored doctor": Robert Zellner, *The Wrong Side of Murder Creek: A White Southerner in the Freedom Movement*, with Constance Curry (Montgomery, Ala.: NewSouth Books, 2008), p. 261.

"I got me one": WATS Line, August 17, 1964.

"ticking time bomb": Nick Kotz, *Judgment Days: Lyndon Baines Johnson, Martin Luther King Jr., and the Laws that Changed America* (Boston: Houghton-Mifflin, 2005), p. 190.

"will lose fifteen states": Michael R. Beschloss, ed., *Taking Charge: The Johnson White House Tapes, 1963–1964* (New York: Simon & Schuster, 1997), p. 516.

"Some of them are beginning to realize": Sandra E. Adickes, *Legacy of a Freedom School* (New York: Palgrave Macmillan, 2005), p. 264.

"We're giving these kids a start": Washington Post, July 20, 1964.

"Don't worry," she was told: Fran O'Brien, "Journey into Light," in Erenrich, *Freedom Is a Constant Struggle*, p. 285.

"This is the stuff democracy is made of": Martinez, *Letters from Mississippi*, pp. 250–51.

CHAPTER 10   "THE STUFF DEMOCRACY IS MADE OF"

"If you seat those black buggers": John Dittmer, *Local People: The Struggle for Civil Rights in Mississippi* (Urbana: University of Illinois Press, 1994), p. 290.

"If our case is fully heard": SNCC Papers, Reel 41.

"go fishing on Election Day": *Washington Post*, August 22, 1964.

"eleven and eight": John Lewis, *Walking with the Wind: A Memoir of the Movement* (New York: Simon & Schuster, 1998), p. 279.

"only an hour": Seth Cagin and Philip Dray, *We Are Not Afraid: The Story of Goodman, Schwerner, and Chaney, and the Civil Rights Campaign for Mississippi* (New York: Nation Books, 2006), p. 389.

"white power structure": *Washington Post*, August 23, 1964.

"I have been imprisoned": *Washington Post*, August 23, 1964; and Cagin and Dray, *We Are Not Afraid*, p. 415.

"It was the 31st of August": Fannie Lou Hamer, testimony before the Democratic National Convention, American Radio Works Web site, http://americanradioworks.publicradio.org/features/sayitplain/flhamer.html

"There's Fannie Lou!": Len Edwards, personal interview, October 29, 2008.

"comedy of terrors": Cagin and Dray, *We Are Not Afraid*, p. 383.

"If you people leave us": WATS Line, August 20, 1964.

I can simply no longer justify: Martinez, *Letters from Mississippi*, p. 265.

"I wasn't going to stay": Fred Winn, correspondence, September 1, 1964.

"What's this all about?": Winn, interview, November 13, 2007.

"I didn't try to register for you": Hamer, testimony.

"On this day nine months ago": Taylor Branch, *Pillar of Fire: America in the King Years, 1963–65* (Simon & Schuster, 1998), p. 460.

"it is in these saints": Branch, *Pillar of Fire*, p. 460.

"power-hungry soreheads": Murray Kempton, "Conscience of a Convention," *New Republic*, September 5, 1964, p. 6.

"vote for the power structure": Susie Erenrich, *Freedom Is a Constant Struggle: An Anthology of the Mississippi Civil Rights Movement* (Montgomery, AL: Black Belt Press, 1999), p. 312.

"I was carried to the county jail": Hamer, testimony.

"I don't think that if this issue": Marilyn Mulford and Connie Field, dirs., *Freedom on My Mind* (Berkeley, Calif.: Clarity Film Productions, 1994).

"honored guests": Kotz, *Judgment Days*, p. 201.

"back of the bus": *Los Angeles Times*, August 24, 1964.

"he better not let": Kotz, *Judgment Days*, p. 208.

"way out of line": Branch, *Pillar of Fire*, p. 461.

"Support the Freedom Democrats": *Christian Science Monitor*, August 26, 1964.

"1964, Not 1864": *Los Angeles Times*, August 26, 1964.

"no future in this party": Kotz, *Judgment Days*, p. 200.

"accept no less": Kotz, *Judment Days*, p. 211.

"Senator Humphrey": Chana Kai Lee, For *Freedom's Sake: The Life of Fannie Lou Hamer* (Urbana: University of Illinois Press, 1999), p. 93; and Olson, *Freedom's Daughters*, p. 320.

"We can win on the floor": *New York Times*, August 25, p. 23.

"made no headway": Kotz, *Judgment Days*, p. 211.

"the Negroes have taken over": Michael R. Beschloss, ed., *Taking Charge: The Johnson White House Tapes, 1963–1964* (New York: Simon & Schuster, 1997), p. 527.

"The Freedom Party has": Kotz, *Judgment Days*, p. 213.

"The times require leadership": Branch, *Pillar of Fire*, p. 468n.

"would throw the nation": Branch, *Pillar of Fire*, p. 468.

"salute" and "lily-white babies": Johnson, Robert David, *All the Way With LBJ: The 1964 Presidential Election*, (New York: Cambridge University Press, 2009), p. 186.

"To step out now": Lady Bird Johnson, *A White House Diary* (New York: Holt, Rhinehart, and Winston, 1970), p. 192.

"Your funding is on the line": Kotz, *Judgment Days*, p. 215.

"The President has said": Kotz, *Judgment Days*, p. 216.

"You cheated!": Kotz, *Judgment Days*, p. 216.

"Atlantic City was a powerful lesson": James Forman, *The Making of Black Revolutionaries* (Washington, DC: Open Hand, 1985), pp. 395–96.

"The kids tried the established methods": Lynne Olson, *Freedom's Daughters: The Unsung Heroines of the Civil Rights Movement from 1830 to 1970* (New York: Scribners, 2001), p. 325.

"horsewhipped": *New York Times*, August 27, 1964.

"cheap, degrading insults": *Jackson Clarion Ledger*, August 27, 1964.

"All we want": Mulford and Field, *Freedom on My Mind*.

"We've shed too much blood": Lewis, *Walking with the Wind*, p. 281.

"We didn't come all this way": Unita Blackwell, *Barefootin': Life Lessons from the Road to Freedom*, with JoAnne Prichard Moore (New York: Crown, 2006), p. 115.

"You have made your point": Kotz, *Judgment Days*, p. 221.

"Being a Negro leader": Kotz, *Judgment Days*, p. 221.

"We're not here to bring politics into our morality": Eric R. Burner, *And Gently He Shall Lead Them: Robert Parris Moses and Civil Rights in Mississippi* (New York: New York University Press, 1994), p. 187.

"moral and political victory": *Los Angeles Times*, August 27, 1964.

"nothing short of heroic": *Washington Post*, August 26, 1964.

"Fine" to "completely out of control": Mississippi State Sovereignty Commission Files, Mississippi Department of Archives and History, Jackson, MS, SCR ID # 2-61-1-101-5-1-1.

"I knew I had been right": Hollis Watkins, interview, June 16, 2008.

"very fine people": Mendy Samstein Papers, State Historical Society of Wisconsin.

"battle fatigue": John Lewis, *Walking with the Wind: A Memoir of the Movement* (New York: Simon & Schuster, 1998), p. 273.

"Our very normal": Doug McAdam, *Freedom Summer* (New York: Oxford University Press, 1988), p. 136.

"the best people I ever met": Elizabeth Martinez, ed., *Letters from Mississippi* (Brookline, MA: Zephyr Press, 2007), p. 259.

"not a very creative guy": McAdam, *Freedom Summer*, p. 165.

"I didn't realize yet": Fran O'Brien, interview, November 12, 2007.

"Well, what was happening": McAdam, *Freedom Summer*, p. 134.

"everything was awful": Linda Wetmore, personal interview, March 27, 2008.

"I could never kiss anybody" and "Then I guess": Wetmore, interview.

"welling out like poison": Dorothy Abbott, ed. *Mississippi Writers: Reflections of Childhood and Youth*, Vol. 2, Nonfiction; (Jackson: University Press of Mississippi, 1896), p. 329.

"We must decide": Clayborne Carson, *In Struggle: SNCC and the Black Awakening of the 1960s* (Cambridge, Mass.: Harvard University Press, 1981), p. 146.

"too many people high on freedom": Casey Hayden, in Constance Curry et al., *Deep in Our Hearts: Nine White Women in the Freedom Movement* (Athens: University of Georgia Press, 2000), p. 364.

"hardly caused a ripple": Hayden, in Curry et al., *Deep in Our Hearts*, p. 365.

"a different kind": Muriel Tillinghast, interview, December 16, 2008.

"I got the feeling": Don Whitehead, *Attack on Terror: The FBI Against the Ku Klux Klan in Mississippi* (New York: Funk & Wagnalls, 1970), p. 161.

"I'll kill anyone who talks": Federal Bureau of Investigation, Mississippi Burning Case, File 44-25706, (hereafter MIBURN), 4-50; Jackson Clarion-Ledger, July 12, 2005.

"Save one for me!": MIBURN, 4-45-48.

"Ol' Rainey could be elected": Los Angeles Times, December 11, 1964.

"a feeling that we hit": Jack Bales, ed., *Conversations with Willie Morris* (Jackson: University Press of Mississippi, 2000), p. 103.

"They did better": *New York Times*, October 21, 1967.

"I was quite delighted": Seth Cagin and Philip Dray, *We Are Not Afraid: The Story of Goodman, Schwerner, and Chaney, and the Civil Rights Campaign for Mississippi* (New York: Nation Books, 2006), p. xv.

AFTER   ORDINARY PEOPLE MADE A DIFFERENCE

"After Freedom Summer, we met black people": John Howell, personal interview, March 11, 2008.

"I never dreamed I'd live to see": Frederick M. Wirt, *Politics of Southern Equality: Law and Social Change in a Mississippi County* (Chicago: Aldine, 1970), p. 160.

"What is in the hearts": Hodding Carter III, email interview, September 26, 2008.

"Not in Mississippi!": Susie Erenrich, *Freedom Is a Constant Struggle: An Anthology of the Mississippi Civil Rights Movement* (Montgomery, AL: Black Belt Press, 1999), p. 409.

"There has not been meaningful change": Sandra E. Adickes, *Legacy of a Freedom School* (New York: Palgrave Macmillan, 2005), p. 163.

"It's a good thing they got that Communist": Fran O'Brien, interview, November 12, 2007.

"It was like going to war": Muriel Tillinghast, December 16, 2008.

"Other people went to Vietnam": Chris Williams, interview, September 21, 2008.

"I am prouder of being there": Adickes, *Legacy of a Freedom School*, p. 159.

"Like working with sharecroppers": Bob Moses, personal interview, December 10, 2008.

"changed Mississippi forever": Charlie Cobb, Oral History Collection, University of Southern Mississippi.

"the greatest sociological experiment": Eric R. Burner, *And Gently He Shall Lead Them: Robert Parris Moses and Civil Rights in Mississippi* (New York: New York University Press, 1994), p. 166.

"Freedom Summer injected a new spirit": John Lewis, personal interview, September 12, 2008.

"the closest thing to a perfect day": Fran O'Brien, email correspondence, January 21, 2009.

"It took forty-five years": Linda Wetmore Halpern, email correspondence, January 21, 2009.

"At the end of it all": Chris Williams, email correspondence, January 21, 2009.

Numerous integrated kindergartens grew out of Freedom Schools started in the summer of 1964. Students and teachers in these schools were often the first participants in newly integrated grade schools. Here, teachers Faye Cauley (right) and Ms. Annette Benson (left) and students (left to right) Annette Benson, Timothy Hill, and John Cauley are setting up for the first classes in a community-created Head Start daycare program in Clemson, South Carolina, in 1967. This school recently celebrated its fiftieth anniversary.

Further Reading

SELECTED AUTHOR'S SOURCES

Adickes, Sandra E. *Legacy of a Freedom School.* New York: Palgrave Macmillan, 2005.

Cagin, Seth and Philip Dray. *We Are Not Afraid: The Story of Goodman, Schwerner, and Chaney, and the Civil Rights Campaign for Mississippi.* New York: Nation Books, 2006.

Dittmer, John. *Local People: The Struggle for Civil Rights in Mississippi.* Urbana: University of Illinois Press, 1994.

Erenreich, Susie. *Freedom Is a Constant Struggle: An Anthology of the Mississippi Civil Rights Movement.* Montgomery, AL: Black Belt Press, 1999.

McAdam, Doug. *Freedom Summer.* New York: Oxford University Press, 1988.

Martinez, Elizabeth, ed. *Letters from Mississippi.* Brookline, MA: Zephyr Press, 2007.

Zellner, Robert, with Constance Curry. *The Wrong Side of Murder Creek: A White Southerner in the Freedom Movement.* Montgomery, AL: NewSouth Books, 2008.

BOOKS FOR YOUNG READERS

Mitchell, Don. *The Freedom Summer Murders.* New York: Scholastic, 2016.

Mooney, Carla. *Freedom Summer, 1964.* Edina, MN: ADBO Books Core Library, 2015.

Rubin, Susan Goldman. *Freedom Summer: The 1964 Struggle for Civil Rights in Mississippi.* New York: Holiday House, 2014.

ONLINE RESOURCES

https://kinginstitute.stanford.edu/encyclopedia/freedom-summer

The Freedom Summer page of the Martin Luther King, Jr., Research and Education Institute, Stanford University.

https://snccdigital.org/events/freedom-summer/

The Freedom Summer page of the Student Nonviolent Coordinating Committee Digital Gateway.

https://www.pbslearningmedia.org/resource/amex26.soc.fsintro/whatwasfreedomsummer/

"What Was Freedom Summer?" A collection of videos from PBS Learning Experience.

Image Credits

Photo by Bess Adler: p. 396 (above).

© AP Photo / Jack Thornell: p. 162.

© George Ballis / Take Stock / The Image Works: pp. 332 (above), 348, 360.

© *Boston Globe* / Getty Images: p. 396 (below).

Photo courtesy Florida Memory, photographer unknown: pp. 72–73.

Photo by Harris & Ewing Inc., courtesy Library of Congress Prints and Photographs Division: pp. 62–64.

© Matt Herron / Take Stock / The Image Works: pp. 70, 295, 298, 336–338.

Photo by Dorothea Lange, courtesy Library of Congress Prints and Photographs Division: p. 61.

Photo by Russell Lee, courtesy of the Library of Congress' Prints and Photographs Division: pp. 118–119.

Photo by Warren K. Leffler, courtesy of the Library of Congress' Prints and Photographs Division: pp. 170, 322.

Photo by Mark Levy, permission by Wisconsin Historical Society: pp. 190–193 (above).

Photo courtesy Library of Congress Prints and Photographs Division, photographer unknown: pp. 98–100, 301–305, 313–316, 325–326, 352–354.

© Danny Lyon / Magnum Photos: pp. vi, 6, 364, 377.

Lithograph by Alfred Edward Mathews, Strobridge Lithographing Company, courtesy Library of Congress Prints and Photographs Division: pp. 52–53.

Photo by John B. Maurer, John B. Maurer Freedom Summer Photographs, McCain Library and Archives, The University of Southern Mississippi: pp. 84, 90–91, 96, 132–133, 157–160, 272–275, 404.

Photo courtesy Mississippi Department of Archives and History, photographer unknown: pp. 48, 83, 148–152, 170, 214, 235 (above and below).

Don O'Briant, *Greenville News*, 1967, p. 426.

Ted Polumbaum / Newseum Collection: pp. 12, 373–374.

Photo by Herbert Randall, Herbert Randall Freedom Summer Photographs, McCain Library and Archives, The University of Southern Mississippi: pp. 16, 19, 22–23, 40–42, 142, 167, 169, 177, 204, 226, 260.

© Steve Schapiro / Corbis Premium Historical / Getty Images: p. 31.

Photo by Marion S. Trikosko, courtesy Library of Congress Prints and Photographs Division: p. 79.

Document permission by Matthew Zwerling Freedom Summer Collection, McCain Library and Archives, The University of Southern Mississippi: p. 106.

Photo permission by Iain Whyte Civil Rights Collection, McCain Library and Archives, The University of Southern Mississippi, photographer unknown: pp. 172–175.

Photo courtesy Whittier Daily News, photographer unknown: p. 193 (below).

Document permission by Wisconsin Historical Society: pp. 15 (image ID:146337), 95 (image ID: 147189), 195 (reel 3/00356), 219 (micro N71-508).

Photo permission by Wisconsin Historical Society, photographer unknown: pp. ii (image ID: 97475), 111 (image ID: 147188), 148–152 (image ID 97437), 180 and 208–211 (image ID: 97712), 190–193 (image ID: 98742), 214 (image ID: 97484), 248–251 (image ID: 97888), 332 (below, image ID: 97928), 388 (image ID: 98008).

Photo by Marion Post Wolcott, courtesy Library of Congress Prints and Photographs Division: pp. 59, 236–240, 264–267, 280–283.

Zoya Zeman Freedom Summer Collection, McCain Library and Archives, The University of Southern Mississippi, photographer unknown: p. 44.

Index

M

MacLaine, Shirley, 231, 305

Magee, Sylvester, *142*

Marshall, Thurgood, 72

Marx, Karl, *246*

McGhee, Laura, *168*

McGhee, Silas, 312

McKellar, Tillman, 86

media coverage, 43–45, 120–121, 123–124, 126–127, 131–134, 138, 287, 288

Meredith, James, 78–80, *79*, 277

Miles, Bob, 87–88, 257, 331, 389

Miles, Mona, 87–88, 257

Miller, Wallace, 378–379

minstrel shows, 62

Mississippi

  against black progress, 75–76

  civil rights progress in, 382–384, 389–390

  during the Civil War, 50–53

  dangers at night, 94–95, 97–101

  Democratic party of, 67–68

  early 1900s, 65

  on news of deaths of Chaney, Goodman, and Schwerner, 289

  as "police state," 20–21

  poverty in, 60, 89, 92–93, 208, 276, 279, 347, 391 (*see also* sharecropping)

  racial division, history of, 4–5

  racial violence in (*see* harassment and attacks)

  reputation of, 245, 382–383

spy organization of, 76

state constitution after Civil War, 54–55

state constitution in 1890, 58

"tough towns," 146–147, 153

Mississippi Caravan of Music, 309

Mississippi Economic Council, 383

Mississippi Freedom Democratic Party (MFDP)

  "at large" solution, 343–345

  canvassing for, 307

  Credentials Committee and, 327, 328–330, 335, 339, 343–351

  at Democratic National Convention, 324, 327–331, 335, 339–351, 355–359, 360–363

  50/50 "seat both delegations," 344

  formation of, 236

  illegal infiltration of, 345–347

  members of, 323–324

  national support for, 342–343

  planning of, 232–234, 253–254, 305, 319–322

  two-seat compromise, 350, 351, 355–356, 357–358, 361–363

  Victoria Gray and, 168

Mississippi Greys, 52

Mississippi John Hurt, 310

Mississippi Southern College, 196–197

Mississippi Summer Project. *see* Freedom Summer

Mississippi: The Closed Society (Silver), 135

Montgomery bus boycott, 14–15

Moore, Amzie, 28, 75

437

W

Wallace, George, 134–135, 325

Wall Street Journal, The, 221–222

warning systems, 98, 101

Watkins, Holly, 367–368

Waveland conference, 375, 376, 377

Wetmore, Linda, 374

white backlash, 220–223, 274, 276–279

White Citizens' Councils, 69–71, 70, 72, 76, 77, 102, 230, 265, 274

White Community Project, 276–279

White Folks Project, 276–279

White Knights of the Ku Klux Klan, 200

whites against segregation and racism, 280–284

white youth, inclusivity of, 278–279

Wilkins, Roy, 7, 361

Williams, Chris, *396*

    about, 22–23

    after Freedom Summer, 395–398

    arrival in Batesville, MS, 85–86

    on Barack Obama, 402, 403

    at Democratic National Convention, 331, 347

    during Freedom Summer training, 26

    letters home, 45, 90–91

    police harassment of, 157–160

    voter registration and, 271–275

Williams, Rosa Lee, 93

Winn, Fred "Bright," 148–149, 150–152, 208–211, 264–267, 336–338, 393–395, 403

wiretapping and bugs, 241, 253, 345–347

women, local civil rights heroes, 168–169

women's liberation movement, 376

women's rights, 11, 372, 375–376

World War I, African Americans and, 65, 323

World War II, African Americans and, 68, 296, 323

Wright, Richard, 198

Y

Young, Andrew, 242

Z

Zellner, Bob, 39, 120, 134–135, 144, 293